Nothing Like a Nice Cuppa

Nothing Like a Nice Cuppa
Three Accounts of Y.M.C.A. Volunteers
Who Served During the First World War

The Canteeners

Agnes M. Dixon

Red Triangle Girl in France

Cairns Collection of American Women Writers

Betty Stevenson, Y.M.C.A

Edited by C. G. R. S. and A. G. S.

Nothing Like a Nice Cuppa
Three Accounts of Y.M.C.A. Volunteers Who Served During the First World War
The Canteeners
by Agnes M. Dixon
Red Triangle Girl in France
by Cairns Collection of American Women Writers
Betty Stevenson, Y.M.C.A
Edited by C. G. R. S. and A. G. S.

FIRST EDITION

First published under the titles
The Canteeners
Red Triangle Girl in France
Betty Stevenson, Y.M.C.A

Leonaur is an imprint of Oakpast Ltd
Copyright in this form © 2014 Oakpast Ltd

ISBN: 978-1-78282-299-8 (hardcover)
ISBN: 978-1-78282-300-1 (softcover)

http://www.leonaur.com

Publisher's Notes

The views expressed in this book are not necessarily those of the publisher.

Contents

The Canteeners	7
Red Triangle Girl in France	101
Betty Stevenson, Y.M.C.A	191

The Canteeners

ZOUAVES

Contents

Troyes   13
La Toussaint   29
Troyes Again   42

To
The French Poilu
As I Have Known Him
To His Courage, Patience, Modesty and
Chivalry
To His Doggedness and Grim Determination
To Rid His Beloved Patrie
Of the Foul and Cruel Invader

Troyes

Monday, Oct. 12, 1915

I write in bed at the end of our first day of work. Truly we have not achieved much! We have given 300 men each a quarter of a litre of coffee! And we have spent, four of us, the clock round in doing it. Breakfast, 7.30; out at 8, to wrestle with ironmongers and wholesale grocers, as our *marchandise* from England still has not come, though sent off ten days ago. Our shopping resulted in buying and taking with us 100 kilos of coffee, 100 kilos of sugar and some boxes of biscuits, and as the shop horse and waggon were at the door, we annexed them, stowed the sacks inside, were kindly lent two empty packing cases by the grinning staff, upon which we seated ourselves, and so drove off along the Croncels road; the amazed sentries admitted our equipage on to the platform with open mouths.

But at least we had the wherewithal to start. Of course, nothing went right at first; the fire would not burn, the water would not boil, the coffee would not grind fast enough—it takes a good while to grind coffee enough for 300 men. In the middle of everything being at sixes and sevens, at about 11 came a message from the *médecin chef* to say about 500 men would go off by train at 1. We could not give them anything but coffee, because we had not got it; but we were on the way to make enough for 400, and we did get that ready, and in the end we only had 240 to supply, and twenty-five *infirmiers*. Another train was to follow, so we continued to grind, grind, grind. By 2 o'clock we had time to think of having some lunch—we wanted it. We had bread and butter, ham, potted meat, cheese, grapes, pears, and our own excellent coffee.

Our recipe, a French one, is 100 litres of water, 14 litres coffee, 6 litres sugar. No chicory. Chicory should never be mixed with black coffee, only with *café au lait*.

We waited until 6 for that train that did not come, by which time we gave it up, and returned to the hotel, but during dinner came a message that 100 wounded would pass through at midnight. No train, pouring rain, and a two-mile walk in the dark.

Such is war.

The Grand Hotel St. Laurent must be the noisiest place in the world. There are only three sorts of noise that we have not got—cats, dogs, and cocks. We have all the rest. My room is over the kitchen; the hotel is a typical old French provincial inn, with a partly covered courtyard behind it; the back part of it is covered with glass, and forms a carpentering shed and a garage and a repair shop. This morning we had an assortment of vociferous workmen, sawing wood, hammering metal, and knocking in nails; a chauffeur (I think one of the ladies of the Scotch unit, who tomorrow are all posting off to Salonika) testing the running of her engine and practising the exhaust; Madame la Patronne screaming into the ear of the very deaf Monsieur le Patron, and Madame Mère shouting at short intervals down the telephone; much coming and going and shrill talking of early birds and worms; clattering of cups and saucers; grinding of coffee machine and cleaning, raking out and stoking of kitchen range. In the middle distance, quite inaudible separately, the ordinary street noises of a busy market town with cobbled pavements. There may have been other noises; if so, they were drowned. I have just changed my room, which looked on to the courtyard, to one higher up. which looks on the street. It may be quieter; it could not be noisier.

Our colonel is charming to us: his manner is both friendly and paternal, as though we were daughters of the regiment, and he makes us feel that we are welcome and honoured guests. One could imagine him a descendant of the Vikings, with his far-seeing blue eyes, his fair hair, and his great height and breadth.

He received us at his *bureau* with effusion and delight. He expatiated on the beauty of our hut, its dryness, strength, and convenience. He had almost built it with his own hands, and planted plants in front of it, and fixed British and French flags on the top. When at a loss for a word in conversation he uses the word *chose*, and introduced me to another officer as Madame Chose. He evidently loves his men, and equally evidently is loved by them. He took us at once to see our hut, whisking us off in a motor car—somebody else's, I think. His face shone when we reached it, and he sort of waved us together with both hands, as though we and the hut were long lost brothers. Truly the hutment was a darling, just like Wendy's in *Peter Pan*. He pointed out all its perfections; like a child with a new toy—the double walls, the space filled with cinders under the floor for dryness, the garden in front (two yards of mould with three plants in it!). It had been run up in five days, and was ready for immediate use: a range, two tables, cupboard, shelves, and all the necessary cooking apparatus—saucepans, marmites, plates, knives and forks, colander, coffee-grinder, pails, basins, etc.; electric light laid on and a pump just outside. The hut is divided in two: the kitchen, very well lighted, is the bigger part, and behind is a small room, where we keep our stores, and which contains a bed for our soldier servant who guards the place at night. Coals and wood are given us. and we are to buy our vegetables and bread cheap from the army contractor.

We have "*2me Armée*" posted up on our canteen, also "*Dames Anglaises de la Goutte de Café.*" In front of our big window is a wide sort of shelf, where we call serve out our wares. But we prefer to serve the soldiers direct in the trains, as it gives us a chance of talking to them and hearing their stories.

The colonel told us we belong to the 2nd Army, whose base is at Troyes, and invited us to move forward with it, and promised we should occupy a "*palais*" in Germany. Of course we said that where he went there we would go too.

Our *marchandises* from London have still not arrived, though they are at the station. But military necessities come before ours, and they are hung up there till tomorrow. So we had to start by buying in coffee and sugar, etc., wholesale, to go on with. Madame la Patronne at the hotel recommended us to a warehouse where we got what we wanted: prices very high—coffee 3.90 a kilo and sugar 1.14.

On Friday night, just as I was going to bed, I had a note from the commandant to say that wounded were expected from the front at 7 a.m. Juliet and I arranged to go early as Miss Gracie seemed tired, and we got up at 5.30 and reached the canteen at 6.30. I started out with a stick of chocolate to eat on the way, but as I noticed a baker's shop was already open, I plunged into the dark doorway to buy some rolls. M. the *boulanger* was apparently in his bath behind the counter; it seemed odd, but it is best to take no notice of foreign habits, so I asked for two halfpenny rolls and finally made out in the gloom of the dawn that he *had* a pair of trousers on. He was enormously stout, and beautifully clean, and he was powdered all over with flour just like a nice clean baby after its hot bath. We neither of us took the slightest notice of the *contretemps*.

It was very pleasant in the early morning: cool and fresh and quiet, slightly misty. Our excellent Bourgeot had got the message we had telephoned through the night before, although the exchange had utterly denied that the Quai Croncels was on the telephone at all; and he had been up since 4 stoking the fire and heating up our coffee and *bouillon*, all of which has to be made ready overnight.

At 12 came another note that over 300 more were expected about 11, but they only required coffee, as dinner was going to be given them. Tables and benches were arranged all along the platform, and when the train got in (two hours late, of course) all who were well enough sat down there in the warm sunshine, weary, depressed, silent, dirty, grimed; some with torn clothes, dried blood on them; others with sleeves cut out to make room for splinted arms. A sad, sorry crew they looked as they sat there waiting to be fed; all had been in the train since 7, and many since the night before, without food. A small table was set at a little distance, laid for six, and after a time, when all the French soldiers had sat down, six wounded German prisoners came along and occupied it, guarded by two soldiers with fixed bayonets. They had faded, stained and dirty uniforms on; one was an officer, and all wore round service caps. They looked fairly decent men; three wore spectacles, and all spoke politely.

I said to *the médecin-chef*, "Don't you think our coffee is much too *strong* for those Germans?" and he agreed that we might fairly water it a little. However, we didn't. We gave them each some, and all thanked us politely. No doubt they supposed us to be French. But we drew the line at cigarettes; they didn't get any of those. It was wonderful to watch the men's faces change as they ate—they were so silent and depressed at first; then the hot *bouillon* took a crease or two out of their faces; next came a plate of meat and a quart of wine; finally a cup of hot coffee which made them smile; accompanied by two cigarettes each, which made their eyes fairly gleam.

Poor human wreckage! And to think that this goes on every day of every month. And to think what it must be in wreckage of German lives, who now have a fighting front of 1,400 miles. These men all came from Vitry le François; the train before from Tahure. I fancy the next attack is developing, and we shall have our work cut out.

It was a pretty sight—the long tables in the sunshine, with the lines of men in every shade of blue; it is nearly the same colour as our blues, but a little lighter. Their enjoyment was evident, and it was

SERVING TRAINS AT TROYES

easy to start them talking and gesticulating by asking them if they had killed many Boches and how many prisoners they had taken. The bad cases remained on their stretchers, or were carried in to the dressing-stations to be attended to. We went along the train afterwards and fed the poor things with coffee and cigarettes. How heavy men are, if you want to lift their head and shoulders to drink! We must get some proper drinking cups for them with spouts.

When all this was over, at about 5, we had to make coffee for next morning.

A pretty long day, but worth it all for the pleasure we gave.

Miss Gracie told us an amusing story of her last canteen. Early in the proceedings the *médecin-chef* came to see them with one or two others, and Miss M. only heard the word "*chef*" of the introduction; she was a little flustered as her French was not fluent, so Miss Gracie carried on an animated, and, I do not doubt, a friendly, conversation. Miss M. looked worried and finally said tartly to Miss G.: "You had better go into the other room and go on with the coffee." Miss Gracie meekly went at once. Miss M. said, "*Bonjour*" firmly to the *médecin-chef* and turned away.

Presently she went in to Miss G. and said severely: "I don't know how it is in *your* country, but we don't think it at all *convenable* to be so *decidedly* friendly to a *cook*" (Miss G. is American).

The colonel, after several *pourparlers* with the mayor, commandeered an empty house for us; the inhabitants had fled in terror on September 5, 1914, when it was expected the Germans would reach Troyes in two or three days. He offered it to us as a rare gem—a *bijou*: "*Tout ce qu'il y a de convenable et pratique; grand, avec onze chambres,*" big enough for both canteen parties; then added it was "*complètement meublé; mais—pas de lits.*" "But," he said hurriedly, "*des lits, on peut les commander; ou les louer; rien, rien.*" We thought ourselves frightfully lucky to step into such a prize without price, as we were to have it free. Alas! it turned out to be the kind of gift-horse you dare not look in the mouth. It was not *meublé* at all; it had not even a kitchen range. But it was well-built, dry, and convenient in position. It had a weed-grown garden; it had water laid on; it HAD A BATHROOM.

It sounds rather mad with winter coming on, but six of our party have taken it—the youngest members. They have hired beds, produced like rabbits from a conjuror's hat, by the doctor, when the whole of Troyes could not produce a bed, because the hospitals had bought them all. They have bought the absolute necessaries—such as a chair, a table, a wash-basin, a strip of carpet, and so on. Army blankets have been lent them, and coal is to be supplied. Each girl will have a fire in her bedroom, and a candle. It does not sound comfortable, I know, with winter coming on, and I am hazy about what they are going to eat. But it is really simpler in war time, and if you are busy, not to eat.

We have had no trains today, so have been rather slack, but we had a sheet worry instead. The colonel came round to us, much disturbed. He found the ladies had beds and blankets, but no sheets; they must have sheets. He gave a hurried order to the doctor that he was to provide them, and hurried away in his motor. Then the doctor became disturbed. He *had* no sheets; anyway, we had no right to hospital sheets, because we were not the army, only *volontaires*. Yet the colonel had commanded. What *could* he do? There were only two pairs of sheets, and they were in use. He paused in distress. Suddenly he brightened; an idea had reached him. He called for a bicycle, leapt upon it, and dashed away. Incredibly soon he was back again, glowing, panting; begged me to come with him at once to the house of a friend a short distance away, who would *lend* sheets to the six ladies.

"*Monsieur*," I said deprecatingly, "five *paires de draps; c'est impossible.*" But he said No; she had promised, and I must come immediately and be introduced to her. So off we went, walking at a furious pace it was all so vitally important, you know till I was obliged to remind him I could not walk as fast as the French Army can, at which he slackened at once, but had increased almost to a run before we got to the house. However, we got the sheets all right, willingly lent by his friend, who turned out to be his landlady, and when I got back I sent off a soldier to fetch them. But that was not the end of the sheet worry. In half an hour the doctor was back again, accompanied by an orderly, whom the colonel had sent to him about the sheets. The orderly would not believe that the doctor had actually *found* sheets already, so he had been dragged to me for my additional evidence. The orderly said the colonel was "*bien agité, très dérangé à cause de ces draps.*" Between us, however, we did manage to calm the orderly down, and I sent such a message to the good colonel that I trust he has been able to sleep in peace between his own sheets.

Aren't they nice?

The colonel easily gets *agité*, but I must say it is mostly about our comfort. He takes up little points, and his whole mind is engrossed by them for the moment. One point was a "cabinet" for our use. He insisted on it; he *exigeait* it; he gave orders about it to every official, always in our presence. We must have a key to it; we must have the exclusive use of it, and so on. He has forgotten about it now, but for days it was dragged into every conversation, he always using the English word.

We had also today a visit from quite a swell, the man next above the colonel—I think the *Commandant d'étape*. He also came to ask if there was anything he could do for us—he was afraid we must be *triste!* But of course there was nothing. Our coal is bad, and we want a pig-pail, but one does not ask the *Commandant d'étape* for a pig-pail!

Miss Gracie made us all laugh last night. She told a story of her and her people travelling in Cornwall. She told it three times over, because the party round the table only heard bits at first, and each insisted on hearing it over again from the beginning. Miss G. herself was so overcome each time with emotion she could hardly articulate. It seems an old Cornish farmer in the train became friendly with these Americans: he lauded his county, its inhabitants, and its merchandise. Finally he pulled from his pocket—which apparently also contained snuff, tobacco, tarred twine, onions, peppermints, and other powerful items—a Cornish pasty, which he proceeded to cut in sections and offer round. Each politely took a piece, and wondered mutely *how* they could eat it. At that moment they plunged into a tunnel, and each was seized with the same brilliant idea. They one after the other leant across the old man and threw their portion out of the open window into the friendly darkness of the tunnel. At length they emerged to find ... the window had been shut after all!

It is a pity to go on after the end of a story, but we did ask her what her unfortunate countrymen did next. Did they not get out immediately at the next wayside station?

"Heavens, no!" she said; "we were in an express, and the train did not stop for forty-seven miles."

She said it was the most awful thing that had ever happened to her, and she has never got over it. The old farmer's gentle dignity would have moved a stone to weep, and the pasty was to have been his dinner.

We had another fearful swell to visit the Hôpital d'Evacuation on Saturday—a general of some sort. I am seldom able to catch their names. They are all dragged to see us and introduced, and we act the *Entente Cordiale* and offer them coffee, which they usually accept, and always praise. When we have warning of the approach of these luminaries we are as tidy and neat as a new pin. We knew about this one coming, because every soldier in the place was frantically cleaning *something*; if he couldn't find something to clean he polished something that somebody else had just done, or swept imaginary leaves from the platform. We could not get the slightest attention from anyone. Most of them were buzzing like wasps round honey over, under, and in a Red Cross train, which stood waiting near by. They swept, scrubbed, polished, and scoured: and as far as I could see the general never even looked at it.

Our hut was exquisite—cleaned, garnished with fresh flowers, the stove newly blacked. Juliet had a coffee stain down one side of her apron, so she had to be careful and keep her other side turned towards him.

The *infirmiers* often want to buy things from us because they are not allowed to go into the town, so we have now a little stall of chocolate, tinned milk, and cigarettes, which they buy from us at wholesale prices. We have a crowd always round our window in the morning, as we bring papers out with us and discuss the news, and I have spread out some large maps of the war, which they pore over, searching the names of the places they read about, and trying to pronounce the English versions. They are all dreadfully concerned about poor little Serbia, and are terribly afraid the Allies will not get to her aid in time, but it looks today as if they had.

We have a constant visitor in a man called Bourgeois, a French-Canadian, who speaks English in a refined, gentle, low voice; he is curiously attractive. He brings us little offerings in the way of coloured leaves, branches of wild strawberries, and moss. Once he brought me some of his cider. In return we give him *bouillon* or barley broth, as he has *mal d'estomac*.

When our soldier servant, Bourgeot, goes into the town to do any errand for us I have to write him out a military pass, or he might get into trouble.

It seems to me that life can be very cheap in Troyes, considering it is war time. I pay 60 *francs* a month for my bedroom, with a little dressing-room off it—electric light, coffee, rolls, and butter in the morning. My fire is extra. We always lunch, and generally have tea, at our canteen. My evening meal I get for myself, and have eggs, bread and butter, fruit, dried figs and raisins, cream-cheese, chocolate, etc. In the market one buys beautiful cheeses. You can get a penny roll of sweet cream cheese, which I like better than butter, and is enough for two meals. I can buy as much bread as I can eat in two days for 1½d.

New laid eggs are 2d. each, but scarce. Fruit is very plentiful. I bought nine large crisp red apples today for 2½d., and enormous juicy pears are 1½d. each. Champagne grapes are very nice. They are large, of a transparent warm yellow, dusted with bloom, but where the sun has caught them they are almost apricot-coloured. Butter is dear, 2.25 *francs* a pound, but cakes and sweets are no dearer than usual, and at the *pâtisserie* they have a large variety of penny tarts and cakes of all sorts, including chocolate *éclairs*. We can get decent chocolate for the soldiers at 3.10 *francs* a kilo, but that is wholesale price.

Alas! All the photographs Miss G. took of us when we first began work at the canteen, and of the picnic lunch and the German prisoners, are all spoilt because she did them on a roll she had used before!

On the morning of our second Sunday I went to the mass at the cathedral. There was a very small congregation, and nearly everyone was in black. The music was poor, but the singing good. There are two organs, one close to the choir, which plays accompaniments, and another at the west end; when an effect is needed, or great noise, both play together, but all the big stops are in the west organ.

The preacher, covered with beautiful old lace, was conducted to his pulpit, and locked in, by a glorious beadle clad in scarlet cloth coat and breeches, white silk stockings, and buckled shoes and a Napoleonic hat; he carried a mace, and was much bedizened with gold lace, gold braid, tassels, cords, and epaulettes. In the midst of the service a lady stood up in the middle of the church, caught the beadle's eye, beckoned him to her, and handed him her umbrella. He took it respectfully and went away with it out of the south door. I puzzled much over this. Could the beadle off duty be an umbrella-mender, and be thus improving the shining hour of the sermon?

Troyes has a delightful market. There is the outdoor market, where booths and stalls under awnings are ranged in rows in a great open square. Here are sold all the necessities of life, so that I cannot see why there need be shops as well. Here you can buy fruit, umbrellas, cakes and sweets, envelopes and bootlaces, pottery and children's frocks, socks, shoes, slippers and boots. Here the chestnut merchant roasts chestnuts at so many a *sou*, the knife-grinder sharpens cutlery, the umbrella-mender mends, the cobbler cobbles, the cheap jack calls his wares. The wrinkled old women sit behind their stalls, with spotless white frilled caps on their heads, endeavouring to attract attention from the passer-by.

Close by is the huge covered market hall, where the principal wares are vegetables, poultry, cheese, butter, and eggs. It is curious to step inside and gradually distinguish the prevailing word in the babel of noise. It is "*Madame,*" ... "*Oui, Madame; Non, Madame; Bien, Madame; Bonjour, Madame; Combien, Madame? Ici, Madame; Deux pièces, Madame; Quat' sous, Madame; Pardon, Madame; Voilà, Madame; Au revoir, Madame.*" The emphasis is so much on the last syllable that one really hears little but "*Dame, Dame, Dame.*"

In the early morning (I am often out between 7 and 8) Troyes is a town of running water. Water pours down each side of every street and alley, bursting out of iron tunnels every few feet at the edge of the path. The water flows out often to a width of a yard. The paths, except along the main streets, are absurdly narrow, often only a foot wide. The windows of the ground-floor rooms are all guarded with iron grilles, which project at least six inches about the height of one's shoulder. This does not leave one much room to walk, even if one has the footpath to oneself. Add to this the fact that at the time when I go to the *Bureau de Poste*, to fetch my letters before going off to the canteen, all householders place outside their doors their dustbins and pails of refuse to be collected by the municipal carts. So one is incessantly brought up by the Scylla of an impassable side-path and the *Charybdis* of a flowing and eddying stream, unless one leaps all the dustbins in succession. The streets are badly paved with old and irregular, on the highest of which one picks one's rather painful way, if one's shoes are thin.

There are a few Belgian dogs which help to draw carts, running underneath with a broad band round their chests. They never pull alone. There are beautiful horses here—quite remarkably so, broad and sleek and well fed; well-treated also. I have never seen an overloaded or badly treated horse; every one seems kind to their animals, and proud of them. The dogs are of course taught to howl at the word "Boche."

The streets, being cobbled, are very noisy. One is sometimes awakened in the morning at perhaps 5 by what sounds like a machine-gun outside one's window; but I have found from observation that it is a handcart being drawn over the excrescences of the pave, the iron wheels bumping from stone to stone. I think they are the carts from the country round, which send their produce early to the market.

The time to see Troyes is between 5 and 7 in the evening. In the daytime Troyes looks much like any ordinary French town; it consists principally of bare-headed, black-shawled women, going about each armed with either a string bag or a market basket, out of which protrude leeks, carrots, turnips, apples, eggs, cheese, etc., and from which a vivid imagination can construct the future dinner of the family. There are also a few soldiers, some children (if they do not happen to be at school), and plenty of old men. But at 5 the soldiers are allowed out from the barracks, and all Troyes joins them in the streets; the whole of life is immediately keyed up to a higher note; the shops turn up their lights, the hot chestnut man in the *Place de la République*, whom nobody has noticed all the afternoon, immediately becomes besieged by ever-increasing waves of infantry—like German assaults. As soon as the first line is dealt with the next springs up ready, till the supply is exhausted. The evening paper-boys scuffle and struggle across the square, and their editions are sold out before they reach the other side. How the French Tommy can afford an evening paper on ½d. a day I do not know. He is going to have 5 *sous* in the future, but not till November 1.

It is amusing to be about in the town at this time in the evening, but not if you want to get anywhere, as you simply can't get through. It is a quiet, well-behaved crowd, but not a sad one; there is no horseplay, and no drunkenness. The soldiers go about in groups, or with their friends and families. By 7 it is all over, and Troyes looks like London early on Sunday morning.

I like to see the soldiers drifting into the churches. They stroll about very quietly, and gaze at the beautiful glass windows; often they kneel for a few minutes, and reverently cross themselves before they go out. I have seen one or two kneeling motionless with bowed head and shut eyes for perhaps half an hour. Were they communing with their dead, or praying for their souls? Or were they putting up a prayer for themselves when their days of danger should come?

People drift in and out of the churches a good deal. There are eight large ones—right in among the streets. They are so quiet and peaceful, and death and one's dead seem so near these days—so many widows, and obvious mourning mothers, pass up and down the streets. If it were not for the soldiers in their gay blues and reds, the streets would look very sombre.

The uniforms are beyond my comprehension. I took notes of several: —

1. Dark brown corduroy suit; scarlet hat.
2. Khaki suit; red *fez*.

THE PIPER

OUR CORNER.

3. Light blue suit; khaki *puttees*; black hat.
4. Dark blue coat; purple breeches.
5. Dark yellow tunic; light yellow breeches; dark blue *puttees*; crimson cap.
6. Light blue coat; scarlet breeches; brown gaiters.
7. Light blue tunic; light blue velvet cord breeches with yellow piping; scarlet cap; dark blue gaiters.
8. Yellow tunic; yellow breeches; dark blue *puttees*; yellow cap with scarlet centre and long black tassel.
9. Dark grey suit; scarlet piping; light blue cap; dark red velvet collar.
(*N.B.*—A velvet collar denotes a doctor.)

If the *Kaiser* keeps his promise to his bankers he has to bring the war to an end in two days.

Mrs. Sollas went yesterday to buy a small piece of meat. She went to a butcher and asked for a little piece of *boeuf*. They shook their heads indulgently. Well, then, a piece of *veau*? "*Mais non, Madame*," they smiled back. "*Nous n'avons en vente ici que du cheval.*"

Mrs. Sollas has found a very nice little apartment, "*deux chambres avec cuisine.*" I went in to see her installed, and found it very pleasant and homelike. Her floors are of dark polished wood, and slope in every direction except the horizontal. She has one stove between the two rooms, but it is fierce enough to heat a church. Her "*cuisine*" consists of a gas ring in a cupboard one foot deep by three and a half wide.

Last night the great bourdon bell of the cathedral boomed out for ten minutes most impressive. I had not heard it before. One could imagine the requiem of a saint or an archangel.

I have been to see the St. Bernard canteen at work. Its work differs mostly from ours in that it is absolutely regular and unremitting, and according to a regime ordered by the doctors; whereas ours is spasmodic and irregular. We have periods of great activity followed by periods of inaction, and we supply practically, within limits, what we like. The St. Bernard canteen is supplied with all its raw material; we find ourselves in everything except coal, wood, and water.

I got there by invitation in time for tea, which took place quite leisurely in the room behind their kitchen. Now and then one of the girls would dash to the range to see nothing was burning, or to mend the fire. At about 4.15 the work of dishing up and distributing the dinner was begun. The great marmites, each holding 100 litres, one full of hot milk, the other of *bouillon*, were lifted down on to the floor. Presently the *infirmiers* began to collect at the open window, which looks across grass and trees on to the hospital. Each *infirmier* was armed with two pails and a written list. The soldier servant stood by the window, the girls each at her appointed place—one by the milk marmite, one by the *bouillon*, and two at the range. The scene was a lively one to watch, as everything must be done rapidly to insure the men getting their rations hot. I stood on the mat by the door, as a child stands on a sand mountain, with the waves lapping the sides of it. My waves were milk and soup. The soldier servant took the lists one by one from the gesticulating, impatient mob of *infirmiers*, who reminded me of Arab porters at Cairo railway station, and presented them to the girls who were serving out, calling each out loud:

"Five litres milk";

"Two eggs, two biscuits, one rice";

"Four macaroni, two beefteks";

"Ten litres *bouillon*";

"Six *purée de pommes*";

"Three rice, three biscuits";

"Two *bouillon*, two eggs," and so on, until all the patients had had their portions measured out into the tins, and the last *infirmier* had left the window. Everyone worked at high pressure, and it was all over in ten minutes. Then I came down off my refuge and tasted all the dishes, and the girls took stock of what was left, decided what should be used again for tomorrow, and what should be used up for their supper. While I was waiting for tea to be ready two of the doctors had come in and had tasted everything too. I presume they approve of the cooking, as the girls find more and more patients are put in their charge. The day I was there they had seventy to cook for. We both have the same trouble with the coal—it is very bad, and it is very difficult to get a really hot fire.

Needless to say, it is French coal; all the good coal comes from England, as the good coal district of France is in the enemy's hands. Not only is decent coal very dear, but it is often impossible to get, as it gets hung up somewhere or other on account of military precedence. For instance, I have had a small stove put in my room, to burn anthracite; but now we can't get anthracite for love or money, so I sit tireless. However, as the French say, "*C'est dur, mon Dièu; mais que voulez vous? C'est la guerre.*" If you hear that once, you hear it a dozen times a day.

If I am ever asked where I live in Troyes I say "*chez Madame Pa-*

ton, à l'imprimerie." But perhaps they don't know it, and then if I am pressed for time I say shortly "*Rue Geoffroi.*" But if I have plenty of time to spare I answer thus: "My hostess, Madame Paton, has a front door which opens on to *Rue-Général-Saussier-mille-huit-cen-vingt-huit-à-mille-neuf-cent-cinq*, but the private door I use opens on to *Rue Geoffroi de Villehardouin-Chroniqueur mille-cent-soixante-sept-à-mille-deux-cent-vingt-huit.*"

Time waits, not only on speech, but on trams in Troyes—unlike England, where Time and Tide wait for no man. It would often be quicker to walk the two miles to Croncels than to go in the tram, not because the tram creeps, because it doesn't—when it isn't standing still it goes quite fast—but because it spends most of its time waiting at spots where there are double lines for another tram to pass by. I have waited a quarter of an hour for this to happen, and by a curious mischance I am invariably in the tram which waits, and not in the one which is waited for. Then there is the Bureau de Poste, where endless Time waits its turn to be wasted. I have seen, in the space of a quarter of an hour, at least five hours of Troyes time being wasted, at four *guichets*, each with a long tail of people waiting their turn to be attended to, with unvarying patience.

Most of the business done is in registered letters and parcels sewn up in white calico for soldiers at the front. Each parcel takes about ten minutes of steady writing in a book before it is finally stamped, postmarked, and thrown into a basket; then the payment has to be calculated and made, then the next person moves along in front of the *guichet*. When there are fifteen in front of you it takes a good while to call for your letters. Not very long ago a sharp-witted person in France suddenly discovered that for months and months a steady supply of cotton had been going into Germany, as all parcels for the French prisoners had been sewn up in white cotton; now that has been stopped, and parcels are wrapped in paper.

In the tram today an oldish man, after looking at me earnestly for some time, slid along the seat nearer to me and began asking me if I was working at St. Bernard. When I had told him I was at Quai Croncels, and what work we were doing, he burst out, "*Ah, Madame, cette bataille de la Marne—les soldats anglais, c'est l'Angleterre qui a sauvé la France.*" He kept repeating it, and put his hand out and clasped mine, and when it came time for him to get out he shook my hand again and bowed and hurried out speechless.

La Toussaint

All Saints' Day (a public holiday) and All Souls' Day (*le jour des Morts*) are over. Both have been raw, wet, and gloomy, with the unspeakable chalky mud of Champagne Pouilleuse under foot. It is hard, because La Toussaint is almost the greatest day of the year in France, specially a day of family reunion; and this year doubly so on account of the many losses by death. For days past every tram has been crowded with women carrying wreaths, bouquets, and pots of chrysanthemums: almost every other shop in the town, whatever it usually sold, displayed flowers, real and artificial, plants, mostly heather and chrysanthemums, wreaths and trophies of beads and glass, metal urns and pots. I saw a regiment of soldiers march out of the barracks on the way to the cemetery, each man carrying a pot or bunch of flowers. I too wended my way to the cemetery. Useless to think of getting into a tram—every one was crammed to overflowing with people and pots. So I tramped along in the mud. Needless, too, to ask one's way—one followed the pots and the wreaths. The avenue that led to the cemetery was lined on each side, like the road to San Lorenzo and the Campo Santo in Rome, with banks and piles of flowers for sale. Inside the first thing that caught one's eye was a great round bed of chrysanthemums surrounded by all sorts of trophies and wreaths; the most important had a bow with this device on it:

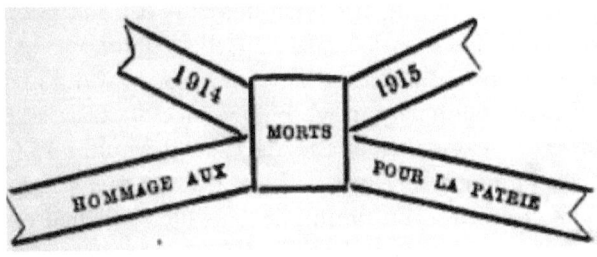

I wondered how many bows there would be in the knot before war is over.

A piece of ground had been set apart for soldiers: one became aware on the left of a fluttering mass of red, white, and blue. A place about the size of four tennis courts was planned out in long rows of neat graves, with little wooden edges, a plain white cross at the head of each and a tri-colour flag fastened to the cross. All the graves were smothered in flowers; the whole scene somehow struck me as being indescribably gay—not like a cemetery, not like the "*jours des morts*," rather like a pageant, a military review, a day of rejoicing. The little flags were so clean and fresh and young-looking, they fluttered so courageously, so cheerfully, it almost seemed to me that the dead were rejoicing that they lay so still and quiet after the din of battle, so painlessly after all their sufferings, so peacefully after the disappointments and troubles and suspense of life. "*Morts pour la Patrie*," wept over and tended and remembered by France. Could anyone wish a better end? If those young lives had not ended like that, could they have ended better?

A railway man with "*Est*" on his cap came and ranged himself beside me; his tears dropped freely. Unabashed, he murmured, "*Ah! les pauvres; non, non, les heureux, les heureux.*" He had lost a son at the Battle of the Marne; and all these dead soldiers who rested in the soil beneath our feet were those who had died in the hospitals of Troyes after the Battle of the Marne, and in the fourteen months of fighting in the Champagne country since.

By the end of the week the sheet worry has nearly ceased to disturb us, though I have an occasional deputation to ask for a receipt, which I refuse to give, as it isn't I who have the sheets. If I give a receipt, I may be asked later to produce them. We have had a coal worry, but that, I hope, has now crystallised itself. It began by our good colonel giving us permission to use coal which apparently he had no jurisdiction over. I gather that after a time the cooks at our station, from whose store our soldier replenished our coal-box, got into trouble for using so much coal. A coal-general, or some sort of luminary, descended upon us and told us it was impossible we should use that coal till a higher authority, in whose province the coal lay, had given his permission; it was merely a formality, and would unquestionably arrange itself immediately.

It didn't, however, and meantime our soldier filched coke for us and broke up packing-cases. I pointed out to the coal-luminary that one could not make bricks without straw, and at last one morning coal appeared in our box. We are now told that when a train is expected the cooks have orders to provide us with coal, but on a day when no train is forthcoming we may only have coke and wood.

Simultaneously with this trouble our servant Bourgeot was suddenly deprived of his *nourriture*. The cooks found out he had been dining with the forty odd men who made up the personnel of Quai Croncels without their receiving his rations, and the sergeant said he could not countenance his being nourished there any more till he had received orders. So poor Bourgeot tramped off twice a day to a restaurant in the town and nourished himself at his own expense. I felt it was better not to interfere, as feeding him was not our business, but after four days of this I did go round and interview the Colonel both on the subject of Bourgeot's nourishment and our coal supply, he is a dear man—ample, generous, large-hearted. All difficulties were swept away with a comprehensive wave of both arms. He literally sweeps all troubles away to the winds.

All is now well, but I shall make it my business to find out if Bourgeot has been indemnified against his outlay.[1] He beamed two or three days ago, because for the first time he had received his pay at the increased amount: it used to be ½d. a day, and from October 1, 1915, it became 2½d. I have not told any of them what our men get.

Mrs. Sollas told me how narrowly they escaped the *Emden*,[2] coming home from Australia. They were warned at Bombay that she was in the neighbourhood, and about twenty-four hours out the captain received a wireless telling him to put back to Bombay. For some reason he disbelieved the message, asked to have it repeated in code; but no reply came, so he continued his voyage to Aden, keeping a very sharp look out.

Afterwards he found no message had ever been sent him, and in all probability if he had gone back he would have walked straight into the jaws of the *Emden*. No doubt it was a trap.

The woods are nearly bare of leaves. Day by day the great avenues of poplars have shown more and more clearly the huge colonies of lumps of mistletoe, which look in the distance like gigantic rooks' nests. A fortnight ago, one sunny day when we penetrated far into the

---
1. After a fortnight he had not been reimbursed, so I paid him myself.
2. *The Kaiser's Raider!* by Hellmuth von Mücke - Two accounts of the S. M. S. *Emden* during the First World War by one of its officers: *The "Emden"* & *The "Ayesha" Being the Adventures of the Landing Squad of the "Emden"* is also published by Leonaur.

Bourgeot, our orderly

A.M.D.

woods along the Seine, the tops of the poplars (not Lombardy poplars) were hung all over with a delicate tracery of golden yellow—each leaf glittered and trembled in the sun like gold. And looking through the delicate grey stems of the nearer trees one saw beyond other lines of more distant poplars, each with a fine cloud of golden dust hovering among the topmost branches. Behind, a deep stormy blue of banks of clouds low on the horizon. In front the Seine flowed gently between banks edged with guelder-rose and crimson-leaved cornel, and the clean grey poplar stems rose out of a tangle of red and scarlet bramble leaves.

On the bank, below the wooden bridge we stood on, two old women in faded blue gowns scrubbed their linen in the river, each kneeling in a wooden box, and shouted questions up to us as to what we were doing, why we were there, and where we came from. When we said we were *infirmières* and worked for the *blessés*, they said, "*Mon Dieu, que vous êtes braves.*"

Yet probably, if their lot had been to live and do their work in a bombarded village, they would callously have washed daily at the river, with shells falling in the neighbourhood, and not have deemed it brave.

If the French woods were within speaking distance of the English market at Christmas time I could make my fortune by selling mistletoe. We often try to pick some, but it is always out of reach, and the bare, smooth poplar trunks do not lend themselves to swarming up in a nurse's cloak. But we have a pet soldier who arrives at our canteen sometimes completely hung round with great branches of it tied to a pole over his shoulder; he looks like a man as trees walking, and I told him he was illustrating a Shakespeare play. Inside and out our canteen is hung with huge lumps of it.

On the wide shelf outside in the winter live a party of wooden soldiers, jointed and supplied with bayonets, each dressed in the uniform of his country. We have a Tommy, a Piou-Piou, a Russian, a Belgian, an Italian, and a Boche. Every soldier at Quai Croncels, every cook, guard, *infirmier, menuisier, peintre, facteur, vaguemestre*; even occasionally the doctors, officers, and visitors, amuse themselves by arranging these figures in battle array. Always the Boche is hopelessly outnumbered; generally he is arranged doing the goose-step in self-conscious pride, while the Allies ether threaten him with drawn bayonet behind, or are in ambush in the surrounding woods (pots of young fir trees and moss). Often the Boche is in his favourite position of arms held aloft, while he shrieks "*Kamerad, Kamerad!*" Or he lies outstretched down on the ground, with every bayonet of his foes planted in his breast.

The men never seem to tire of this game, and nearly every time I arrive I find a new battle progressing.

An Anglican bishop, on a visit to the Front in Flanders, motoring one day along a road encountered a regiment of French soldiers returning to the trenches. He stopped his car, and begged the officers' permission to bless the men before they returned to their dangerous duty. Having got out of the car, he raised his hands over the soldiers, and said solemnly but genially, "*Dieu vous blesse, mes enfants.*"

I was pleased to find one day a shop near the market which sold delicious-looking crisp tin loaves—the kind one buys to cut sandwiches from. I bought a loaf, and took it with me to the canteen, thinking to indulge in the treat of hot buttered toast. We used every implement we had, including a tin-opener, a hammer, a saw, and a case-opener, but nothing would pierce the crust of that loaf. It turned out to be special prisoners' bread! baked so slowly and thoroughly that it was crust, or rusk, right through, and consequently would keep without going mouldy for months. We did eat some, though it was a great strain on one's teeth, and as rusk with plenty of butter it was very nice.

In the course of my labours I have to interview all sorts of people: unfortunately they are nearly all of the *bourgeoisie*, so I fear my French will become very provincial, and when I next go to Paris I shall hardly be understood. We learn expressions and phrases from the soldiers and never know if they are slang or not. Apart from generals, *commandants d'étape*, colonels, captains, *médecins*, and *médecins-chef*, I have had to deal with electricians, *fumistes*, *menuisiers*, *imprimeurs*, photographers, chemists, ironmongers, bankers, sergeants, *infirmiers*, military censors, and franchise officials, wholesale tobacconists, grocers, merchants, and *pain d'épice* and biscuit manufacturers, not to speak of every kind and shape and sort of railway official connected with the goods department of the railway.

Yesterday I had an amusing evening. I have just acquired a Kodak camera, and as I don't understand a single thing about photography I asked Madame Paton if her son would give me a little help in learning the ways of the machine. So after dinner I went through into the next house, where Madame Paton, junior, has her *ménage*, and we all sat round a large table, with a big chandelier overhead and a red rep tablecloth, in the most approved early Victorian style—*Madame*, junior, young and buxom and very good-looking, at one end, *Madame*, senior, old and bent and withered, at the other. Myself and young Monsieur Paton, who is a "simple *soldat*," and extremely good-looking and well set-up, at one side and opposite us the parents of *Madame*, junior. I found myself obliged to translate aloud into French the book of rules of the Kodak game, and I must say it strained my French resources. They all listened devoutly, and almost without a smile, while I made hashes of such words as spring, hinge, lens, reel, film, focus, sight adjustment, and so on, but in the end we worried it out pretty well between us.

These old houses are all very Victorian. My room is panelled at one end, and the rest is hung with a fine old cretonne; the floors are uneven, and of old polished oak; my bed is an old double mahogany one. Young *Madame* has a beautiful bedroom. I went through it last night on my way to her dining-room—a wide expanse of dark polished floor, with no carpet; good old furniture, and a great poster mahogany bed, hung with soft green satin curtains.

Old *Madame* told me that during and after the Franco-German war my room had been occupied by a Prussian officer. He had been quartered upon the family for two years, and, though of course they hated having him, he had always behaved with entire discretion and respect. The Prussian Army occupied Troyes for two whole years, and as instalments of the indemnity were successively paid they withdrew from town after town, till finally Verdun was the last occupied spot of French territory.

It isn't very nice walking home from our canteen in the middle of the night—unless it is moonlight. There are no lights left burning at all; and whether one chooses the road or the path, each has its peculiar pitfalls. The road has large holes in it, which fill with water after rain, and the points of the tramlines are badly joined, and the lines themselves stand up at times above the roadway and catch unpleasantly an unwary toe. The path is even worse; there are puddles there too, but not quite so deep. But the worst thing is that each house has a private waterway between the end of its drainage pipe from its roof and the gutter along the roadway, and, instead of being conducted by a pipe or culvert underground, the water flows to the road in a little trench, which is either paved with bricks or simply cut down into the soil. On a dark night it isn't possible to see them at all, and one's progress is a series of stumbles, splashes, slips—and language—about every twenty feet.

One day our *médecin*-chef came in beaming. I can't think, or could not at the time, why he came. Ostensibly he came to dry his hands, that he had washed at the pump, on our towel, and incidentally informed us, beaming, that he was treating himself to a special *déjeuner* with his wife. We have since heard that he has just been given a military medal, and the lunch was in honour of this. He wanted our sympathy in anticipation—*escargots!* He was going to lunch on *escargots*, very special, yellow ones, from the south of France, ancient Romans, I think he said. He beamed and expanded. "You catch them and place them in a well-warmed and lighted apartment, and for three weeks you *starve* them."

"Oh, *Monsieur*," we said, "how cruel!"

"Not at all," he replied, "they taste better that way. Next you boil them in milk, and when they drop out of their shells you chop them up, mix them with cream and butter and green flavourings, such as mint, parsley, sage. They must be eaten *boiling* hot, and when they are served you pick out the contents with a special fork. Of course," he continued airily, "I am not *gourmand, moi*, I only eat one dozen and half—a *gourmand* he eat four five dozen."

"What a lovely *déjeuner*," we murmured. "We hope you and your wife will enjoy it. *Bon appetit, Monsieur!*"

"*Merci*," he replied, "but *that* is not the *déjeuner*, that is only the *hors d'oeuvre*. After that we have *jambon, mouton, dinde, salade, pâtisserie, dessert!*"

He swelled himself again, and beamed at us and departed.

In mid-November we are just beginning to realise the convenience of working in a wooden hut which has been run up in five days, and of which all the wood has shrunk visibly since. The weather has been very wet the last few days, and our soldier has decided he had better sleep under an umbrella, and have Macintosh sheeting fastened to the wall behind his bed to keep out the "*courant d'air*" We were obliged this morning to move and examine every single case of stores we possess, as the rain was coursing all over the floor. In opening a case we believed to be ship's biscuits we found a long-lost treasure—a dozen or more large tins of Huntley and Palmer's fancy biscuits, which had been sent by a friend to Mrs. Sollas, and which she feared had gone to Le Tréport instead. All the boxes now are stood upon wooden blocks high and dry out of the swirling floods.

One of the *infirmiers* has just passed his examinations and become the first grade of *médecin*. So the personnel of the station had a feast;

they had *soupe cresson*, in the making of which we assisted; then vermicelli; then fillet of beef, *salade, petits pois, pâtisserie,* extra good wine, and finally coffee with rum in it. I do not call that bad rations for "simples *soldats.*"

We helped in the making of the soup, because I had begged the *chef* to show me how it was made. He sent us in a canful one day, and we had all thought it so good. So we all went in to the kitchen and had a lesson, and gave him an English lesson in return. For those who have plenty of watercress I recommend it.

Melt a piece of butter the size of a walnut in a frying pan—throw in three handfuls of cress, let them reduce to one-third as you toss them about; add three more. When reduced add six large potatoes cut up, and salt; put them all into a saucepan with a quart and a half of water. Boil till soft enough to pass through a colander. Then add milk and a walnut of butter, and serve.

N.B.—The *chef* used cocoa butter for frying the cress in, because cheaper than butter. Nut margarine would do, of course.

Bourgeot spent his afternoon next day bringing me small driblets of coal to my lodgings. Even if you can buy coal, which is difficult, you can't get it delivered, as horses, carts, and labour are all scarce. So Bourgeot is making several journeys and bringing what he can in a bag. It is necessary, as the weather is bitterly cold. Mrs. Sollas was so hard up the other day that when she succeeded in running some coal to earth, she carried seven kilos off with her in a bag!

Even when some coal can be procured to go on with, the stove will refuse to work.

On the very coldest day of all I was reduced to a hot-water bottle, placed alternately at my feet and on my lap, because although I had a whole scuttleful of best anthracite with hardly any coke in it, the stove was possessed by a devil. Three several times it was lighted; delicate sticks of charcoal placed on pieces of rag dipped in petroleum, and reverently fed with tiny bits of coal, a piece at a time, like feeding a very sick man. Yet, after burning fitfully and sadly, each time it slowly went out. Other days, when there is scarcely any coal to feed it with, it will burn fiercely and madly.

Troyes is somewhat fantastic in its nomenclature of shops. You have a pastry-cook who calls himself "*Au fidèle Berger*"; a draper, "*Aux 100,000 Paletots*"; and a boot shop styled "*La Chaussure de Luxe*"; a baker calls himself "*Le Petit Troyen*," and a blouse shop "*Aux Bonheur des Dames*"—"*Au Grand Chic.*"

Several shops put out this enticing notice, "*Ici on consulte le Bottin.*" I long wondered who M. Bottin was, and wished to consult him in leisure moments. Was he a doctor, a chiropodist, or a palmist? I know now that he is a directory, but I was glad that I refrained from consulting him, for M. Bottin, they assured me, was a beer.

"*The way of transgressors is hard.*" So is the way of return from France to England in war time. France does not want to lose you; England does not want to receive you. But neither does France want you back, if you once leave her soil. She is quite clear about that.

It took me hours of patient effort to try and get a "*permission*" to come back to Troyes after going over to England for my son's wedding. I started a good ten days beforehand, and visited every bureau I could hear of, beginning with the *état-major*, passing on to the Direction of the Service de Santé, being handed on with a polite letter to the *médecin-chef*, M. Bergasse, who read the letter, destroyed it, wrote another one, and handed me on with it to the *Commandant d'étape*. But even he failed me: all were courteous, friendly, and painstaking, and all professed their delight at seeing me back at Troyes again, but no one would take the responsibility of giving me the necessary *permission de retour*. The *Commandant d'étape*, I am certain, funked an interview. I saw the *capitaine d'étape*, whom I knew quite well, and I gathered from his embarrassed manner that the commandant was behind the folding doors all the time, though he sent a polite message that he was regrettably and unavoidably absent!

So I left Troyes and have no means of knowing whether I shall ever succeed in getting back. I did get a military *sauf-conduit* out of the *état-major* with considerable trouble, only to be told at the station when I left that I need not have bothered about it as my Red Cross railway pass was sufficient. Troyes is in the "*zone des armées*" and everyone has to have permission to leave it—civilians from the *mairie*, the military from the *état-major*. The *commandant* de Waubert at the *état-major* has a curious liking for making travellers to Paris go round by Sens, which in the only train there is now takes nine hours. I was terribly afraid he would write "*par Sens*" across my *sauf-conduit*. But I was saved that. Even with going to Paris in an express, which was only three quarters of an hour late, it took me from Sunday afternoon to Wednesday evening to reach London.

If civilians *will* travel in war time they must expect to be kept a whole day in Paris to get their passports *visés*; they must not be surprised if there is a break down on the main line, and they are taken a slow circuitous route which brings them in to Boulogne, after an eight-hours' journey, an hour after the boat has left for Folkestone; neither ought they to be annoyed to find that that particular way across the Channel was closed to the public from the day before, and that the authorities tried to send them back to Dieppe. Rather ought they to be very thankful that the courtesy and persuasiveness of the M.L.O. officer on the quay succeeded in overcoming the red tape of the South Eastern Railway chief and persuading him to give them a promise that they should cross the following afternoon. And they ought to be (and were) very grateful to said M.L.O. officer for recommending a decent and moderate hotel to spend the night in.

And they ought to be (and were) very grateful for being allowed to cross (even in a gale) in a troopship, carrying 600 men going home on leave, even though they were required to remain below all the voyage; even though the ladies' cabin was found to be crowded with sleeping forms of muddy officers straight out of the trenches and occupying every available inch; even though every ordinary convenience had been removed till the Days of Peace come once more, such as stewardesses, carpets, cushions, chintz covers, and so on. Lifebelts there were, dealt out to each person; and stewards there were, and very busy they were kept. And storm pans there were too, but whether there were enough to go round the 600 men who covered every available spot on deck or gangway and sat two deep on every available chair and stair I can not say, because I was not allowed on deck, and by the time a scratch committee had been collected up in the smoke-room of doctors and passport examiners, and we were summoned to go before them, it was pitch dark, and all the troops had departed to London by a special.

And another thing civilians ought to be thankful for, *but were not*, was that only about 150 P. & O. passengers were allowed on board at the last minute, who had travelled overland from Marseilles, and that *only* three babies were of the party; and that of those three babies, who howled all the way across, *only* one of them shared the same straw bolster.

I am sometimes afraid the supply of packing paper that is used for prisoners' and soldiers' parcels may run short, because the French have suddenly begun using it in large quantities for wrapping up their plants and bushes in the gardens for the winter. It is the universal habit at Troyes. The first garden we saw decorated in this fashion we concluded was a lunatic asylum—every plant of every size, every rose bush and tree and small shrub, was wrapped in coloured waterproof paper and tied neatly and firmly round the waist with twine. The colours were tastefully arranged. One path would have alternate pink and green on one side and purple on the other, the parcels resembling huge cabbage heads. Another bed might be nothing but green and white, or there would be a series of black shiny blobs varied with yellow and orange. The larger bushes, young conifers, and peach or almond trees, were swathed in straw.

The gardens, thus prepared for the winter, looked neat and interesting, but hardly beautiful. About this time the pump outside our hut was also arrayed in its winter dress, even its handle being so thickly twisted round with straw that it is thicker than a man's arm and the pump itself thicker than a fat German's body. It appears that Troyes always expects a cold winter, and is quite prepared to have its main water supply and its gas cut off by frost. Those who depend on gas fires and gas light feel rather apprehensive, as all weather prophets foretell an unusually cold winter.

When I was applying for my *sauf-conduit* I had to fill up a paper with description of my appearance, height, age, birthplace, etc., and I was sent with it into an inner room in company with two sergeants. We sat down at a table—I on one side, they on the other—and earnestly discussed my personal appearance. The difficulty was that my passport which already contained all these details, and which we might otherwise have copied, had already gone on in front to the *état-major*. So we had to describe me afresh, and hoped the two would tally. We all agreed about fair hair and blue eyes, only I suggested blue-grey, but was outvoted. Then came nose, mouth, chin, shape of face; the two sergeants studied me attentively and conscientiously, and though I gave them every possible help, and even suggested suitable words such as "*ordinaire*" they would not acquiesce, and finally decided that the more elegant word "*moyen*" applied to chin, nose, and mouth, and wrote down that I had no distinguishing marks.

Anyway, the thing worked; but I should be sorry to have to identify anybody by the paper those two sergeants made out.

Here are two more long-winded streets at Troyes, which I noted down in passing:

"*Rue-Charles-Fichet-Dessinateur-Archéologue-1817—1903.*"

"*Rue-Charles-Dutreix-Fabricant-de-Bonneterie-Député-de-l'Aube-1848—1899.*"

I had a letter from Bourgeois which ended thus:

Please to accept the hommage of the profound respect with which I have the honour to be, L. Bourgeois.

Troyes Again

Dec. 17, 1915.

Back at Troyes, having been away from November 28 till December 16—two weeks and a half, out of which almost one week was taken up in going to and fro. From rue Général Saussier home to Roke, four days all but three hours; from Roke to rue Général Saussier, two days and three-quarters. The public can travel if it likes, but neither at its own time nor its own convenience. The worst thing about the journey was the delays. We got to Folkestone beautifully; then, after a sort of Black Hole of Calcutta business outside the passport office, while I should imagine the officials, instead of sitting waiting for us at their post, were being called, shaving and breakfasting at leisure, while we hapless passengers remained outside the door flattened and compressed ever more densely by the converging crowd behind. . . . My sentence has grown out of all bounds. We will start a new one. We, the first trainload, got through at last to the boat, and I managed to secure a berth up against a porthole; but the second trainload of people, whom we were able to watch going through all their convolutions, had to put up with accommodation on the floor. There was a crowd of people, and certainly we had the smallest steamer in the British Empire to cross in. I suppose the idea is if the boat has to be mined or torpedoed it may as well be only a small loss.

We reached Folkestone at 10.30. We did not leave it till 1.30. All that time we might have got most of the crossing over. For nearly five hours I held out against the horrible assortment of noises that sea-sick ladies can make. It was too rough to get down off one's bunk, as one could not have stood up, and the floor was covered with paralysed and convulsed forms—those who feared they would die, and those who feared they wouldn't. Every few minutes the bows came down with such a thud upon the water that it sounded like a violent explosion each time, but I am thankful to say nobody screamed. But it was easy to imagine them to be mine explosions.

At Dieppe an officer came below and ordered us all up on to the starboard deck—we supposed for passport examination again. But we were simply kept waiting there, in the dark and in the rain, jammed close together by people always crowding closer behind, for about an hour. The barrier was kept closed, and no one could imagine why we were not allowed to land. perhaps the passport committee was having tea. At last came the welcome order, "Military off the boat first," and by virtue of my uniform I crushed out with a handful of soldiers who were on board. The first question put to me was, "Why did you not obtain a *permis de séjour* at Troyes?"

How they found out I had not got one I can't imagine. The only answer I could think of was, "I suppose because I did not ask for one." This did not seem to satisfy, and I was firmly told that I must apply for one directly I got back to Troyes. I did not see why I should be trampled on, so I said I had never been told by anyone that it was necessary. But *how* did they know? The moment they opened my passport they pelted the question at me, as though they had been awaiting my arrival. Have I a black mark against my name?

The next *contretemps* was that I and four English Tommies who were bound for the other side of Paris were all told to go up into the town to exchange our *ordres de transport* for tickets. That is the worst of travelling with a military pass—you are always having to search out military *bureaux*, which take a pleasure in hiding themselves in obscure corners, and waiting on very insecure chairs while your passport is again examined; a clerk proceeds to write out a long complicated form in duplicate which you have to sign, and which has to be countersigned always by some invisible person who is either to be found in an inner room or somewhere outside out of sight. From experience I knew this would take much time, especially for five people, so I treated myself and the four Tommies to a cab; it was pouring with rain, and we were also afraid of missing the train. We need not have feared; the train did not leave for two hours, and we got back and had an excellent dinner on it before even we started from the port. They certainly gave a good dinner for five *francs*:

Barley soup.	Bombe of ice.
Tarts of *foie gras*.	Cheese.
Savoury rice.	Fruit.

Chickens. Coffee.
Peas.

Reached Paris at midnight, instead of 9.50, which fellow-passengers said was very good, as it was often 2 or 3 in the morning.

The result of the protest at Dieppe was that the first day I got back to Troyes I presented myself at the *mairie* and asked for a *permis de séjour*. They looked at my passport and Red Cross papers, and said, "Why do you want one? It is not necessary; you are authorised to be here by the French Red Cross." I explained what had taken place at Dieppe. Somewhat unwillingly they said I could have it if I liked, and directed me to another *bureau* hidden inside an *octroi*, where I again made my application and finally overcame official reluctance. Forms were produced, my papers laid out, and a searching catechism followed. The details asked for were puerile. How could it help the war for them to know my father's name, my mother's maiden name and Christian name, my husband's age and occupation; and where both he and I were born? The official could not grasp any of the names or places. I had to write them all down for him on a piece of paper, from which he copied them letter by letter on to his form—Old Charlton, Kent, Powell, Marten, Thomas, Edgbaston, Charles Wolryche, etc., etc.

Then we came to personal details. Was I married? When I said "Yes" he looked doubtful and distressed, and I could see the idea working in his mind. If I was married, why was I not at home minding my *ménage*? The next question was, had I any children? But without waiting for me to answer he drew a line through that column, and when I firmly said "Yes, I have three," he swivelled round in his chair, gazed helplessly at me, threw out his hands and waved them several times in the air, as though to say, "These English are beyond me; if she has children, why is she not with them?"

"*Majeurs ou mineurs?*" he queried.

"*Deux majeurs et un mineur*," I replied. He again gesticulated silently. Finally he turned himself back to his form and firmly drew another line through the space left for *enfants*. After that we got on splendidly, and he wrote submissively anything I liked to tell him. He did ask at the end if my husband was also in Troyes, and when I said "No" he only made one little shrug, as though to say, "A woman who has deserted home and children would of course not have her husband out here with her."

I breathed a sigh of relief. It was done, and I signed my name and prepared to depart. But not at all: he proceeded to write it all out again in duplicate, and I had to sign that too. One paper was presented to me, and I was requested to return with it to the *mairie*. But before I went I let drop a bomb on his head.

"*Monsieur*," I said, "I have three other English ladies with me at my canteen, and besides that there are two other canteens at Troyes, with eight English ladies working in them. Shall I tell them all to come to you for *permis de séjour?*"

He turned quite pale. "For Heaven's sake, *Madame*," he cried (or words to that effect), "do nothing of the kind. I assure you, *un permis de séjour est facultatif. Ce n'est pas obligatoire, du tout, du tout, du tout*," his voice rising in shrill *crescendo*.

I felt I had got the best of that episode.

Now back to the *mairie*, where my paper was taken and carefully copied, English spelling and all, into a book, and a fresh form was taken out and filled in, given to me to keep, with a space in it for a photograph, which I was asked to provide. This I firmly but suavely refused. I hadn't got any, and if I had—— They then suggested tearing one out of the three or four I had plastered on my passport and identification papers, but I told them to tamper with a passport in war time was high treason in England, and I could not think of permitting it; so they gave way on that point, and drew a line over where the photograph ought to be. Now it seemed to be really finished. I was charged to keep all the papers carefully, and we parted, doubtless mutually hoping never to meet again.

CHRISTMAS.

This is not much of an affair in France; the churches keep it by midnight services and masses; some of them have a decorated and illuminated *crèche* somewhere near or behind the altar. They are rather prettily arranged, though somewhat theatrical in effect, with fairy lights in saucers to give the necessary light; there are usually about eight figures, Mary, Joseph, St. John the Baptist and the three *magi*, and sometimes three shepherds as well. The child, laid on straw in a manger, is nearly always at least three times too large in proportion.

A good deal is done for the wounded soldiers, too, rather as a custom adopted from the English. We selected an out-of-the-way military hospital, which did not seem to be having anything done for it, and asked permission to give the men presents all round. They were very grateful. We made up eighty parcels, in blue, white, and scarlet paper: each had a small present—pocket-book, knife, tobacco-pouch, or purse; each had a piece of *pain d'épice*, ¼ lb. of chocolate, an orange, a packet of cigarettes, a tooth-brush, some postcards, and a large *"friandise"* (some kind of marzipan or chocolate pennyworth).

We went into each ward and gave them ourselves. The hospital was dull and cheerless: the walls were painted brown, and the beds had brown army blankets as counterpanes. Our gaily coloured parcels made a delightful contrast to the sombre wards and the gloom of a pouring wet dark morning outside. Being a military hospital, there were no nurses, only orderlies.

"What do the men occupy themselves with? "I asked the captain who took us round. "Have they games, or books?"

"Alas, no," he replied; "they buy themselves papers to read, but we cannot afford to get games for them."

"May we send you some for an *étrenne* for the New Year? Games and packs of cards?"

His face lit up. "*Mais, Madame*, it would be too good of you. We should accept them gladly."

The Red Cross hospitals are much pleasanter places. They are managed and run by the *"Dames de France,"* and are more like our English hospitals, being bright and cheerful, with red counterpanes, and nice nurses dressed in white.

At Troyes the *lycée* had been turned into a Red Cross hospital and was admirably suitable, the big dormitories forming spacious sunny wards, and the gardens round the building ensuring quietness; the soldiers look contented and bright and cheerful. In the military hospitals they look apathetic, dreary, bored.

The men at Quai Croncels marked Christmas by having a specially good dinner. We added to this a dessert in the form of oranges, apple tarts, and cigarettes, so that the complete menu was a very respectable one. We invaded the kitchen in the morning, as we and the cook-*chef* take a mutual interest in each other, and the turkey was liberated from the oven for a moment for our approval.

Our humble Christmas dinner was a contrast. We had barley soup, somewhat burnt, as we had had to leave it to itself while we went to the hospital; and cherry tart. We could not even leave Bourgeot to mind the soup like King Alfred, as he was occupied in wheeling our eighty parcels along on a handcart, packed in two enormous marmites as the best method of keeping them dry in the pouring rain.

It does not quite always rain here, only nearly always. By today (the

29th) the roads had got nice and dry, and Dorothy and I went to outlying villages on an egg hunt. Eggs are still difficult to buy in the shops, as the hospitals take so many, but out in the country we can pick one or two up at the various cottages. Almost every cottager keeps fowls; wherever we see any we go in and ask. Today we were most successful and came home with twenty-two beautiful new laid eggs—most of them pullets' eggs, it is true. The Seine is all out in flood, and walks we are accustomed to take to the woods have disappeared under water.

Dorothy's activities are various: she teaches English at our station, and receives French lessons in return. Her pupils are the *sous-chef de gare*, Bourgeot, and a doctor major whom we call the Bison Boy, because the first time he came to see us he talked a little broken English and told us he was learning out of the *"Bison Book."* Tactful inquiries revealed the fact that he was trying to say the *"Boy's Own Book."* Dorothy writes out exercises for them to learn by heart, and hears them in turn every morning. The *sous-chef* learns the quickest, but he cannot grasp the pronunciation, whereas Bourgeot pronounces very well. Dorothy's dictionary, which she brought with her to learn French from, is nearly always out on a visit. The Bison Boy grabs it in the morning, if it has come back from the *sous-chef*, who borrows it overnight to study while he is on night duty. Bourgeot endeavours to get the use of it for the evenings, when he is left alone at the canteen. The result is, when I say to her on a fine afternoon, "I think you must go on an egg hunt today," she replies, plaintively, "Oh, dear, I was just going to have a good go at my dictionary."

The *sous-chef* has a passion for making lists. He is at present copying out the dictionary[3] (the English half of it), and is in the middle of the letter "C." Today I lent him a book which contains lists of all the navies of the world, which he promptly began to copy out, and in a short time sent me round by the porter, Charles Robin (or it might be Robin Charles—he gives his name both ways, and says it does not matter which we call him), a list he had compiled of all the ships which had been sunk during the war. A good many amenities take place between the *sous-chef's bureau* and the canteen: he develops and criticises our photographs and corrects Dorothy's French; he invites us to the warmth of his stove on days when we are only allowed coke; and on a wet afternoon entertains us with his stereoscopic photographs, of which he has taken many excellent ones at the French front.

A few days ago a railway notice arrived for me, informing me that

---

3. He finished it before we left Troyes.

eight cases awaited me at Troyes Station. I was not expecting more than two or three, so went down in the evening to investigate. But nobody could find any at all.

My particular friend, M. Colin, was off duty, and nobody else there has a head on his shoulders. So I made an appointment to meet him the next afternoon at 3, and asked the St. Luc ladies to meet me there as well, as *they were* expecting goods from London.

We all turned up, and M. Colin speedily found the group of eight cases. Three were for me, three for St. Bernard, the others for St. Luc. That was all plain sailing, and we all noted down our respective numbers, and said we would send our *vaguemestres* to fetch them. I sent mine this morning, and he returned empty-handed with a message from the *chef de gare* to say I could not possibly have only three cases: eight cases I might have, but not three. In the meantime the St. Luc ladies, having found out by advice from London that their consignment consisted of 200 plum puddings, where they had only ordered fifty, took their *vaguemestre* with them, went down in force to the station, stormed and took possession of the platform, opened their cases, abstracted the puddings they wanted, repacked and sent away the rest, and retired in triumph. I did not see this episode; I wish I had. But now, if I *were* to claim those eight packing-cases, how would the station-master justify his position?

NEW YEAR'S DAY, 1916.

We did not want to minister to our men's physical needs again, so for a change we gave them a variety of games to play in their leisure hours—draughts, dominoes, and cards—with which they seemed very pleased. These we presented during "*soupe*" on New Year's eve, and felt that now all the amenities were well over.

On New Year's morning we noticed that the men, instead of drifting out of their tent after "*soupe*" by twos and threes as usual, all came out in a body together, and made straight for our canteen. The door opened itself, as it were, and a large plant appeared in the doorway, propelled by the head sergeant, Jouzeau, and a perfect sea of faces was visible behind him. The plant was tastefully festooned with ribbons of the Allied colours, and it was presented to us by the sergeant on behalf of the whole station, and accompanied by a well-spoken and grateful little speech, in which he thanked us for all we had done and were doing. We shook hands with everybody we could reach, and those who were too shy to come inside shook hands through the window.

We all talked a great deal about the "*Entente Cordiale*" and "*Le Bonheur du Nouvel An*" and promised to be "*Alliés pour toujours*," and then the deputation departed. They have a special dinner again today, which includes *poulets* somewhere on its menu, and the government gift of a bottle of champagne to every four soldiers, an apple and orange, and two cigars each.

A good many old friends who had been sent some time ago to another station, turned up and called upon us; one came in the middle of lunch, so we invited him to join us; we had reached the stage of chocolate *soufflé*, *mocha* cake and coffee, all of which he enjoyed. He brought me two souvenirs from the battlefield in Champagne where he had been for a week on *ravitaillement* duty (carrying medicinal and other Red Cross necessaries to the field hospitals), a piece of shell from a *soixante-quinze* gun, and a piece of chalk in the shape of a tiny tombstone from the military cemetery of Vitry-le-Francois, on which he had carved his initials, the date, and the words "*Mort pour la Patrie*"; the whole thing was only an inch and a half high.

This man, Leopold Bourgeois, is delicate and probably dyspeptic; also possibly something of a "*malade imaginaire*" He always talked a great deal to us about his *estomac*, and once asked for some boiling water to wash it with—whether externally or internally he did not say! We often used to cook him an egg or give him barley soup on days when he had "*mal d'estomac*" He asked us today if we did not think he had got very thin since he had left here, and certainly he did seem to have become rather hollow below his chest. He smote himself gently in the *estomac*, and in the middle of his chocolate *soufflé* said quite calmly "You know I think I have a tapeworm (*solitaire*). I am always hungry and I eat, and eat, and eat, and I always get thinner."

Juliet said: "You look very well in your face; better than when you were here"; at which he looked rather disappointed, and said: "Ah! but *underneath* I am much thinner."

Afterwards, when the two girls had gone out, Bourgeot came in, and he and Bourgeois conversed very intimately, to my great edification, on the subject of the possible presence of a *solitaire* and how best to deal with it. They were both entirely without any false shame.

Jan. 4. Again today it is like summer. I have had no fire in my room for three days, and the temperature is 60°, even in the evening with the window wide open. Dorothy and I have been for a walk and found ordinary indoor winter clothes too hot: it was a relief, when the sun went behind a cloud. Yet in London they told us only strong people ought to come to Troyes because it was such a very cold place.

Jan. 10. The last two days we have had a new kind of train passing us, going east: always we have trainfuls of troops, largely, I believe, *permissionnaires* going home; but now it is trainfuls of young recruits, all still in civilian dress, going off to Verdun, where they are to receive their training—lads of seventeen, of the *dix-sept* class, cheering lustily as they pass our canteen, and waving their caps to us. How many of them will ever fight, I wonder? And what a strange place to choose for their training—Verdun, almost the first place in France to be attacked in this war, and the last place to be held by the German Army of Occupation in the war of 1870. At least these lads will learn to know the sound of guns.

Jan. 11. Yesterday afternoon we heard the guns plainly—so plainly that we almost thought it must be something else. But in today's paper is an account of a German attack in Champagne—an effort to take the Butte de Tahure from the French, which failed. That was what we heard.

Our castle of cards has fallen about our ears. Signs were not wanting that it was tottering; this morning it came down with a run. Perhaps the first sign was the lessening of work; the next was the rumour that the 2nd Army was going to leave Troyes; then the 19th Regiment left us, to whose colonel we owed our installation; next came rumours of the closing of the Evacuation Hospital. Then one morning we arrived to find the notice board of "*2me Armée*" on our canteen had been removed in the night! The 2nd Army had vanished, leaving no trace behind it except our soldier Bourgeot; and the 107th Regiment took the place of the 19th. New, unfamiliar, unsympathetic faces met us everywhere; the station, which had blossomed like the rose, became a desert. And then there came a sergeant and fetched our Bourgeot away.

And that was the beginning of the end. The semi-final stage was that the personnel of the station was reduced by one half, and the final scene took place this morning, when at my request Captain Weill came round to let us know what decision the *Commandant d'étape* had come to about our work. We are to shut it up, and the canteen is to be moved bodily away to another hospital where it is badly wanted, and where we are to follow it, or not, as the spirit moves us.

And in the meantime, after being untended for two days, and left

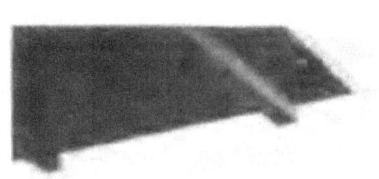

CLÉMENT (*LE DIABLE*) AND PAUL GODET.

to light our own fire, and scrub or leave unscrubbed our own floor, we are accorded the services of the dirtiest-looking man on the station, a shepherd of the name of Clément, but who is familiarly known to everyone as "*Le Diable.*" He is really a very nice man, and is perhaps not as dirty as he looks. He bounces into the canteen, uncouth and noisy, but willing; what he can fall over and knock into he does, and his voice is exactly like the barking of a dog, of his own sheep-dog. His other duties appear to be to wash up and fetch water for the cook and to be the butt of every other man on the station. His home occupation is that of a shepherd, and he has 450 sheep to tend. He is accustomed to work at all hours of the day and night, specially in lambing season, and he considers being a soldier is a very soft job. We think he has acquired a sheeplike face through long association with them.

The Troyens do not love their river, as we do ours; they look askance at it and have banished it outside, where once their walls stood, and have made in its place through the middle of their city a wide, perfectly straight canal, with a fine avenue of trees on each side and shady walks underneath. The disregarded Seine wanders and meanders around half the city; it loops and curves and curls and takes up as much room as it possibly can. It also divides itself up and probably joins its parts together again, out of pure perversity; so that if you walk along a mile of road you cross seven times over a river, and each time you ask a passer-by what river it is, to be told always it is the Seine. The Troyens adore bridges. Probably they have built canals for the pure pleasure of putting bridges over them, and they have certainly arranged their railway system on the same principle. If they can't get their canals to hold water, they just excavate ones that won't, and then throw a bridge across about every 100 yards. One is impelled to think that a Professor of Bridges lives at Troyes, and that his pupils build a bridge every term for practice.

The countryside, then, consists of canals and railway bridges, and the looping of the Seine. If anyone wanted a pleasant holiday, he might hire a boat at Troyes and row steadily down the river for about a week, sleeping every night in the city. He would never have far to walk.

On the 16th we left Troyes for Héricourt. Juliet and I nearly missed our train, as the taxi she had ordered never came, and she had to dash down to Troyes in the tram and pick up the first one she could find, and then go the whole mile back to fetch her luggage. It was abominably greasy, and we dashed along and ran down a considerable part of the French Army and slid round corners, only to meet with exasperating slowness in the military *bureau* where they laboriously wrote out our *ordres de transport*. We were so occupied in waving flags and handkerchiefs to the whole personnel of Quai Croncels as we passed through the station, and throwing out last souvenirs to them In the form of tins of cigarettes, that we nearly missed getting any *déjeuner*. The train certainly thought we were throwing bombs out of the window.

It was quite a change to have a meal we had not cooked for ourselves. It was a beautiful sunny day, and it was a pretty journey. As we neared Belfort it got colder, and snow lay lightly on the northern slopes; in the distance to the north we could see snow-clad ranges.

We had two hours to wait at Belfort, so proposed to go and see the town. But we met with considerable resistance from the uniformed person who kept guard at the exit of the station, because we had not got *sauf-conduits* for the town. I did my best with him: I pointed out that we were Red Cross (no good); that we were English (no good); that we were Allies (no good); that we were travelling with a *sauf-conduit* from Troyes to Héricourt, signed by the *commandant* himself! He began to waver here, so I pushed my advantage home. It would be so *ennuyant* at the station for two whole hours, and besides, we did so want some tea! He shrugged his shoulders, smiled, and waved us through the turnstile.

Troyes was of course in the "*zone des armées*" but Belfort is a yet inner shrine and is "*zone interdite*" There was nothing to do there except have tea at a shop of "*degustation*" and look at the fort which is forbidden ground, and watch an aeroplane which was circling overhead. The German Taubes are incessantly trying to come over Belfort, but they are chased away.

We arrived at Héricourt Station to find nothing but a platform, a station-house, and an ambulance. The ambulance kindly offered itself, and it and we and an *éclopé* rattled together over awful roads to the "*Hôtel deux Clefs*," which was expecting us. It was quite the most uncomfortable vehicle I have ever been in, worse even than the garden cart. If I were really *éclopée* or *blessée* I would prefer a wheelbarrow. The seats were very hard, and so high one's feet could hardly reach the ground.

Having left our luggage in the hotel, the ambulance took us on to the *Dépôt d'Eclopés*, where Miss Blaine has her canteen. The state of affairs was even worse than I had been told. Miss Blaine, the *directrice*, was in bed with severe tonsillitis; two of her party had gone home, and the other, Miss Graham, was valiantly running the canteen with the occasional help of a French lady. I found there was enough to do to keep all my party of four busy, so I decided to telegraph back to Troyes at once for Mrs. Sollas and D. Knowles.

They arrived on the evening of the 20th, and I am glad of them, as it is hard work for two. Juliet and I were alone today, as the other ladies have now given the canteen over to us. The routine is this: Arrive at 8.30, start making a dish for about twelve to twenty-four men; they vary in number every day. It may be a pudding, or a vegetable: we provide what we like. The oven is very bad, and what would take an hour to cook in England takes two or three here. In the meantime, the big marmites are heating, and we start to make coffee. By 11 the dish we have made, and hot milk, have to be ready for those men who are on a special *régime*; by 11.15 the whole lot come pouring out from their dinner to our canteen to be served with coffee—any number from 600 to 1,000. The doctor comes in every morning with a list of numbers, and signs the paper with the amount of tea, coffee, and sugar we are entitled to from the stores. The pouring out goes on as fast as we can pour till about 12.15, when it slacks off, and we can lay the table for lunch and eat what we can find time for: the men keep on coming, and sometimes we recognise the same man two or three times.

Almost immediately the afternoon dishes have to be made—two for the evening meal—and the water started heating for tea. Tea begins to be served from 2.30, and the great rush is from 3 to 4, when again it slacks off, and we can get our own. Then at 4.45 hot milk has to be ready for the *petite régime* when the *infirmiers* come in for the dishes. We may always go with our "*plats*" if we like and see the men eat them, and one can note which "*plat*" they seem to like best. If they like it very much there is an awful scuffle to get their tin dish handed up quick for more. I love going up and seeing the soldiers at their meals, and we go into the infirmary, too, when we like. The sorts of dishes we make are simple: rice, semolina, and sago puddings, lemon pudding, bread and butter pudding, apple and bread crumbs, stewed apples, prunes, cut up oranges, custard, etc.; also buttered eggs, poached eggs, *purée* of potatoes, cauliflower *au gratin*, cheese macaroni, etc., etc. Our dishes are supplementary; they do not form the whole meal, though certainly the larger half of it.

After their evening "*soupe*" at 5 the men are apt to try and sneak in again and get final cups of tea, but there is usually a sergeant about who comes to us and asks us to shut, so we murmur, "Captain's orders,

The canteen at Héricourt

il est défendu," and reluctantly shut down our shutters and turn the light out. The men may not drink the water; it is not "*potable*": so they only get the drinks we give them and two "quarts" of wine a day. A "quart" is a quarter litre.

    D. Knowles applied to the *maire* for a *laissez-passer* to Belfort, and I went with her to help in case she got stuck. He made her pass out for her, and wrote down a description of her appearance, after a careful study of her features, instead of copying it out of her passport, as he had done in my case. Afterwards we tried to read what he had put, and found his writing almost indecipherable. Her hair appeared to be "chat," her complexion "drab," her height 167 feet, and her forehead we could make nothing of. So I appealed to the little Alsatian maid, Odile, to read the word for us. She looked at it, stammered, and blushed so furiously, but refused to say what it was, that we thought it must be something dreadful, like idiotic, or senile, or wanting; and we searched the dictionary in vain for a clue. Dorothy wanted to go back to the *maire* and ask him. But we found out in the end that the word was "*découvert*," and we found out also that the reason why Odile blushed and refused to speak was that she could neither read nor write! And she was born and brought up in German Alsace! What about *Kultur*?

    It was a week later that we went a beautiful walk up one of the hills that is crowned by an outlying fort of Belfort. The view was magnificent, and we thought we could see the Hartmansweilerkopf. The wind was east, and the guns were continuous, and sounded rather louder than usual. It was as warm as May. At the top we found quantities of spring squill flowering among the dead leaves, also stinking hellebore and sweet daphne. Last Sunday a German aeroplane came over Héricourt, and the shots from the French guns bursting near it could be plainly seen.

    I have offered a prize of a scarf to the first soldier who brings us a violet from the woods. We have found already oxlips, periwinkles, and coltsfoot and daphne, and the fields near the station are starred with daisies.

    For two whole days all the men have been "C.B." or "*Consignés*." They have told us so each day at coffee with very long faces, and every evening when we go home, and are let out of the barracks by the guard, we are followed by the wistful eyes of half the depot, who stand with their faces pressed against the bars of the great gates, like animals at the Zoo—deprived of their liberty. It seems that they have been slow and unpunctual and slovenly, and the captain got into a rage and docked them of half their wine and all their liberty. The result was they drank more tea and coffee than usual, so *we* had to work harder!

We hear that on the 27th, the *Kaiser's* birthday, the Germans tried to break through the French lines at Delle, the frontier town between France and Switzerland; and failed, fortunately for us, as Delle is not many miles away. The flare lights of the attack could be seen from here between 6 and p.m. I think the French must be retaliating, as the rumble of the guns has been continuous the last two afternoons.

On a perfect cloudless morning in early February Dorothy and I started off at 8.30 up the hills with two and a half hours in hand before we need be at the canteen. There was hoar frost on the ground, but the sun was well up, and by the time we had reached the woodmen's hut we were glad to leave our coats in their charge and finish the climb without them.

Thin, delicate mist filled the valleys, and shrouded Héricourt at our feet; but the hilltops rose clearly silhouetted against a pale blue sky. The larks would have been singing in England, but in France they shoot their larks and eat them in little pies, so even the woods were empty and still, except for the occasional screech of a magpie and the occasional hum of a bee visiting the catkins for pollen.

Near the crest we picked bunches of blue scilla, which was flowering freely among the dead leaves, and at the top the first violet. Violets and wild daphne growing up against the most murderous wire entanglements you can possibly imagine! How could the violet choose such company? But it had its back to them, and its little face was turned to the sun and the woods—perhaps it was unconscious of their proximity, and did not even hear the drone of the guns going on almost without ceasing. To the pure all things are pure, and perhaps the guns sounded to it like the distant humming of bees.

Dorothy said, "I want to go to the very top." Now the top is crowned by the fort, and I did not suppose we should be allowed close to it, as the ground is marked "*Terrain militaire; interdit au public.*" So when we met two soldiers we expected to be turned back at once, but it is always a good plan if you expect an attack to hurriedly attack first and so upset their strategy. I therefore asked if we might go on any farther, as we particularly wanted to see the view on the other side—it was in fact what we had come up for. The one soldier said, "It is *very* irregular," and looked extremely shocked; the other, who was probably a lieutenant, offered to accompany us and show us where we might go. We accepted his offer gladly, and . . . he took us all over the fort!

We saw the great deep moat that separated the inner fort from the outer, and from the inside we saw the guns that were fixed so as to rake every spot of it in case the enemy *did* set foot in it. We were conducted through long dim passages with iron doors at each end, lighted and aired by electricity. We were taken down a never-ending stairway to remote bombproof regions below, where there was a bakery and a butchery, enough stores to last three years, a huge room 300 metres long, furnished with two tiers of iron bedsteads, enough to lodge 800 men, and lighted by electric light, and warmed by stoves and aired by electric fans and huge pipes carrying fresh air from above. When we emerged again to the surface up a series of sloping tunnels we were shown the guns, with their piles of ammunition waiting ready, then the telephone and telegraph rooms, the guard-room, the prison, and finally we scrambled right up to the very top where our lieutenant pointed out to us the principal landmarks, and the other forts which ring Belfort round, and are all in communication with each other, and with the one we were on.

The place is absolutely deserted, but it could be very quickly manned, and would be, of course, if the Germans were ever to break through the French lines. Till then the troops are wanted elsewhere. We also learned how in the 1870-1 war a battle had raged in the valleys round Héricourt (January 26, 1871) and how Belfort had capitulated to the Germans. Above the station are still to be seen the emplacements the enemy made for their cannon.

Feb. 8. Yesterday at 3 I was in Belfort for the afternoon, having to go to the bank and do some shopping. Today at 3 the Germans began bombarding Belfort with high explosive shells from an Austrian 42 cm. howitzer. I did not hear the first shell, but al 5.15 I was walking home along the Faubourg Montbéliard when I heard a tremendous bang. I thought it must be an aeroplane being fired at, but could see no sign of one; then I met an excited group of people and asked them if they knew what it was. Belfort is about eleven kilometres distant.

It was just a chance that I went to Belfort yesterday and not today. It happened that the men at the depot had been behaving very badly, staying out late, and going into the town after hours, among other enormities, so the captain cut them off, not only their wine, but their tea and coffee as well. At 11 he came to the canteen and ordered us to close our doors! This practically gave us a holiday, except for some cooking, so I chose the opportunity of an afternoon in Belfort.

Already when I got back to the hotel some refugees had arrived, including a young woman who had walked over, wheeling her baby in a perambulator.

It was not till I had to lie in bed for several days in the grip of *"la grippe"* at the "pub" where we live on the main street of Héricourt, that I learnt what the noise could be in a village inn, in war time, on a main road not far from the front. I had never spent any part of the day in Héricourt before, as our canteen lies a mile out on a country road.

Out of doors there was, just those few days, February 11 to 16, an almost incessant passing by of troops, going to reinforce the front in the neighbourhood of Delle, where the Germans had begun an attack. Regiment after regiment passed by, with the usual accompaniment of army carts, field kitchens, guns, ammunition, Red Cross motors, and so on. A special lot of new motor vans, with R.V.F.[4] painted on their green canvas covers, took a whole morning to go by. And a convoy of new cars, some hundreds, all marked with an English name, took the better part of a day. They were all Fords, and went comparatively quietly. The road under my window had just been newly metalled before I retired to bed, but had not been rolled in. My windows look on a side street, which comes down a fairly steep street from Lure and Vesoul, over the Vosges: convoys are very apt to stop just outside before turning into the main street, and motors going the other way also change their gears just beneath my window.

All this, however, is beyond and above the ordinary every-day noises. About 5 a.m. the sirens and bells begin to clamour for the early workman, and he himself, in considerable numbers, accompanied by his sisters and daughters, tramps past shortly afterwards. The church bells ring at short intervals for services, and two clocks chime each quarter of an hour, one doing it twice over. The clocks are about five minutes apart, so that for really a considerable part of the twenty-four hours one can listen to bells and clocks.

The life of the inn begins at an early hour—sometimes shortly after midnight, when belated or lost soldiers hammer at doors or windows and clamour for food or drink or beds. But usually 6 is the hour when life stirs again. Through the drowsiness of early morning one is conscious of banging of doors, opening of windows, rattling of milk vans and bakers' carts; of weird noises connected with shutters

---

4. *Ravitaillement de Viande Froide.*

being rolled up; of teacups and saucers; of *monsieur's* rich bass voice rolling about below like a barrel of old wine; of coffee being ground; of much violent banging and chopping going on in the kitchen. I have come to the conclusion that all French food is prepared for the table either by being repeatedly banged with the flat of a hatchet, or by being chopped into mincemeat. These two processes continue for hours before both *déjeuner* and *diner*. The strident voices of Madame and Mademoiselle Marguerite fill any gaps there may be by calling for either "Odile" or "Rose," neither of whom ever seem to be there, and a shrill canary trills above everything else.

The schoolchildren clatter into school, or clatter out again, in wooden *sabots*: the front door bell, specially on market days, jingles constantly, and officers, soldiers, workmen, market women, stump in and out with their *sabots* on the flagged passages and converse in loud and shrill voices. A despatch-rider on a motor bicycle flashes through the town, warning all and sundry of his approach by a raucous horn, and at intervals a ridiculous train, incessantly tooting a sort of foghorn, meanders down the street.

One of the days I was ill we had a really heavy gale, and above the howling and shrieking of the wind and the lashing of rain against the windows, shutters flapped and banged all down the street, or were wrenched off their hinges and dashed against walls; chimney-pots came down with sundry crashes, and sheds and leanto's were lifted up and blown bodily away. When there might otherwise be an occasional moment of peace, the maids shut themselves in next door to me and turn a mangle for an hour or two; or they turn out the contents of a bedroom into the passage and bang everything with sticks to get the dust out; or it is *déjeuner* and the *élite* of Héricourt, including a good many officers, come in and lunch just under me and spend most of the meal scraping their chairs.

If it isn't one thing it is another. We have several times had soldiers come to the canteen who have been in English hospitals at Le Tréport, Dieppe, and so on, and who speak in the highest terms of them. "*Nous étions bien soignés, en effet,*" they say; "*très, très bien soignés; c'était un vrai paradis, l'hôpital*"—which is very pleasant hearing. And they generally want to shake hands with us because we remind them of their nurses.

Yesterday a procession passed through Héricourt and on past our barracks which lasted all through the afternoon and on into the dark. It was the 98th and 99th Regiments, with all their travelling paraphernalia—army carts, supply-waggons, ammunition-waggons, gun-carriages, ambulances, field-kitchens cooking as they went, and leaving the odours of the next meal behind them. The men march for fifty minutes, and rest for ten, but as the roads were ankle-deep in melting slush, they could but stand still when the rest time came. They looked a very determined, dour, serious set of men, hardly any young ones among them.

We stood out in the snow, catching chilblains and colds, for a long time, watching them go by, and wishing we could give them all hot coffee. Mrs. Sollas ran about among them and distributed acid-drops to all she could reach. She has had 250 lbs. sent out by Prof. Sollas!

When we started home at about 6, another halt was going on, and endless Red Cross ambulances were drawn up head to tail. As we passed one we heard English voices, and of course stopped to remark into the dark hood, "Oh, how nice to hear English spoken!" They turned out to be English Red Cross volunteers serving with the French army, and they had come from Rougemont through Belfort. They did not know in the least where they were going, so we were able to inform them that they were going to Seppois and Delle to reinforce the lines where the Germans were attacking violently. So, at least, our captain had told us.

Early the next morning these boys were to be seen still in Héricourt. They had got on as far as Montbéliard, but had been unable to find beds, so had returned here on the chance. They were very cheerful as they fared forth again into the unknown upon roads sodden with melting snow and water.

Coming back from a walk at dusk I met a workman who civilly called out *"Bonsoir, ma soeur"* as he passed. Then he stopped to ask me which hospital I was working at and if I came from a distance. When I said *"Je suis anglaise "*he beamed all over, and said "Will you shake hands with me for the sake of the *Entente Cordiale?"* We pump-handled cordially for quite a long time. He told me he had three boys in the trenches; they had been there since the beginning of the war, and none had been wounded. He asked me if England was as beautiful as France, and when I said "Yes," he hoped it would never be invaded or injured by the Boches. An aeroplane circled over the fort while we talked, but it must have been French, as it was not fired at. Yet I certainly heard the sound of machine-guns from Belfort while I was on Mont Vaudois.

Madame said to me tonight: "If you hear guns in the night, don't be frightened; we are going to attack the Germans, probably near Belfort." I suppose that is to draw troops off Verdun and Seppois, both of which are being attacked. The news from Verdun is better tonight. An officer who was at dinner told us that all the guns had been taken out of the fort at Douaumont long before the Germans got into it; they found nothing there. I gathered the guns were on rails, or were movable in some way. It is pleasant to be everywhere saluted in the neighbourhood. Even the tiny boys salute or take off their caps, and all the children say "*Bon jour, ma soeur,*" or "*Ma mère.*" All the peasants confide their doleful stories to one, often in such bad Alsatian French or German that one can hardly understand.

Horrible stories all of them:—An old grandmother injured by an explosive shell who had to have both legs amputated above the knee. A young soldier, not long married, whose arm was cut off at the shoulder, and his silly, hysterical young wife refused to see him when he came home because she was afraid of the disfigurement. A young woman, hourly expecting her baby to be born, took refuge in a church in an invaded village in France; shells fell into it and she was badly injured, both her legs being broken. The German soldiers refused to allow anyone to go to help her for two days, even to give her water. Finally, an officer, less brutal than the rest, had her carried away to a German hospital. No more is known of her.

Odile, our handmaid, has a brother, who, being an Alsatian, has been swept into the German Army, though he is at heart a Frenchman. As the Alsatians are not to be trusted to fight on the Western front the regiment he is in has been sent to fight against Russia; she has had no news of him for many months. Her father was ill six months ago, but she was unable to get into Alsace, and he died without her seeing him.

A *curé* from Paris has lately been staying at the inn. He was sent for to the "*Hôpital Temporaire,*" where his only brother was dying from a wound received in the fighting near Delle. Day and night he remained with him to the end. Two days later the funeral procession passed me as I was on my way to the canteen in the early morning. The *curé* walked alone as chief mourner; and indeed, except for the personnel of the hospital, as only mourner, for his brother had been his only relation; and the two, men of forty-five and forty-eight, had lived together in Paris.

Every soldier who dies at the military hospital is followed to the grave by such patients as are able and willing to walk; by all the school children of Héricourt, both girls and boys, with their teachers; and by some of the nurses and orderlies. It must take a good deal of the time of these latter, as there are, alas, many "*poilus*" who have fought the good fight, and have finished their work for France. As the processions wend their way through the town, and up the steep hill to the church, the followers are greatly increased in number by the townspeople, and the little church is nearly full for the last service for the dead.

The *curé* was sitting alone in the bar when I returned to the hotel, and I tried to get the poor forlorn-looking creature into conversation. He responded courteously, but not effusively, so I left him to himself. He left the same evening, a *marquis-chauffeur*, who dines here often, motoring him into Montbéliard to catch the Paris train. Even now his troubles were not over: the ambulance he drove in caught fire in some way, and the poor priest, interned at the back, was heard to scream, "Let me out, let me out. I am on fire." It was difficult to extricate him quickly, as he was stout. The rest of the journey had to be performed in total darkness, as for some reason the *marquis* was afraid to light his lamps: the petrol had ignited, I think. It was a pitch-dark night, and they had simply to feel their way along.

March 3. It is nearly a month since I first went into Belfort to get some money from the Crédit Lyonnais, and the very next day the bombardment began. They were to send me some money as soon as they received it from London, but I have not heard from them since. I wrote to them a week ago, but have had still no reply. Last night I went to the *maire* to get a *laissez-passer* for Belfort, in order to go to the bank myself, but the *maire* told me that since March 1 there were new regulations, and I must write to the *général-gouverneur* for a permit, stating my reason for wishing to go, which I did the same evening. For all I know, the Crédit Lyonnais may be blown sky-high, and then where do I come in?

This evening I had to go to the *maire* to get a telegram *visé*, and he asked me had I written to the *gouverneur* of Belfort?

"Yes," I said; "I wrote last night."

"Let me see, *Jeudi, Vendredi, Samedi, Dimanche*; you may get an answer on Monday."

"As soon as that?" said I, trying to look surprised. (Belfort is seven miles away.)

"Yes," he replied, quite seriously. (Officials never *can* understand sarcasm or exaggeration.) "You may hear on Monday, and he may tell you the Crédit Lyonnais is shut, and has moved to Montbéliard."

"Oh, and in that case can you give me a *laissez-passer* to Montbéliard?"

"Oh, yes, we can do that in this office."

"And are there any trains?" I asked.

"If military necessities permit, there is a train at 5.30." (a.m.).

"Oh, thank you," I murmured.

"And another at 11.30," he continued.

"That would do nicely," said I. "And how about coming back?" (Montbéliard is six miles off.)

"There is a train back at 7.30 in the evening."

"Oh, indeed," I remarked. "And what would I do in Montbéliard for eight hours?"

He looked rather blank and pulled his moustache, and seemed to consider a little. Then he brightened, and said with conviction: "*Que voulez-vous, Madame? C'est la guerre. La guerre ne s'arrange pas pour les civils.*"

Very true.

As a matter of fact it took exactly six days to get the answer from the governor of Belfort, and then the *laissez-passer* was for one day only, the 10th.

The next time I asked for a *laissez-passer* it took ten days to get the answer, and then it was for three days later than the day I had mentioned. Suppose it had been an appointment at a dentist's—or, say, one's wedding?

Here is a letter we received at the canteen from one of our *poilus*.

Mes très chères dames,

Quoique n'étant qu'un tout petit soldat de cette guerre mondiale, je ne peux pas laisser passer de telles preuves nouvelles de nos alliés d'outre mer, sans venir moi aussi vous prouver toute ma reconnaissance, et mon admiration, pour tout ce que vous témoignez de dévouement aux soldats de la vieille France.

Notre coeur serait trop ingrat de ne pas être touché de tant de bonté, et d'abnégation, qui seront surement le prix de la victoire des alliés.

Très chères mesdames, je peux vous assurer, que la mission que vous avez enterprise, et que vous menez avec tant de zèle, a été, parmi nous petits pioupious, un encouragement considérable, et une nouvelle confiance qui nous rend plus forts à l'heure de danger.

Comment voulez-vous ne pas vaincre le pirate commun, lorsque de puissants peuples, comme l'Angleterre et la France, en un mot tous les peuples alliés, oublient tout le passé, sacrifient tout leur être en commun, leur avoir aussi, et qui, maître d'une patience et d'une volonté insurmontable, luttent pour un droit, et une justice, qui ne doit, et ne peut, aboutir qu'à la victoire?

Oui, mesdames, oui, nous y croyons tous, tous, à cette victoire, à la démonstration des cruels empires du centre; et comment serait il possible d'en croire autrement alors que si près de l'ennemi on a une confiance qui a tué tous les sentiments sauf celui de la joie, par l'accomplissement du devoir, combien de fois a-t-il pensé d'être malheureux, le soldat? Jamais si parfois, il a un moment de tristesse, tout est guéri par la seule idée qu'il se fait d'en avoir eu davantage, serait il malade il dira 'Ah ce n'est rien, j'ai été plus malade, mon camarade qui est tombé devant l'ennemi, a souffert davantage, et le voilà consolé à tel point qu'il ne se sent plus souffrir, ni fatigué, et ne pense pas même aux mauvais jours des demains.'

Seules, quelques idées sombres viennent troubler la pensée du brave bibi; un père infirme, qui se trouve encore dans la terre sacrée du domaine pour qui le poilu se bat; une mère qui pleure les malheurs de ses pauvres petits, et fait son possible pour boucher le point d'une chaussette commencée depuis des mois, et que la pauvre martyre n'a pu achever encore; enfin le souvenir de deux frères, l'un tombé glorieusement dans un assaut, l'autre, qui dans une tranchée, comme lui, attend l'attaque prochaine, tout à coup, un essai de l'âme tire le petit soldat de son rêve, et dans un élan suprème, il machonne en syllabes incompréensibles, 'Vive la patrie, vive la France, vive l'Angleterre, vive les allies.'

Antoine Rigal, poilu,
81e de ligne 34e comp. de bataillon,
Secteur postal 161.

Mrs. Huntington and I got back to the inn last night, covered with snow, and freezing cold. We sat down in the bar by the stove to dry and unfreeze. In the bar were Monsieur Roth, at his desk, Madame Roth, and Mademoiselle Marguerite; the Marquis de ——, who is the chauffeur of an ambulance; a *commis voyageur*, having a glass of wine, and one or two *poilus*. The *marquis* was having tea *à l'Anglaise*. We discussed everything in the world—French dinners, English breakfasts, bacon, Boches, religion and politics, and the new law for cutting off beards in the army. France is republican by nature as well as by name: everybody is on an absolute equality, and there seems to be absolutely

Entrance to the Artillery Barracks.

no consciousness of difference of rank or station. After a while Odile, the little Alsatian maid, came in, and the *marquis* got up and placed a chair for her, and she joined our circle and our conversation.

This morning I brought my writing into the bar, where I found an acquaintance, an ambulance driver, who had just come in for his coffee, having been out all night in and round Belfort. He spent nearly an hour expatiating on the war—in a large sense. He is evidently a Catholic, and a religious man. His views are interesting, and I will record a few of them. He believes that God (*le bon Dieu*, he always calls Him) has willed this war as a punishment to the nations, but specially to France, for their atheism and materialism. That the war must go on for a long time, because none of them (again specially France) are yet punished enough; they have not suffered yet sufficiently. He thinks that all the fighting countries will be ruined in the end, and that out of the ruin purer and better and simpler lives will be built. He loathes the Serbs, and despises them: he calls them treacherous, cunning, deceitful, full of all evil. I asked him would he not concede they were brave and patriotic?—to which he replied, Yes, but so were all the other nations.

He says there have been of late three great diplomatists: King Edward VII., Leopold II. of Belgium, and Ferdinand of Bulgaria. Then he lamented the loss of the monarchy in France, principally, I think, because it gives a peg to hang loyalty on. "What are the French fighting for? a president, or a minister, who can leave his job whenever he likes, and nobody even remembers his name? Liberty? We have no liberty. Where is liberty in this country, when a dying soldier in a hospital may not have the priest in to shrive his soul?" He marched up and down the room all the time, and in moments of excitement his voice rose almost to a squeak, broke, and disappeared. He went off after his coffee, and only got back at about 9, frozen stiff; he had bread and cheese and coffee, and departed again into the bitter night.

"Alas!" he said, as he struggled into his third or fourth layer of leather coat, "there will be many '*pieds gelés*' after this."

The following afternoon we had a tea party: the horse captain, M. de Chanay, and his lieutenant, M. de Marne, came by invitation, and shared a beautiful English cake that Mrs. Sollas' cook had sent her out, iced, almonded, decorated like a wedding cake.

We had a nice boy in today who had been with the English troops in the trenches at (or near) Dunkirk. He could not say enough in praise of them. "*Il sont bons camarades, ma foi, bons enfants, toujours gais.*"

According to him the Tommies were perfection; they never grumbled, were generous to a fault, gave away everything they had.

"What did they give you?" we asked.

"Cigarettes, *oh, la, la, confiture; oh, la, la, la, tabac, gâteaux, chocolat, bonbons; oh, la, la! et nous causions tout le temps vite, vite, moi je parlais français, eux ils parlaient anglais, mais n'importe, et nous parlions sans mots, avec les mains, avec les yeux, avec la bouche. Oh, la, la, de bons camarades!*"

Some went home on leave while he was there, and they all came back from home loaded up, hung round, with presents of all sorts, and everything was divided up and given away with impartial generosity to French and English alike.

The guns have been louder and more continuous than we have ever known them. We stood in the snow in the barrack yard and listened, while five aeroplanes scouted overhead, and could hardly tear ourselves away.

March 10. This morning I went in to the Crédit Lyonnais at Belfort in an ambulance: I took a lot of trouble in getting a *laissez-passer* from the *general-gouverneur* of Belfort, and then it was never asked for, though we twice entered and left the town. The *marquis* would have taken me in, but yesterday he brought an infectious case back to Héricourt, and his car was spending the day being disinfected.

The Crédit Lyonnais had removed itself since the bombardment into a village to the north of Belfort, where, after much searching and many inquiries, we found it established in a school with a personnel of three—a sort of director with two schoolboys under him. They were thrown into a perfect panic by the presentation of English cheques, and made me write all sorts of things upon them, which I am sure will render them invalid in England. However, I have got the money, and the production of it evidently taxed their resources to the utmost.

I saw a Taube being fired at this morning by the Belfort guns; at least, it is incorrect to say I saw it—it was too high; but the air round was full of little tufts of what looked like cotton-wool. I am afraid it was not hit. A great aeroplane came soaring up from near where I was waiting for my chauffeur at the *Hôpital d'Evacuation.*

March 16. Last night Mrs. Huntington and I drove into Montbéliard with Juliet to see her off by the Paris train. The trains *via* Belfort are "*supprimés*" at present, on account of the Verdun battle, so she has to go *via* Dijon. The *hôpital temporaire* lent us an ambulance and an escort: Mrs. H. and I got leave to go too, as we wanted a drive. The escort consisted of the chauffeur, a "Russian bear," and two orderlies. Juliet insisted on sitting in front in the "Russian bear's" place by the driver, so he had to come inside, and it was all he could do to squeeze his vast furry overcoat through the opening. It was a wonderful, still, brilliant moonlight night, as warm as summer: the beautiful Vosges country of unhedged green fields and wooded crests and slopes lay serene and peaceful and bathed in moonlight, as if such a thing as war had never been known. Yet only a few folds of the hills away the guns were growling and snapping at each other, and men were being killed and mutilated.

An officer came out as we passed the barracks and crowded himself in with us, and we were rather glad of him when we got to Montbéliard, and the sentry came out to examine us, as neither Mrs. H. nor I had troubled to get a *laissez-passer*, and you can't go in or out of any town in the war zone without one. We therefore retired into the innermost darkness of the ambulance, and the officer and the "Russian bear" blotted us out from the sentry's view.

Coming back our driver lost his way. He had only come from Alsace two days ago, and I fancy was not accustomed to this particular make of car, judging from the noises and smells he caused it to emit. He chose to attempt to turn it round on a very narrow road, bordered on each side by sloping, squelchy, marshy grass, and, having managed to get it at right angles to the road, could not move it for love or money. We all got out, and the orderlies and the "Russian bear" applied themselves to pull and push and tug and shove—to do everything except swear. I have never yet heard a French soldier use a bad word. They were so polite, and so sorry and so apprehensive for our comfort, so we got in and sat down, while they tried fresh combinations of handles and levers and plugs and gears. We had had an excellent dinner (soup, sardines, omelette, *vo-au-vent*, French beans, beefsteak, dessert), and we had the hotel key with us, so we said we would as soon stay there all night as not.

However, we did not have to. Some chance movement on the driver's part started the machinery, and we suddenly plunged forward; and, to an accompaniment of quite new varieties of noises and fresh smells of burning and frying, we regained the main road and were taken back in safety to our hotel.

March 18. This evening at 7 another *obus* fell in Belfort. The whole population of Héricourt immediately thronged into the street, and we waited almost in silence for the next. It came in five minutes, and then no more. We waited for some time, but finally decided that, even though Belfort was being bombarded, we might as well dine, as—who knew?—it might be our turn next; and as *Monsieur* had thought it his duty to go back to his kitchen and dish up the dinner, it was clearly our duty to go in and eat it.

The first shell, I was told afterwards, fell in the middle of a garage and blew into little pieces three Red Cross ambulances which were stabled there. Two others just entering the yard at the moment were untouched and their drivers uninjured. The next fell into the Escompte National, and I felt quite glad that *my* bank, the Crédit Lyonnais, had had the wisdom to move into the country with the £5 I have lent it. The third shell did not burst at all.

Général Joffre and President Poincare were both in Belfort at the time, and one bomb fell very near the house they were in.

Early in the morning of the 20th the little family of twenty-five Ford ambulances departed for the front. But, alas, they no longer numbered twenty-five—there were three poor chauffeurs who had no cars, for three had been blown to pieces at Belfort. So only twenty-two set out this morning. We are to have twenty-five others, I am told. I think the chauffeurs have been learning to drive and repair them, and that is why they have been here all these weeks.

Ten days ago we had a day and night of heavy rain, which swept most of the snow away, and for the last week we have had weather like summer. Less than a week ago I went up Mont Vaudois, and found the ground carpeted with *scilla bifolia*, almost as blue as our English bluebell woods: here and there an anemone or an oxlip. Today, six days later, there is not a *scilla* to be seen, but the ground is thickly starred with white anemones, and there are great clumps of oxlips, rows of lungwort along the dry ditches, and little groups of fumitory, ranging from crimson to white through every shade of pink and lilac. The woods seemed to be almost Swiss in their rapid transformation of dress. Ten days ago the whole countryside was deep in snow.

An officer called out through our window, "May I tell my dog to jump in here?"

"Surely," I replied.

So he told him to, and a great *chien de loup* was silhouetted in the window frame, and the next moment was on our counter, which he had taken in his stride, all among our flowers and coffee-glasses and papers and ink-bottles. The officer told us that one day the dog had

DISTRIBUTING CIGARETTES TO TROOPS.

pursued a cat into a pastry-cook's shop, and had succeeded in doing nine *francs'* worth of damage.

"An expensive dog to keep," I remarked.

"Yes," he said; "but as he and I ate all the damaged cakes between us, it was not as bad as it sounds."

This officer was in the garage at Belfort on the evening when the bomb fell: he said the colours of the flames that burst from it were most beautiful—blues, purples, pinks and violets.

Yesterday morning we were startled by a sudden explosion close to our kitchen. A fool of a soldier, who had come in wounded to the hospital, had brought a souvenir from the trenches in his kit in the form of an unexploded grenade. One of the chauffeurs had handled it or let it drop, and it exploded and wounded him badly in the face.

The master of Fuchs, the *chien de loup*, insisted on photographing us this morning. I begged him to do one of Captain Blanc for me, as I had not got any of him, but the captain refused to be penalised unless we were in the group too. The captain came in a little while ago to ask if we had the *Commandant d'étape* concealed on our premises, because he had mislaid him. He apparently was on a visit of inspection to the depot, and the captain was supposed to be trotting him round—I do not know if he was ever found. The master of Fuchs is a most exquisite photographer; he showed me some snow scenes he had taken in Alsace that I have never seen surpassed. He has been in the trenches since the beginning of the war, but had a severe chill and laryngitis: his laryngitis has become chronic, and he has been sent back to the depot as an *éclopé*, and is in charge of the ambulance department next door. We like him very much, and have been treating him as a boy. I guessed his age today at twenty-three; and he is thirty-five, with a daughter nearly as tall as himself!

In answer to Antoine Rigal's letter Mrs. Sollas sent him a tin of sweets. Here is the response:

Mes très chères dames,

J'ai reçu il y a deux heures et votre lettre et votre magnifique cadeau.

"Oh, Madame, vraiment, c'est trop de gâterie et de bonté, je m'empresse de vous offrir en deux mots toute ma sympathie et ma reconnaissance.

J'ai fait part à mes camarades de vos bonnes actions et de vos délicieux bonbons, ils vous envoyent d'ici toutes leurs sincères bonjours et leurs félicitations.

En un mot recevez de nous tous, jeunes soldats de la France, toute la reconnaissance qui vous est due, et que nous ne pourrons jamais assez vous témoigner.

De tout son coeur, de la part de ses camarades et pour votre dévouement, merci de votre bon coeur.

Celui qui se signe votre tout devoué et reconnaissant

Rigal, Antoine.

April 4. I think rumours of war are quite as interesting as wars themselves. All sorts of rumours go about here, and we never know what is true. There has been a general belief that the crown prince is at Mülhausen and is preparing an offensive against Belfort, as Verdun has proved a failure. Others believe that the French will not wait to be attacked, but are themselves preparing an offensive. Certainly there are great movements of troops, etc., going on. I was in Belfort today (having sneaked in in an ambulance, as the governor took no notice of my request for a *laissez-passer*), and saw miles of helmeted men going off towards the north, and other miles of artillery coming in: Héricourt is simply packed as full as it will hold of troops, carts, horses, etc. Every open gateway reveals rows of horses tethered to something or other and eating hay; the square is densely packed with covered supply waggons; every yard, open space, and back street is the temporary home of ambulances, motors, tumbrils and lorries, and the streets are so full of bluecoats one can hardly get along. There is a general feeling of expectancy and of confidence. Mrs. Huntington's "nephew," a nice young chauffeur who drives a doctor about, and who lives in a beautiful *château* in Versailles, whispered as he passed us at dinner tonight, "I don't think it will be more than a fortnight before you will hear of great events."

The last four or five days a new kind of gun has made itself evident—very loud, and apparently nearer, but I believe not nearer actually. You can feel it shake the ground; even in our kitchen we can feel the reverberation through all the noise of talking, putting coals on the fire, and the feverish activity of Lavet, the substitute for Thomas, who is away on "*permission*" We are told it is a new French gun—larger than any they had before, and of greater carrying power. We had feared for a time it was German shells bursting at Belfort. An aeroplane came down, or was brought down, three days ago near Héricourt. Both the occupants were wounded—one in his head; the other had an arm broken. They were removed to Belfort in an ambulance, and the *éclopé* aeroplane followed them through Héricourt on a motor lorry.

Our new orderly, Lavet, gets through his work at tremendous speed, washing up and cleaning with a will, and with a noise, in order to have time to read. I have never seen anybody read so fast. The moment he has finished his job he is to be seen sitting on a packing-case covered with a sack, his elbows on the table, buried in his book. I do my best to supply him with decent literature. There is only one thing that will take him from his reading, apart from his work, and that is the gramophone. The moment that begins he runs to it like a needle to the magnet. He is a nice lad, and I fear will soon leave us, as he has nearly recovered from his injury: a shell burst near him and wounded one side of his face, and when it was nearly well eczema broke out on it.

Here is another example of the rapid change in the wild flowers here. A fortnight ago a certain clearing close to the fort was covered with oxlips, and a delicate large fumitory that grows about a foot high, and white anemones. Today all have vanished except a few anemones, which meantime have turned pink, and will also vanish in a few days. Instead the place is a lush thicket of a tall crimson vetchling and Solomon's Seal, and among them incredibly large plants of incredibly large dog violets. The fields, too, where a few days ago only daisies could be seen, are now covered with cowslips, with stalks eight inches long, and purple orchis.

Two soldiers came into the canteen: one leaned confidentially across the counter and whispered persuasively, "Haven't you a little rum?"

"I'm afraid not. It's not allowed here."

"Just a little," he pleaded, holding up two fingers to show how much. "I can't sleep without rum. Why, I woke three times last night because I hadn't had any. This depot is a poor place."

"Rum tomorrow," I said, "and rum yesterday, but never rum today."

He liked the joke immensely and promised to come every tomorrow for it. The other man chimed in "*Mais non*—this is not a bad place. I had a good bed last night, with sheets. Why, I have seen neither bed nor sheets for twenty months."

I left Héricourt, with great regret, on April 9 in an ambulance, just as I arrived there three months ago. The driver did not spare his petrol, and I was thankful I was not a *blessé* returning from the front as we leapt and bounded and plunged over the appalling road that runs between Héricourt and Montbéliard. There is no available labour to

Returning to the Front.

mend the roads, and it is a wonder they are not worse. The very worst holes do get filled up after a time.

The train was so crowded that for a little while a French lady and a soldier and I had to stand in the corridor till the guard came along and unlocked an empty carriage marked "*Réservé.*" So we each got a corner. But the soldier lay at full length and immediately snored, and there were times in the night when after violent stretching and plunging in his sleep his head landed in my lap and rolled about there. I thought perhaps he had come from the trenches, and this was comfort! he was "*en permission*" The little French lady became confidential: she sat opposite me and shared my rug and coat. She told me she was on her way back from her honeymoon; she had gone to meet her *fiancé* at some tiny place near Belfort, and had had great difficulty in getting there, having to travel by peasants' carts, as the trains were reserved for the military. She had been married just six days: she was nineteen and he twenty-two. She had evidently met with great opposition on her family's part, but was so thankful she had overcome it. "Now," she said, "I can do everything for him; and if he is ill I can nurse him."

It seems he had been *réformé* early in the war on account of his lungs; then he had been unable to bear the remarks of people who called him an *embusqué*, and he had re-enlisted. He had been working as a cyclist in his regiment, and now he had ruptured a blood-vessel in the lung, and she thought he would be sent to the south to recover. In which case she could join him and live with him, and all would be well. She beamed at me as though her future was all rose leaves. Poor child! But she is better off than some who are left widows at nineteen.

If Parisians live after the war by taking in each other's washing, they will find it an expensive life. An apron costs .60 and a nightdress 1.25. At Héricourt an apron cost .15; but then it wasn't washed!

I wanted to visit a friend at Meaux, which is in the *zone des armées*, and went to the *commissaire de police* to get a *laissez-passer*. But I was confronted by a tiresome thing called a "*carnet rouge.*" Had I got one?

"No, certainly not, at least not to my knowledge. What is a *carnet rouge*."

"You can't go into the zone of the armies without one."

"But, *Monsieur*, I have only today come from the zone of the armies—nay more, from the *zone interdite*; and I have never heard of a *carnet rouge*."

The police were shocked. "Never heard of a *carnet rouge?* How, then, did we exist in those parts? How had I got to Paris?—for you can neither enter *nor leave* the zone without one?"

I could only smile and say, "Well, here I am to prove the contrary. Now I want to go to Meaux."

"But that is quite impossible, if you have not got a *carnet rouge*."

"Very well, then, give me a *carnet rouge*. Do I buy one?"

"Oh, not at all: you have to get one from the Minister of War, and it takes eight days—fifteen days perhaps. Since two months *all* foreigners have had to possess a *carnet rouge*, if they are in the war zone, or wish to enter or leave it."

"Then it would appear that I am not a foreigner, as I exist, yet have no *carnet rouge*."

"How, then," asked the *commissaire*, "did you leave Belfort without a *carnet rouge?*"

"Well, I just left, you know. My captain gave me an *ordre de transport; et me voilà!* Moreover, he gave me an *ordre de transport* to go back to my post; now can I go back with that without a *carnet rouge?*" I produced this and showed it him, and he was obliged to admit I could. "The fact is," I said, "we are all much too busy in the *zone interdite* to bother about such things, and we get on very well without them."

However, I had to give up going to Meaux.

I find there is a worse thing than having no *carnet rouge*, and that is having an incorrect one. I have just met Miss Wallace, of the St. Bernard canteen at Troyes, and she tells me she has been hung up in Paris for eight days on her way home, because the *état-major* there wrote "Troyes to Paris" on her *carnet rouge* instead of "Troyes to London," and so she has to stick here till the War Minister has time to attend to her case. I think the *état-major* ought to pay her hotel bill.

From Paris I paid a visit to Miss Grade's canteen at Le Bourget, about an hour's tram ride from the opera, for which treat I paid 40 *centimes*. Miss Gracie and her three helpers live in a minute hut built in the yard of a *usine electro-mécanique*, where soldiers collect after illness or leave to be refitted for the front; they never stay more than a night, often less, and there is perpetual coming and going. Their canteen is open from 6.30 a.m. till 10.30 p.m., and when they are not serving the foremen and workmen of the factory with tea and coffee they are giving odd meals and drinks to the coming and going soldiers. There is never a pause, so they work in two shifts. Everything is free—tea, coffee, writing-paper, tracts, soap, biscuits, meat and bread, and one cigarette a day to each man after his coffee. One day Miss Gracie remarked to the *médecin-chef* how lovely it would be if the money which went in coal smoke could go in cigarette smoke instead—after which the coal for their fires mysteriously appeared without charge.

On the boat between Le Havre and Southampton I met the same Scotch unit who left Troyes in October for Salonika. They told me a little of their journey into the interior of Serbia, and of their hurried retreat before the German troops: then the struggles in the *douane* separated us, and I never heard the end. All had escaped, however, safely.

I got home without incident: we might have been torpedoed, but were not. I was told in the morning, after the calmest crossing I have ever experienced, that a submarine did have a try for us, but was chased away by a gunboat. I did leave my luggage at Le Havre, but that was not my fault, but the fault of the authorities at St. Lazare: the military *bureau* would not give me a railway pass till I had had my luggage weighed, so that they could enter the weight of it on the ticket, and the registration department would not weigh, or even look at, my luggage till I could produce a ticket. I did manage at last to reconcile the two *bureaux* to each other, but it was not easy, as they were about a quarter of a mile apart, and much time was taken up running backwards and forwards.

In the end they only registered it halfway instead of to London, and did not tell me. I travelled part of the way home with two young English aviators, who had been in prison in Germany for five months. Five of them had escaped together, and then had divided into two parties of two and three respectively. The party of two got safely across the Swiss border, by dint of hiding in woods in the daytime and travelling at night only, on foot or hanging occasionally on to trains in the dark. Somebody gave them civilian clothes: they ate turnips in the fields and occasionally begged a drink. I have never seen two faces more cheerful and jolly: I travelled in the same train with them from Berne to Paris.

One day I had what I must really call a *"succès fou"* I had brought out with me from England half a gross of penny soap tablets, coloured and scented, and I put some out in a box on our counter. The next soldier who came in spotted them at once. He took them up one by one, examined them carefully, and then asked the price.

"*C'est libre*," I said. "*Tout est donné ici.*"

He was thunderstruck. "*Madame! je puis en prendre une, sans rien payer?*"

"*Oui, Monsieur. Servez-vous en.*"

He lingeringly and affectionately picked out the colour he preferred, and muttering "*Savon! libre!*" he retired into the courtyard. Through the window I was able to observe what he did. He waited about till a soldier came in sight, then beckoned him mysteriously, and showed his booty. There was much gesticulation, discussion, and sensing of the soap tablet; four senses out of the five were applied to it; lively satisfaction and hand-shakings terminated the interview, and soldier No. 1 departed, while soldier No. 2 remained on the spot to repeat the performance with soldier No. 3. This went on all the afternoon, the latest tablet always being displayed for the benefit of the last comer.

By evening all the soap had gone, and the men displayed the greatest degree of gratitude, as soap is not included in their rations. After that I used to buy soap of a dull household variety by the hundred kilos, and cut it up for them in small pieces. Another pleasure we had was giving away 1,200 pairs of hand-knitted socks which were sent us out by some war depot in England. The socks were used for all sorts of purposes other than the legitimate one—as cholera-belts, chest-protectors, scarves, or gloves, with the ends stuffed up their sleeves.

Sunday was a sort of gala day. After "*soupe*" the men had cocoa and English biscuits, which were a great treat: if we called it cocoa they looked rather askance at it, but if we suggested *chocolat* for a change from coffee their faces were wreathed with smiles, specially the Zouaves or negroes; they are all perfect babies about sweet things. Then in the afternoons the gramophone was brought out, and if fine we had a "*café chantant*" outside, often accompanied by dancing and singing.

CANTINE DES DAMES ANGLAISES,

GARE ECHANGE,

LE BOURGET, SEINE.

If you asked me, would I choose to spend June at Spa Road, Bermondsey, I should say No. But that is practically what I have done. I was offered a post at Domrémy, which I should have loved, and at Le Bourget, which I knew I should loathe, because I already knew Le Bourget. I chose the latter, because Domrémy is so far, and I might have had to wait for weeks to get a *carnet rouge*, which has now become a *sine qua non* for getting into the *zone des armées*. The amusing thing is, that the first time I went to Le Bourget Echange Station, with M. Desmarquoy, the commandant told me I was in the zone of the armies, because it is a purely military place, and that *really* I ought to have a *carnet rouge*; however—and here he bowed and waved his arms.

It takes me a quarter of an hour to walk from the house where I have a bedroom, close to the civil station, to my canteen: first I go through the station, thread my way across the main line of the Chemin de Fer du Nord, and over endless tracks which lead to the military Exchange Station which connects the Nord, Est, Lyons, and Grande Ceinture trains. It is a wilderness of lines, points, signals, engines roaming about, strings of goods carriages, trucks, etc. (left lying apparently derelict), long platforms, and military *bureaux*. Soldiers with fixed bayonets are also stationed very freely about. After a final walk of about a quarter of a mile along a cinder platform one reaches our very dingy, dirty little canteen; it is the worst I have ever seen. It may once have been clean and fresh, but the smoke of six stoves going all day and every day inside, and the smoke of perpetually passing engines outside, as well as the fact that there is a kiln close to us for burning refuse, which smoulders all day, have converted it into something little better than a hovel.

It is seldom I do not have to go back some time in the day to my lodging; one day I was particularly bright, and had to go twice. First I forgot to take an apron with me, and as I was expecting a visit from Madame Desmarquoy, I felt obliged to go back and fetch it. And in the evening, having forgotten to leave the key at the *bureau*, I had to go back all the way, almost in the dark, as our orderlies have to get the key early in the morning so as to light the fires ready.

Three times back and forward, added to being on one's feet the whole day from 10 till 8, makes a pretty hard day.

I found the six ladies who had been running the show had all gone home before I came out; two from another canteen which has been having a slack time had taken it temporarily in hand—Miss Worsley and Miss Nancy Roscoe. One or other of them came for a few hours every day during the week I was here alone. Miss Roscoe was a pupil teacher at Miss Bishop's School, and remembers John and Rachel quite well. She was what one of the children called rather contemptuously to her mother one day, "One of the side teachers, mother; we don't mind them."

The work consists of pouring out coffee for any soldiers who happen along and filling bowls with *bouillon* for them; giving those who ask writing-paper, postcards, or pencils, ink and blotting paper; doing first aid to the injured, and washing and bandaging cut or sore fingers. One man came with a very severe knife wound in the abdomen, for which he had been discharged as cured from the hospital. It seemed to us very imperfectly healed and to be in danger of breaking out.

Today a man was brought to me unconscious; he had fallen backwards on to the line on his head. I decided it was wiser to have him carried to a doctor on a stretcher. There is always a Red Cross train sitting somewhere about the station.

The stream of men coming for drinks is quite steady; but besides the regular flow we have wild eruptions—floods, tidal waves—of, it may be, hundreds—who overwhelm and almost drown us for ten minutes, or half an hour, and then recede like a spring tide, leaving us nearly exhausted but triumphant, because the *bouillon* and coffee have lasted out the ordeal.

We have two orderlies—they both answer to the name of François. So I call them François Premier and François Second. The latter is charming, very humorous and good-natured, and rather like Saint Joseph. The former is a lean, tall, powerful man, an untiring and zealous worker, very capable and trustworthy. He practically makes all the soup and coffee, and I taste and criticise and do all the catering. They take it in turns to go off for their meals, so we are never left alone. One comes early and the other stays late. François Premier was a sailor, and he has the blue eyes and the far-seeing look that our English sailors usually have. He is an Algerian.

Our third orderly (*plantons* they are called here) is nomadic and keeps changing, like the guard. Today, I regret to say, he arrived drunk, and got steadily more and more cloudy and stupid and futile, till I was obliged to send him away. The difficulty was to *make* him go without making the other *plantons* use force, or appealing to the commandant; I just steadily stared at him, telling him repeatedly that he was to go away; and finally his eyes dropped, and he went—but not till he had very solemnly shaken hands all round. I believe he retreated into a railway truck and went to sleep.

We have a very simple and efficacious way of supplying ourselves with coal and hot water: we just beg what we want from any stray engine that the station happens to be giving hospitality to. We fill our coal-boxes up with government coal whenever they are getting empty, and fetch pails of boiling water to make our coffee and soup, or to wash our hands and scrub our tables.

Sometimes a soldier who has been on leave brings some eggs to

François I. and François II.

Canteen Gare Echange (Le Bourget)

be cooked; these are lowered in a colander by means of string into the boiling *bouillon* for the requisite number of minutes. It doesn't hurt the eggs, and it doesn't hurt the *bouillon*.

It is simple, primitive, and economical. It is also the only way we can cook ourselves anything for lunch. Meals here are very uncertain and precarious. I have my morning coffee at a restaurant close by, after I have been across to the station bookstall for a paper: I have coffee in a small washing-basin and eat it with a soup spoon; I have more bread and butter than I can eat for 60 *centimes*.

The restaurant is shut by the time I get home in the evening, so I boil myself an egg, and have bread and cheese, fruit, chocolate, jam, and *tisane*. The other meals are jumbled, according to whether one has time or remembers them, or has anything handy to eat at eating time. Sometimes I have two teas and no lunch, or two lunches and no tea. Or I have tea at lunch-time and lunch at tea-time. Or I have *bouillon* in the middle of the morning, and a sort of lunch later on.

The busiest part of the day is apt to be between 5 and 7—though overwhelming floods may occur at any minute. At 5.15 the "Roccarde" is due from Marseilles, on its way through to Creil and Calais. It departs again at 6.45, so generally there is ample time to serve it with coffee, or make the men in it come to our canteen. Nearly always there are British troops in it, generally Australians, sometimes marine detachments, or some English Tommies from Egypt, or Anzacs. They always know where they have come from, but they never know where they are going. Everybody on the station is interested in our "*compatriotes*" and makes a point of coming to tell us if any khaki is observed in the train as it comes in. It draws up at a distance, where we can't see it. The French are always much impressed with them, specially with the Australians, and certainly they are splendid fellows, so keen and eager and agile, and lean and sunburnt.

The two races mingle together most amicably, and clink their cup of coffee and drink to the *Entente Cordiale*. I hear murmurs of "*braves hommes*" "*belles troupes*," "*des hommes magnifiques*," "*de vrais soldats*" which are certainly all true. It is the nicest part of the day meeting these jolly fellows and giving them drinks, writing-paper, and postcards, and, what they value even more, some old magazines, novels and newspapers. I collect all I can for them, and have got two or three shops in Paris to give me bundles of old English magazines. We get the strangest mingling of nationalities in front of our canteen. I have seen all at once French, Australian, Zouave, Belgian, Senegalese, Algerian, Negro,

Zouaves on holiday.

A Spahi

and English. Naturally, the moment they have finished their coffee the Britishers seized the bowls, and before you could say Jack Robinson there was a hot contest going on, Australian on one side, French on the other. Then, alas, the order comes to go—so different from what one imagines would be the Prussian command in similar circumstances! A brown, lean, tall sergeant calls out, "Now, chaps, I guess it's time we were making tracks"; and in no time they are all formed up in fours, three cheers are given, the last caps are hastily exchanged between French and British, and they are gone—all too soon.

One evening we had 300 of them, the next 150. In the course of conversation with the officer of these latter I found that really they were all prisoners, because they had outstayed their leave and missed their train the day before. "But," said the captain plaintively, "what can I do? I have no guard, so I just have to trust them." This unfortunate officer, as soon as he had dumped his little lot down wherever they belonged, had to go back to Marseilles again: already he had been in this train three days and nights, and I must say the whole lot looked pretty grubby and weary, though they were cheerful enough. But they said there wasn't a single lavatory on the whole train, so they could not wash.

One of the men had a tiny fox terrier puppy he had brought from Egypt; it had to have its tail docked, and they had drawn lots as to who should do it; and the man was pointed out to me who had undertaken to *bite* off the end the next morning! Poor little puppy. They fed it on condensed milk.

On the night of June 15 the French clocks were all put forward an hour. I suppose the railways got rather upset, and the trains were apt to be late next day. The "Roccarde" was so behind time that we gave it up and began to shut the canteen at 7.30, when suddenly it turned up, and the faithful porter, whom I call our "*client fidèle*" hurried to inform us it was full of khaki, so we hastened across to invite them all round. But their officers would not let them get out. A few English Tommies who were along were allowed to come back with us and carry pails full of coffee for the rest: we just managed to feed them all round and give them a few books and papers before they were off, cheering heartily, and dropping souvenirs out of the windows to us. The officers were frightfully grateful: it was the first hot drink any of them had had all day; they had all been two and a half days in that train, and they said the sight of English women bucked them all up enormously.

On the top of that we had a very full train of *permissionnaires*, who surged round our canteen and pretty well ate us out of house and home.

That was a very heavy day. We closed at 8.30, and there was only once a pause of about five minutes, when no one came, and we thought perhaps the war was over.

The first week I was here it was bitterly cold, with a raw northerly wind and a good deal of rain. On Whit Sunday we had a tremendous hailstorm; the noise on our roof was so loud one could not hear oneself speak.

The next day, June 12, while we were serving a train, we had a deluge of rain like a tropical downpour, only that the weather was arctic; the soldiers insisted on dragging me and my pail of coffee inside, and that particular carriageful had a very good time. Our canteen leaks at every pore, and when the hail came down we put up our umbrellas, and afterwards it had to be swept up and thrown outside.

Before the rain had finished in came the "Roccarde"; we felt too exhausted after just serving one long train to start on another, so we went round and persuaded the officers of the Australian contingent to let their men come across to us. They were unwilling to let them out of their sight, but I promised to get them all back in time: I said I was sure they would all follow me like sheep when it was a question of hot drinks. The captain said "H—m! I fear some of them may be rather black sheep." However, they came—300 of them—and we got quite hot, and almost dry, supplying them with coffee and soup. As many of them as could crowd into the canteen came in and warmed by the stoves, and had a quarter of an hour of gramophone. We got them all safely back, after three cheers and much handshaking.

Just as we were closing on the 13th we noticed a cloud of blue in the far distance. We watched for a few minutes: then the lower half of it began to twinkle (that means legs in movement). Slowly it got nearer, and we hastily reopened and got things ready. Five hundred men materialised—they were in a desperate hurry; in a quarter of an hour each man had drunk and departed, and the platform was empty again.

June 14. A little sun today for the first time, and if it had not been for the wind it would have been almost warm. A drunken man came up and pitifully asked for wine: he could not believe we had none, and said he would pay me to fetch him some. He came three times at intervals, and was most serious and impressive about his needs, and ended up in tears. The soldiers waiting at the station for their respective trains are all *"consignés,"* which is hard on some of them, who may have to wait twenty-four hours.

We were just closing after a very hard day, when a message came from the commandant to say "Please don't shut, as a detachment is just coming in." Now a detachment may be anything from 50 to 500, and François and I looked at each other in horror, for we had run rather short of coffee, and if 500 came it would mean there would be none left for early next morning. I would willingly stay and make fresh myself, if I could do it alone, but I can't. To stoke the fires the heavy marmites have to be lifted on one side, and I can't move them. And I don't like to keep the *plantons* up very late, as they come on duty at 6.30 in the morning and stay on till I choose to close.

The detachment proved to be only about 100, so all was well, and François' brow smoothed out again.

On the 16th, a long train of *permissionnaires* came in about 5, followed close by a trainful of Australians who about cleared us out.

Next day Miss Wilkinson arrived, and I was very glad to get another helper. The principal advantage is that one can get off for a couple of hours every day, and there is also someone to work the gramophone. It is difficult to manage both that and pouring out without occasionally spoiling discs. I took advantage of her presence next day to accept an invitation to tea at Drançy Farm to meet some Tommies—a detachment who are engaged in mending army boots near by at Bobigny. It is a charming old place, of black and white timber work, with old red-tiled roofs, built round a large open square, with an old walled garden facing the east. In one corner of the yard Miss Worsley and Miss Roscoe have their canteen, where they cook for the infirmary and give drinks to everybody, including the prisoners, of whom there are several. These are not criminals, but merely men who are undergoing sentence for some military misdemeanour, like breaking leave or being late.

One of the walls of the garden had been pierced with holes for rifles during the German advance on Paris; but they have long since been filled up again. Some *Uhlans* had penetrated as near Paris as the next village, no doubt expecting the German Army was close on their heels. The *Uhlans* were killed, and the surrounding houses and farms were put in a state of defence, including the Drançy Farm, whose commodious outbuildings were packed as full of troops as they would

PETIT DRANÇY FARM.

hold. Trenches were dug and barbed wire entanglements hastily set up, which still remain. But the German flood had reached its highest tide, and began to recede, and Drançy was saved. And the *Uhlans* were the soldiers who advanced the nearest to Paris.

As I walked to the farm I stood in the trench and reached over the barbed wire to pick poppies and corncockle and cornflowers in the barley.

I got back to my post just in time to meet and succour 150 Australian and British troops.

June 19. Mademoiselle Comte spent the morning at the canteen and freed me to go into Paris: by going in early before breakfast one can get quite a lot done by midday. I spent most of the time going round to booksellers and begging for old copies of papers and magazines for the soldiers, and had a most gratifying response, specially from Brentano, in the Avenue de l'Opéra, who sent us not only old magazines, but the latest numbers of most of the illustrateds as well.

The Drançy tea party was a great success. The French had decorated the table charmingly with pansies and green boughs, and there was an ample meal spread—cake cooked by the English ladies, bread and butter and radishes, fly biscuits, and strawberries. We all did it ample justice, except the commandant, who unfortunately had an "*estomac*." So many of the French have—it is almost a national failing. The conversation at tea was most amusing—stammering French in English accents, and worse English in French accents; but the two lots of men fraternised delightfully in each other's caps; and the moment tea was over the Tommies seized a football and were out in the fields playing, disregarding the elegant amusements provided for them in the courtyard in the shape of ninepins and a gramophone.

How the Briton sticks to his habits!

One of the men told me he had been through the whole war, landing in France with the first Expeditionary Force, in the retreat from Mons, the battles of the Ourcq and the Marne, the Aisne and Ypres, and had never had a wound or a day's sickness.

We are close to a flying school, and aeroplanes buzz about overhead all day and most of the night. As soon as the cold windy weather was over they came out in great numbers, and every evening as soon as it is dusk they appear in the sky whizzing like huge cockchafers, or darting and wheeling and manoeuvring like swallows. As it gets dark they carry lights: the wings are illuminated with red and green, and

AT THE CANTEEN

below in the middle hangs a great white light. The sky seems to be full of Venuses sailing majestically and serenely at a distance, swimming in a vast silence; but at the same moment that one comes near enough for you to hear it you see also the lighted wings. Then they look like jewelled dragonflies, or exquisite toys made for the illumination of some *fête* or carnival—they look like anything rather than war machines. They manoeuvre together very often in figures of eight and spirals and sharp turns, or they play follow-my-leader round the sky.

On the 17th we saw two aeroplanes which had been playing together suddenly perform the most daring feat—they were apparently looping the loop round each other; but alas, it was nothing of the sort. They had collided with each other, and fell to the ground about a kilometre away from our canteen, rolling over and over and over. It seemed inevitable that both the men should be smashed; but, strange to say, neither was really hurt at all, though the planes were rather the worse for wear.

When the aeroplanes turn sharp corners they go almost over on to one side, like a racing yacht, or a motor tearing round a track. It is very pretty seeing them right themselves after it and sail along level again.

On the 15th a number of men came in from Belfort; they were all very cross, and even coffee seemed to fail to brighten them up. They had gone there from Le Bourget to rejoin their regiment, but on inquiry on arrival it could not be found: nobody knew where it was. Apparently it had got mislaid or buried or sent skywards. So they had to come all the way back, which in a military train probably meant a day and night journey, to Le Bourget, which is a sorting station for all lost, mislaid, derelict, or returned-from-leave soldiers. It is to be hoped this regiment will soon be found, as in the meantime the men hang about and come to us at least once an hour for coffee and soup. The only other attraction we can offer them is the gramophone, which we sometimes work (by request!) for a couple of hours at a time, if we can spare the time to do it.

We also had a number of Belgians, who seemed very pleased to meet some English ladies. Many of them had heard no word of their families since the German invasion. One young fellow, quite good-looking (which few Belgians are), stuck to us all day like a leech, helping us in the canteen, and working the gramophone for us nearly all the afternoon. He was a dear boy, and nearly wept when his train went off and he had to leave us. At the beginning of the war he had been taken by the Germans as a hostage or prisoner and had been sent

A DAILY SCENE

away into Germany, but had escaped into Holland and got back to France through England and enlisted in the French army. The worst of a gramophone performance is that we nearly always have a recitative engine whistle accompaniment, which is not necessarily harmonious, and it always comes in the most unsuitable places. If the engine chimed in in "*Départ du Paquebot*" or "*Chauffeur d'Automobile*" it would be rather suitable, but it never does that. It comes in suddenly with a sustained shriek in the middle of "Carmen," or "God Save the King," or "*Chanson de Rossignol.*"

Sometimes at the canteen it is almost impossible either to make oneself understood, or understand what the soldiers are saying—as for instance when François I. is stoking our six stoves one after the other and François II. is grinding coffee, and the third *planton* is boisterously washing up bowls and spoons, and the gramophone is playing "*L'homme qui rit toujours,*" and several engines close outside are shrieking and letting off steam. "*Mais que voulez-vous? C'est la guerre.*"

Here is a letter one of the soldiers sent to Miss Wilkinson:

The 21th, 6/16.

Dear Miss,
I am arrived yesterday very much fatiguated.
After 36 o'clocks of train we have made 15 kms.
You can think then that has been very dur for us, because in the train we don't sleep many, and when we have been obliged to walk that was not agreable.
We are here in a village at six kms. of the first lines, but we cannot receive marmites.
Our work consists in construction of *tranchées* in third lines. We go to *tranchées* six o'clocks a day, and all the 4 days we go the night.
We are here only for 15 days.
I don't see other things to say you for the moment.
I close my letter in hopings receive quickly of your good news (in French).

I am, dear Miss, yours very sincerely,

Rene Lambert.

Don't make attention at my mistakes, please.
21e Chasseurs à pied,
20e Compagnie,
S.P. 73.

June 21. The most marvellous peace has reigned this morning for a short time, and we keep looking at each other and thinking "Have the reserves of the French army come to an end, and are there no more soldiers to pass through Le Bourget?" It lasted quite ten minutes. I sit beside the coffee marmite at the open window; Miss W. at the gramophone at the other end of the canteen playing select airs (with engine accompaniment) to a quiet group of elderly reservists (territorials). François I. sits at a table peeling and cutting onions, and François II. is perched on a table by my side reading *Le Petit Journal*.

We saw such guns passing through yesterday—monsters: the men travelling with them looked like little ants or flies like a kitten sitting on an elephant. They are 400 and 500 mm. guns, painted blotchily and fantastically in sky and tree colours, with foliage and stems here and there; armoured cars are painted the same, to avoid detection. They look like ridiculous stage-pieces got up for a pantomime.

A soldier told me that the French troops who are fighting among the English wear khaki also to deceive the enemy, but I can't quite see the object.

It has been terribly hot today, really almost unbearable. I don't know what the temperature of our canteen has been; but I went back to what seemed coolness in my bedroom at about 3 o'clock, and that was 80°.

We had No. 3 regiment of Zouaves at mid-day. One of their officers came up and asked if we could *possibly* give them something to drink, and seemed so surprised when I said "Oh dear, yes, any number of you; it is all ready." They came up in orderly detachments, being in a great hurry; the poor things were terribly thirsty; but then *Zouaves* always are, specially for coffee. They were a fine lot, all young and strong and sturdy. Their flag had been decorated three times.

In the evening we had 300 Australians through, as well as a lot of French, and a great many men travelling with horses, who might not leave their trains.

Ten times have I been up and down that platform today in this terrific heat! Miss Wilkinson and I both think we shall see it for ever in our nightmares. I am sure it is worse than trenches!

The key-note of our station is black. Black platforms made of cinders ground to dust; black trains and engines; black smoke. Against this the yellow of Belgians and *Zouaves* and the blue of the French show up to great advantage, but still more so do the picturesque uniforms of the *Spahis*. They have scarlet tunics braided with yellow, very full-

THE *CROIX DE GUERRE*

pleated cloth divided-skirts of a soft blue, brown leather gaiters and boots, spurs, and high brown turbans wound round and round with string like close braiding. Their faces are swarthy, with high cheekbones and dazzling white teeth, and their hair densely black.

I photographed a few of them; they were awfully pleased, but one old chap was in a terrible state about something. I could not make out what, so waited till he was more composed. At last he fished out of his voluminous garments a *croix de guerre* and pinned it on, and then by his smiling face intimated that he was ready.

The thirst of the *Spahis* seemed to be unquenchable. Fortunately they were limited in number, for they were the most expensive clients we have ever had to spend the day with us.

It has been a very "African" day—what with the heat, and the *Spahis*, and the *Zouaves*.

June 23. Today has been pretty much the same as yesterday, nothing but *Zouaves*—this time 300 of the 2nd Regiment, and *all* terribly thirsty. They simply fell out of the train and screamed when they saw us and our coffee-pails, but they were not allowed to go away from the train, and we toiled three times up and down that weary, scorching platform, each carrying two pails, before they were all satisfied. I think our hair will turn grey if this heat continues—yet, if it did, we should still look black.

At about 5 it got cooler, and we had a sudden violent burst of wind, which blew three of our chimneys down on to the roof with a great clatter. Everybody rushed out thinking it was a bomb from a Taube.

At night very heavy rain, and the world has become bearable again.

I have had a charming conversation with François I. today. I explained to him that I was obliged to go home in about ten days; that I could not leave Miss Wilkinson alone to work the canteen, and that unless other ladies came out to take my place we should most reluctantly be obliged to close it, at any rate temporarily.

He considered this for a little while, and then he made a really beautiful speech. He explained how he was a family man (with five children), "*fort sérieux et capable, et tout à fait comme il faut, père de famille,*" etc.; and that the young lady would be perfectly safe in his charge: he would look after her in every way, and would even, if I wished it, daily conduct her to and from her lodging to the canteen. Even, he said, he had once taken a hatchet to a drunken soldier who was not quite *comme il faut*, and he was prepared to do so again for the protection of *Mademoiselle* should it be necessary.

I assured François I knew well that all he said was perfectly true and that he would make the most admirable father to Miss Wilkinson, but, I said (for I did not want to hurt his feelings, and of course her people would *not* like her staying on here alone), the fact is she cannot afford the money to run the canteen by herself, and unless other ladies come to share it with her she must go home with me.

Ever fertile in expedient, he at once had a plan whereby the canteen could be made self-supporting, and offered, if I wished, to run it himself and charge the soldiers the exact cost price of the coffee and *bouillon* they have. We worked it out and found the coffee costs just under a *sou* a cup, or five *centimes*. However, I fear that is out of the question, as the London *comité* would certainly not approve.

The 29th and 30th have been one continuous steady stream of clients, without ever a minute's pause. By the end of the day one becomes mechanical and wooden, one's smile becomes frozen on one's lips, and one's words cease to come when called upon, and all one's little jokes and stock remarks sound banal and witless. One serves in dignified silence.

Tonight we were too busy to think of serving the "Roccarde" when it came in: we ignored it, though regretfully. As it grew close to 7 I almost began to count the minutes, as I had been up since 6.30 a.m., and literally had hardly sat down; 7 struck, and we were just going to put up our shutters, when a message came from the commandant, "Please don't shut yet, as there is a large contingent just coming in." It came, and not a single man-jack of them had a quart—which means double work, as each basin has to be washed before it is given out again.

The longest worm turns at last, and after that we closed hurriedly lest another message should come.

My only diversion today has been to try and run the coy and reluctant coal proprietor to earth: our coal has run out. François has been unable to take French leave (they call it English leave here) and help himself off engines, because for the last four days the engines also have been coy and reluctant: perhaps they have discovered our habits. In which case they get neither coffee nor soup. Both the François went out on a prowling expedition, armed each with a bucket, today, and by dint of searching and picking up unconsidered trifles lying

THE DANCER

about between the rails, they managed to bring in a small harvest. Coal is nearly as difficult to get here as it is in Switzerland. There you take a basket and buy a pound at a time.

Saturday, July 1. Today has almost reached the point of being unbearable. Between 2 and 5 the canteen kept a steady temperature of 94°, and it was a very busy day indeed. One poured and handed out quarts, ladled soup, and washed basins without a break, except for occasionally working the gramophone for a change. Between 5 and 8 the sun shines straight into the canteen, and we stand and serve in the full glare of it till we are almost blinded. It is a relief when the evening train comes in, and we leave the men to take charge of the canteen, and we dash out with heavy pails of coffee—a distance very often of a quarter of a mile. This repeated several times finishes our day's work. It is a pity neither Miss W. nor I have got the particular disease for which Turkish baths are ordered, as we could have them all day long at no charge, and by now we should surely be cured.

We had a little *Zouave* play the violin to us this morning, and with such vigour, sitting in the full sun, that it seemed he must melt. He played really well, and it was a pleasant change after the eternal gramophone. One of the soldiers asked for the British National Anthem, but after hearing it he still was dissatisfied, and began to whistle what he wanted. It turned out to be "Tipperary" he was asking for!

The hottest day coincided with the hardest work. We gave away over 4,000 quarts of coffee, *bouillon*, and "coco," which latter is the soldier's name for tisane of liquorice—a nauseous mixture, but very popular in the army. A quart is a quarter of a litre—about a teacupful.

I left Le Bourget on July 3. Since then the personnel has increased as well as the work. When I was there there was scope for much more than we were able to do in the time, and with only two pairs of hands; the ladies increased first to four and finally to six, and as the heat increased, so did the soldiers' thirst, as well as the numbers travelling, and the hours the canteen was open lengthened out from 6 a.m. till 9 p.m. On their record day fifteen marmites of coffee (each marmite holds 400 quarts), two of *bouillon*, and two of "coco" were made and given: altogether 7,600 quarts!

Red Triangle Girl in France

Contents

Prefatory	105
Introductory	107
1	109
2	110
3	111
4	114
5	116
6	117
7	120
8	123
9	125
10	128
11	130
12	132
13	135
14	138
15	140
16	144
17	147

18	149
19	151
20	153
21	155
22	157
23	159
24	161
25	163
26	165
27	167
28	169
29	172
30	174
31	176
32	178
33	180
34	182
35	185
36	188

Prefatory

Dear Dr. Mott:

May I in a few words explain why I have placed at your disposal the accompanying manuscript? It consists of selections from the home letters of our daughter, written in a Y. M. C. A. canteen "Somewhere in France." They were dashed off rapidly, in busy days, with many interruptions, addressed to members of our family circle; and they bear on their face everywhere the stamp of having been written without premeditation or the remotest dream of publication.

But they tell the story of the daily life in a crowded canteen in France, as experienced by an intensely interested and enthusiastic participant, not only in its outward form, but also in its innermost spirit. The infinite variety of the life, its humour, its pathos, its confidences, its noble, its generous, its picturesque characters, its delights and its privations, its devotions and its gratitudes, its tragedies and its sorrows, the countless services and the priceless spirit of the Y. M. C. A. workers, all this and much more is disclosed in these vivid letters with an art that is wholly unconscious and to which the thought of publication would have been fatal.

For many years as you know, it has been a part of my duty to keep myself informed in a general way about the character and value of the work of the Y. M. C. A, in the army and navy at home and abroad, in peace and in war. I have visited some stations, and listened to many eloquent addresses, and read many illuminating pages on this subject. Yet when it came to the acid test of sacrificing our own daughter, I confess that we consented to her enlistment and forwarded her preparations with great doubt and anxiety. These letters have completely reassured us. They have taken us across the sea to the headquarters at Paris and thence to the camp and into the canteen itself. There we have lived for months. And values have been disclosed to us in this canteen work, in variety and extent never dreamed. And besides no small part of our solicitude about our soldier sons in France has been relieved.

And so the question forced itself on us whether the vital parts of these letters might not perform a like service for others. Friends who have shared some of them have urged this. We remember that thousands of daughters throughout the land, in the coming months, must be anxiously considering whether they shall offer themselves for this work and will be eager to know accurately and intimately what precisely the life is. Their parents will be as hesitant as we were. Men of wealth are to be called on to give and to double their former gifts for this cause. Possibly these letters may give to some of them as they gave to us a new and deeper sense of its value. And then there is the million of anxious mothers of soldier boys, soon to be millions, to some of whom as to us, these letters may afford comfort and relief. And so at last in placing the letters at your disposal, we have yielded to what came to be a duty. Of course all strictly personal or family references have been cut out. We have also concealed our daughter's location in France, the names of her friends and fellow workers and very carefully her own name, from a sense of justice to them and of respect to their delicacy of feeling.

Introductory

A soldier boy's pen picture of the Red Triangle Girl in her canteen

We passed through the door of the Y. M. C. A. canteen, and saw her standing there, dealing out a cup of chocolate, a smile and a few words to each soldier boy as he shambled up. Farther down the counter the Y. M. C. A. man collected their money,—for the chocolate? Not on your life. It was that smile, and that cheery "Good morning" they stood in line for. I know, for I was one of them and did it myself.

Sergt. Bill, who was raised on whiskey and kicks, is generally the first in line. Does he want the chocolate? He does not. Does he like it? Not so that you could notice it. Then why is he there? Just so that he, along with a hundred other boys, can have one of God's own noble women speak three words to him like a human being.

Say! There are twenty fellows just standing around, hoping that some one will say something she doesn't like, so that they can knock his block off. If I ever want to get in the hospital quick, I'll just go up and look cross-eyed at her. The next day they would be sending me flowers and walking slow behind me. When it comes to having bodyguards, the *Kaiser* is a piker compared to her. Is she safe? Well! a ring in a plush box in a safety deposit compartment inside a burglar proof, fire proof vault is in imminent danger compared with her.

Is she happy? If a smiling face and sparkling eyes and cheery words spell anything; if the knowledge that every day is crammed full of little helpful deeds and more helpful words, and that one's mere presence is a constant pleasure to those around, if these things bring happiness, then she is happy.

Is she comfortable? You should have been with us when I was shown her little room by her soldier brother, with its dainty curtains at the window, and the pictures of her loved ones all about her. You should see her hundred soldier friends willing, nay, pleading to be allowed to do something for her. Why! I believe that if she expressed a desire for the moon, fifty young men in this aviation camp would break the altitude record trying to get it for her.

As she is a regular enrolled member of the American Expeditionary Force, and of the United States Army, and as your Service Flag holds four stars, I suggest you enlarge one of them to thrice its present size and mark it "Daughter."

1

One little last goodbye as we are slipping down the bay, and a final assurance that all goes well. The young lady who shares my stateroom, Miss M—— A——, is a dear, and we shall get on beautifully together. I have a nice place for my deck chair beside hers.

The ship is very pretty and French. Most of the passengers are chattering French. I have met four people already and the whole trip is certainly going to be pleasant.

With such a weeping crowd on the dock, I do thank you so much for giving me that cheerful send-off. I was proud of my good sports.

2

Yes, I was seasick for three days, just as usual, but since then I've had a great time. These Y. M. C. A. people are very nice; I like them all and particularly my room-mates, who are peaches.

We are now in the danger zone, and the life boats are hung out over the sides and we have our "lifies" under our chairs. I am assigned to the captain's boat.—Last to leave the ship. Hurrah!—with a collection of the stoutest people on board. If we have a wreck they will make a mighty tight fit. But there has been no occasion for anyone to be nervous a moment. Except for a very few excitable people, submarines are really a joke among us. One distinguished and pampered gentleman earnestly requested the captain, I am told, to allow him to enter the lifeboat at the lowest deck with the ladies, as there was lead in the feet of his patent life suit and he feared he could never get down the ladder.

There are fifty American sailor boys aboard, third class, and we have been looking after them and giving them things. The Y. M. C. A. crowd went down there this afternoon and we all had a service together.

The lights are all dimmed inside the ship, every port hole is closed at sundown, and the halls and stairways are pitch dark. No one can even smoke on deck, and flash lights are everywhere absolutely forbidden. It's been a very interesting trip. We've all studied French a lot and practised it on the stewards. Mr. André Tardeau is aboard and several near-celebrities.

It's getting too rough for writing inside with comfort, hence this short letter.

3

Of course you want to know all about everything, but there isn't much to tell yet.. We spent one night at a pleasant hotel at our port of entry (not to be mentioned) and came to Paris the next day—a beautiful trip through the loveliest country I've ever seen.. I'm appreciating things a lot more than I did when I was here before I was a grown-up.

Some of the Paris secretaries met us here (there were thirty-one in our party on the steamer, twenty women) and we went to a restaurant for a nice little dinner party, partly to be given lots of instructions. Then we came to this hotel and are settled here for about a week, while our uniforms are being made and they decide just where to send us. I have a nice little single room, with all the photographs out, and it feels very home-like.

We have had one whole day of speakers; splendid, inspiring men all of them, and it made us very anxious to get right out into the field at once.

There *certainly* is very great need of us. I wish you could have heard those speeches. You would have been so very happy to have me here. They have all said they wish we had brought ten friends apiece. They could place them instantly.

Last night one of the Y. M. C. A. boys took some of us down to the headquarters to see the canteen there. It is a beautiful building and arranged splendidly, I thought, but they are so crowded they are going to move very soon.

They are to give me a regular army identity book, and take away my passports. I have to wear my uniform or at least a part of it all the time, and am actually a member of the United States Army. My mail (outgoing) is censored at the Y. M. C. A. and will be franked just like the soldiers'. It is a good thing to be in uniform, I know, and I am glad of it; but it will cost me a lot—550 *francs*, about $110.00. It is very good looking—a grey whipcord suit, made Norfolk, with big pockets like the English uniform and with a French horizon-blue collar. There is a pretty horizon-blue hat and muffler, grey or blue flannel waists, a blue necktie, and a long grey cape, with a blue collar. Everything has the Y. M. C. A. insignia in red and blue. I can wear my own dresses in the canteen itself, with the canteen apron and cap over them, but outside and in any city I have to wear the uniform all on. Please send my blue sweater with the grey angora collar. It will just match and will save me getting another one. Also I should like a very plain wool or serge dress in grey or Alice blue, to wear in the canteen. It ought to be *made*, to be plain enough. Just a plain blouse with a V-neck, made so I don't have to wear a white collar with it, long sleeves and a pleated skirt, rather unusually short. They say the mud is terrible at the front.

This morning I had interviews with Secys., Mr. C—— and Mr. S——. Both welcomed me charmingly and they will let me know in a day or two where I shall be placed. I may be in a city, a town, a tiny hamlet, or a place where there is nothing but the camp. Also I may be able to do some hospital convalescent work. I told them I liked to read aloud. I can hardly wait to learn my destination, and do so wish I might tell you right out where it is when I do learn it. But the Y. M. C. A. has strictly to obey army orders.

Our party has some of the most delightful people in it. I sat at the table on the steamer with two unmarried ladies, wealthy, I imagine, from L——, a Miss P—— and a Miss M——, the latter a sister of the celebrated M——. They had brought their own fresh butter along, special bread, hot house grapes, persimmons, etc., and Miss M—— A—— and I got lots of benefit. Then there is a pair of lovely women, in the early thirties, I should think, from P——. I hope I shall draw a canteen with one of them. Also a lady who teaches singing in N——, and has been taking a special course in French pronunciation, has taken me under her tutelage, and taught me a better accent than I have ever had before. I am picking up French much faster than I dreamed I could, and it is very largely due to the clearer and more correct pronunciation.

No matter how halting the grammar and vocabulary, they can at least understand every word I say and that helps a lot. I talk with every one I can and have lost all embarrassment over awful mistakes. I chat with the *femme de chambre* and the garçon *de l'ascenseur* and the *concierge* and even people on the street. Last night I went out to mail a letter and asked the direction of a French girl. She took me to the Post Office herself, talking with *l'Americaine* all the way.

We have to be so careful here. The speakers have strongly impressed on our minds the sensitiveness of the French people, that it is they who have borne the brunt of the war, and for an American to boast about what we are going to do, is an insult and an outrage. We are to be particularly careful to foster a spirit of friendship in the canteens between the French and American soldiers.

Paris is very beautiful. I have walked everywhere I've been, just to see it. At night it is very dark, only about one in six lights going on the streets, shaded above, and no illuminated signs, or headlights on the automobiles. There seem to be lots of taxis and carriages, but every man from seventeen to forty-seven is in uniform. The houses are not heated, but I've been quite, comfortable. The food is delicious and seems to be plentiful. I've really had too much to eat, but probably that is true only in good hotels. There have been no meatless days so far.

My baggage all came promptly and in good condition. No duty to pay.

4

My destination isn't absolutely decided yet. It was to be an aviation camp, but one of the other district secretaries wants me in his artillery camp. So they are undecided again. I shall probably find out this afternoon.

It is so funny to see the American soldiers and sailors who happen to be stopping at this hotel trying to discover whether we are Americans or not. One sailor walked up and down the hotel lobby whistling "Dixie" and "My Old Kentucky Home" and watching to see if we recognised it. Another picked up a French paper and announced to no one in particular, "I guess I'll see if I can read this. I ought to be able to, I've been here seven months." That brought no response, so he said in a pathetic tone, "And I was torpedoed two weeks ago." So we invited him to tell the story, and he talked steadily for two hours. I never saw a man so eager for company. He completely finished off the story of the destruction of the ship A. He was taking a bath when the ship was struck, and was in the water an hour and three-quarters with no clothes and no "lifie." He was finally picked up by a *dory* and rowed to shore for eleven hours, still without clothes or food.

Then he told us all about his family and home, his past and his plans for the future. I never realised before how lonely one can be in the midst of a crowd. It was pathetic to see how pleased and relieved this boy was to find somebody that he could talk freely with. They say a good listener is a great asset in a canteen, and already I am getting glimpses of my future work. Please send me khaki wool, so I can knit while I listen. They are going to be interesting, too, as well as irrepressible and sometimes tragic.

I was pretty homesick the other night; it gets dark at 4:30 and then there is nothing to do till tomorrow; but my reason was saved by a nice district secretary who took another girl and me to the movies—

Douglas Fairbanks, if you please. So I've passed the first hard pull successfully.

The district secretaries, about sixty of them, had a conference at this hotel over the week-end, and they were a splendid looking lot of men. Some ministers, a few Y. M. C. A. men, but mostly fine business men who are too old to enlist but want to help in the war. They are placed in charge of whole districts, with several canteens in each. One of the nicest men on the ship was a Mr. H——, head of —— Motor Co. He is to be put in charge of the motor department of one of the largest Y. M. C. A. districts.

I went down to the Hotel des Invalides (Napoleon's Tomb) yesterday. The courtyard is full of war trophies, guns of every sort and a lot of aeroplanes, most of a Zeppelin, mines, pill boxes and everything I ever heard of connected with war. Captain Guynemer's machine was there, simply loaded with flowers, from tiny bunches of violets to great wreaths. I went into the Hotel Continental yesterday, where we stopped when I was a child, and felt as if I were getting home.

I will tell about my finances in my next letter when I've paid for my uniform and hotel bill.

5

I am still here in Paris, but am to go to —— on Tuesday and will be there indefinitely. I have heard that it is one of the nicest places of all. But again it may turn out badly, or I may be an unsuitable selection. My next letter will let you know all about it . You would be amused to see me smearing my shoes with awful smelling water-proof grease. They say the mud in most of the camps at this time of year is ankle deep and always there, and rubbers get lost off the first step. So I just have to prepare my shoes for trouble.

C—— H—— heard we were here and she came in a hundred miles on a motor truck to see us. Tell her mother for me that I never have seen her looking so well. She is ruddy and husky and enthusiastic and doing great work, I know. We had lunch together yesterday. Her family would certainly be reassured if they could see her.

I went to a Y. M. C. A. show at the Hotel de Pavilion, the Y. M. Hotel for United States enlisted men and had great fun the other night. There was music, and the cleverest sleight-of-hand I ever saw. The boys simply loved it. Afterwards we all stood round the piano and sang. It is curious that absolutely the only music that I have heard has been made by Americans—not one note from a French band. Think of it! There is rarely a laugh, too. It isn't exactly a sad silence, just continuous seriousness, too rarely broken.

6

This is absolutely the first minute I have had to write to you in three hectic, yes, father, hectic days. We came to this camp on Tuesday and went directly to the hospital in town before coming to the canteen. There were a couple of American and English boys there who were pathetically glad to see us.

We find the canteen far too small for the present size of the camp and we are kept going at a terrific rate.

We have a French woman to help with the cooking and a stocky little peasant girl to do the scrubbing. She beams with good nature every minute. There are two men secretaries, one about thirty and the other perhaps twenty-four, both very nice and working their heads off. My companion is Miss H———, the lady of whom I spoke who is so good in speaking French. But there won't be much time for French, or anything else but canteen work, I imagine. There hasn't been any canteen since the French turned the place over to the Americans about a month ago and the boys have had no place in which to read or write letters, or buy anything, or congregate or play the piano. So perhaps you can imagine how they flock in here now. The very ramshackle piano is on the go continually. I love the whole noise and bustle of it, but it is awful not to be able to feed them as we would like. Their mess is good enough, but the same day after day, and of course they want something different.

We started with splendid plans to run a sort of quick hot-lunch restaurant, with ham and eggs, omelette, hot chocolate, steak, French fried potatoes, chops, etc. I laugh when I think of it. We got up at six and tried to start the fire. French coal is about half slate and you can't depend on it a minute. Anyway, our range is a snare and a delusion, with a fire-box about the size of a couple of bricks. We also had a balky little charcoal burner and my sterno. The cook and Miss H———

and I cooked ham and eggs from seven until ten-thirty and the boys served them, cut bread and made change. It was as bad as climbing B—— Mountain at home. But honestly, I loved it. The boys drank eighty gallons of chocolate and milk; and after the hours of serving were over, some of the cadets came in to help wash the dishes, sweep the floor and put the canteen in order. They are the nicest boys! Most of them are college men and the pick of the army without doubt. When one hears I am from the State of ——, if he is from any nearby state he rushes up to ask if I don't know about fifty of his friends.

We have ordered and been promised some wonderful things from Paris: a large portable Y. M. hut, with a stage, Victor, four hundred books, billiard table, new piano, and all sorts of supplies. But it is almost impossible to get anything through in reasonable time. We certainly were fortunate to get our trunks safely and in good condition. Our canteen, though too small, is better than many, for we have floors, a few little heating stoves and, best of all, electric lights.

If I don't write you often, you'll know it is not because I am not thinking of you almost all the time—except when I'm all mixed up making French change—but because I'm busy every second. We go to bed at nine-thirty and the sleeping bag puts me to sleep instantly. It is the best thing I brought, and I don't know what I should have done without it and the heavy grey dressing gown mother insisted on my having. You would be amused at our room, by the way. There are two beds, a small washstand and a little table. There wasn't a drawer or a shelf, or a hook, until a kind soldier came in one day and fixed a bar across one corner and drove in some nails. He also put up a shelf for a mirror so we can do our hair. I repacked my trunk to make it like a bureau and my suitcase has been transformed into a dressing table. I can't say it is much like my own blue room at home, but it's a *perfectly good place*, and I've learned the art of appreciation in these two weeks. Why, I simply love that little shelf, after bracing a mirror against the foot-board of my bed for ten days.

One of the things I enjoy most is watching the way the different boys take the hardships here. The real aristocrats shine out every time. Last night I sold a dry hard loaf of bread and a tin cup full of jam to a New York millionaire and he was so appreciative and glad to get it that this morning he came in to tell me how he had enjoyed it when he was on guard in the middle of the night. And then some other man will wonder why we can't have his particular brand of cigarettes, when the scarcity of tobacco is so great in Paris that the *gendarmes* have to keep the crowds in front of the shops in order.

It is great fun to sell things to the French soldiers. At first they were not sure they were allowed to come in and they sidled up to ask for wine. Of course we had to tell them "*Il est defendu.*" They thought that meant they were not welcome, and stayed away for days until an English boy found out the trouble. Since then we have tried to be extra polite to them and they come trooping in to buy hot chocolate (which they don't like much, just take it to be polite) and tobacco. They always salute several times, talk until my French is exhausted and then go smiling and bowing out. We have cases of chewing gum to sell and at first they wouldn't touch it. Finally one ventured and now they all buy it by the ten packages. I am terribly afraid they swallow it, but don't know how to warn them in French.

There are a lot of German prisoners in camp and every now and then they are detailed to clear up the canteen. They wear their own uniforms with a big P. G. (*Prisoner de Guerre*) painted on their backs. Some of them are just kids. One nice looking boy, about seventeen, I guess, has painted the back door of the canteen at least twenty times. I know he's homesick and just wants to see some people who aren't following him around with a gun.

You wouldn't believe how hard it is to find time to write even a letter a week home. That does not mean that I am worked to death at all, but only that when I have spare moments I use them in rest, which I know is even more satisfactory to you than letters. I'm just as well and happy as I can be.

7

Oh! I wish I could tell you how glad I am to be here. It's just the best thing that ever came my way; so please be happy about me. I laugh when I think of father's worry before I came away fearing that I would have my feelings hurt every day. My word! these boys are the most considerate gentlemen you can imagine. It's like being in a Yale Prom, crowd all the time. Practically every one of the cadets in aviation is a college graduate, at least they are the ones who are in the canteen the most. The mechanics, too, are fine fellows and are specially polished and polite when they come in for anything. You should see me chatting amiably with an ex-prizefighter who gets red, shuffles his feet, and calls me "Yess Mum." He comes in every day for a short call. It's simply fascinating.

Last night we had a Y. M. C. A. concert in the mess hall. I thought I'd given up all that when I left home, but there was a violinist who has been the leader of the San Francisco Philharmonic Orchestra, and a New York concert singer with one of the loveliest men's voices I ever heard. There we sat in that large wooden room, with one stove, a funny upright piano, and all the boys seated on the benches, while these fine artists gave us such wonderful music. We have had several entertainments this week. Professor Nettleton of Yale gave us a good lecture. Mrs. August Belmont spoke. She is very charming, and a young man named Jack Barton sang. He had a "peach" of a voice and got all the boys yelling their heads off in chorus. Tomorrow we are to have Bishop Brent and Walter Camp.

Here is a sort of *résumé* of my day. I get up at seven, and Oh, but the room is cold! At eight we begin serving breakfast to the boys. They come streaming in from the flying fields almost frozen, and that coffee is the most popular thing I ever saw. I usually stand behind the counter pouring it from big pitchers, and dashing back and forth from the pantry for sugar, milk and butter. Sometimes I make change at the other end of the counter where we sell the dry stuff—chocolate, tobacco, Christmas cards, chewing-gum, soap, shoe polish, tooth brushes, and some canned goods. I know the faces of most of the men already and the names of a great many. Nearly all the time there are four or five of them helping us and they are so considerate that it is a joy to be associated with them. We close the building entirely several times during the day, to have our meals and clean up the rubbish. We take turns sitting behind the counter selling stuff (knitting between times), sleeping, and talking with the boys. In the evening the boys sit around and read and write, and I usually join a little group of them.

It is wonderfully interesting every minute of the day. By the way, I have not heard one word of profanity since I've been here, and not a single boy has acted "fresh" in any way. They seem to appreciate having American ladies to talk with and that is very gratifying to us. Five have confided to me that they are engaged, but "It isn't announced yet," and I can't tell you how many pictures of wives and best girls I have admired.

I was doomed from the first to have a cold, for every man in camp is sneezing and coughing. By the way, send me a dozen packages of V. E. M. if you can. I've used up the only one I brought, partly on myself and partly on the camp in general. The boys don't get good care when they are sick; I mean when half sick only. Of course the camp is too full and a miserable and not serious cold cannot be pampered. But it is discouraging for them to cough day and night and not be able to get any remedies. We send dozens of omelettes every day to the sick ones and Miss H—— makes turpentine and lard for them. My aspirin is about used up and some strange boy in the second building on the left has my hot water bag. Really, they get well so much faster, and are so pathetically grateful for every small favour, that it is fun to help them a little.

I have been meaning to tell you how useful the different things I brought are, all of them given me by you and the dear friends. I have worn the wrist watch every minute, and it is the only one I ever had that really keeps time. Everyone in the canteen goes by that watch. F—— can guess from my mention of the doctoring how much I have appreciated his kit. I practice my first aid training by binding up several cuts a day too. D——'s writing case is my only place for writing and this is L——'s pen and ink. Please tell L—— and D—— that the lights all over the camp invariably go out before I go to bed, and I climb into the sleeping bag by the aid of their flashlights every night. Tell C—— I still have some of her generous box of candy left, and am curing one boy of smoking too much by doling him out six cigarettes per day and giving him a little candy at night to help him through. He is really sticking to it, although his friends are kidding him about it incessantly. He used to smoke an average of thirty per day. E——'s sterno has heated many a hot milk for a sick one, and her book is in the library.

Things are going mighty smoothly now, even if they did take away our field army kitchen stove yesterday, and we have to make gallons of coffee on an improvised one of some bricks and a sheet of tin; I still love my job and have never regretted coming one instant

8

This is the afternoon of Christmas Eve, and I'm thinking of you all very specially. This is one of the busiest places in the whole world, I am sure; so busy that it is really a problem to find a few minutes for writing home. All my other correspondence has fallen down entirely. I suppose people will stop writing to me sooner or later, if I never answer their letters, but I simply can't do it. We just have these two hours at noon to ourselves, and that is usually employed in luncheon, cleaning up the canteen for the afternoon's fray, getting really washed ourselves (it is so cold and dark when we get up it is hard to get well fixed, especially when we have to break the ice on the water jars, as we have this last week) and in getting a little rest.

Miss H—— and I went to town since my last letter, and spent a couple of days in a hotel, as we both had colds and were anxious to get entirely rid of them. Both of us were improved by the rest, but really we are beginning to get quite hard now and can stand a lot.

The new Y. M, C. A. hut is being started and will be a tremendous improvement over this one. For one thing it will be about five times as big. If you could see how the boys crowd in here, you could guess how eagerly we are looking forward to it.

I have been trying hard to work up a little of the real Christmas feeling, but I'm afraid I haven't felt a spark of it. Lots of the boys have been pretty blue and homesick, especially as many of them have not been paid for months and are absolutely broke. Be sure to have P—— bring a good big letter of credit when he comes. He may need it badly. I've tried to be extra cheerful and the result may have been nil on everyone else, but it has kept me in good spirits and I haven't been blue a minute—not very flattering to you, but I know you'll be glad to hear it.

(*Later*) We are going to have a Christmas tree! We are to give each man a box of stationery, a hot chocolate and *patisserie*. Ours is to be tomorrow night, for the Red Cross is having a party for them tonight to distribute the Christmas boxes that were made for them in America. I hear they are to have turkey tomorrow, too.

Bishop Brent, whom L—— will remember at Northfield, spoke here the other night and took dinner with us before the lecture, and I found him a charming conversationalist. Bishop McCormick, and also a lady singer, were here last night for a Christmas service.

Well, it is time to go out to the counter. You should see me trying to make change in French, English and American money at once, not to mention travellers' cheques. There is usually a steady stream going from the hot coffee place to where they pay, and my head is one mass of figures. But I still like my job. Don't waste any sympathy or worry on me,—but I do hope you miss me! I am *happy* to have so many wonderful Christmases to remember.

9

I want you to know right away what a very happy Christmas I had. Truly it was one of the best and surely the longest-to-be-remembered of my life.

In the morning Miss H—— and I went in the ambulance and visited all the hospitals in the town where any of our boys are located. In these hospitals we found about twenty Americans. We gave them each a box of stationery, the box holly-covered, a bar of chocolate, and two delicious little nut cakes, all wrapped separately, so there would be as much undoing as possible, and trimmed with sprigs of holly and mistletoe. The boys certainly were glad to see us. Some of them didn't know there were any American ladies in town and hadn't talked to one for months. It really seems to mean quite a lot to some of the men to see and talk with people from home. I wish you could have overheard some of the funny stories, verging often on the very pathetic, I've been told, and letters I've been asked to read. The mechanics here are a lot of thoroughly good fellows. They are not so well educated, of course, as the cadets are, but there are many splendid men among them.

Well, we had our Christmas dinner sent up from the mess, and it was mighty good. Delicious turkey and pie, and vegetables, and nuts, raisins and fruit. Oh! I forgot to say that each of us at the canteen received a Red Cross bag. Mine had a tooth brush, a lot of tobacco and a khaki handkerchief full of American candy. I gave the tooth brush to the little peasant girl who does the scrubbing and sent the tobacco to the cook's husband, who is at the front.

In the afternoon we closed the canteen for a while and about ten of our best friends among the cadets came in and helped us trim the big Christmas tree. The camp electrician strung it with lights, and we had regular home decorations, with a star and flag on the top. We tied up five hundred boxes of stationery, each with a sprig of mistletoe or holly under the string, and piled them up on three big tables. It was great fun and gave me just the good old Christmas feeling. I opened the steamer present from E—— F——, which was not to be untied, you remember, until Christmas, and it proved to be a delicious box of Page and Shaw's. I passed it around to dozens of boys, and you should have heard the groans of delight that invariably greeted the sight of that box. Tell her about it, please, and thank her very specially with my love, for it meant a bit of home to so many people.

None of the packages from home have come yet, but I got a very nice box of candy from S—— in Paris, who is getting an artillery commission, and a perfectly beautiful plant came from A—— S——. It trims up the whole canteen. I only hope it won't die of chill in the night.

How I do get away from Christmas! After the wrapping and decoration Miss H—— and I and three friends as escorts, walked to a tiny French village about two miles away and had dinner at the quaintest little inn in the world. I'll never forget that scene. It was a wee little low-ceilinged room, with funny imitation tapestry for wall paper (soldiers doing all sorts of stunts) and big knitting machines standing about. There was a billiard table in one end, with two old Frenchmen playing; we were in the other. At our table was all the best linen and china in honour of *les Americaines*. The landlord and his wife hovered about and tried so hard and gave us one little, but wonderful steak, and French potatoes, and the best honey I ever ate—sort of petrified. We had to dig it out of the jar. Then we walked home, with a fresh wind in our faces, and a big moon overhead. Oh! it was great.

We got back about 7:30 and had the Christmas party here in the canteen. It was so jammed that one could hardly move. A couple of short speeches, some music and then the presents, hot chocolate and *patisserie* for everyone. Don't you think it was a pretty good Christmas?

Miss H—— is feeling a bit under the weather, and has gone to the hotel to get over a cold. She will probably be gone a few days, but in the meanwhile so many of the boys come in to help that the work is lighter than usual for me. For instance, this afternoon one cadet took the counter for hours while I was resting and talking with a boy who plays the piano wonderfully, and listening to one of the best musical treats I ever had. And tonight B—— is doing it while I am writing in the nice warm office. So it goes—they are the most thoughtful, dearest bunch of boys.

Last night there was a light snow, and after it the moon came out very brilliantly. Mr. M——, the Y. M. C. A. secretary, insisted that I should get some exercise, so B—— and I took a bracing walk—fast and not talking much, just enjoying the glorious fresh air and the beautiful French landscape.

I wish I could describe how picturesque our view is. The flying-school is on one side, and on the other a tiny French hamlet, with nestling little *stucco* houses, all with different coloured roofs, soft shades of green and brown and red, and big poplar trees all about. It is almost too good to be real, and when there are eight or ten aeroplanes in sight, it certainly is a romantic scene.

10

Now don't read "The American Hospital, Paris," heading above and go all up in the air! Because there is nothing to go up in the air about. I am just using my bean in the interest of that perpetual admonition of all of you, "Now, don't take any chances on your health." So here I am with only the meagrest excuse for being here, and feeling a bit as though I were imposing on the hospital, but withal having a most wonderful time. A clean white bed in a clean white room, and a clean white nurse to bring me things, seem heaven indeed after six weeks in a sleeping bag. But just the same I love my own dear aviation camp and I'm going back the first minute the doctor will let me out.

Goodness! After all I haven't told you yet that I just have a cold, one of the common garden, or in other words, canteen variety, which was a little hard to shake off in rather a cold canteen or an unheated hotel at T——. So after it began to affect my voice so I couldn't talk to the dozens who are always hanging on the counter, I was packed off to this wonderful little hospital, where B—— spent a very happy week once. It really is about the nicest place I ever saw—delightful American doctors who have been kind to me, sweet English, French and American nurses, and all American patients. When we want to give away some money sometime this is the place I vote for. I really needn't have come, but I was afraid if I let laryng—(can't spell it, the thing that gets on your vocal chords) go on indefinitely, I might not be able to sing for a long time. They give me cough medicine every few minutes, and I inhale some sort of steaming stuff, and I have had a fine hot bath and tea, and Oh! I feel just great. Whoever thought of having a hospital for Americans in Paris had a peach of a hunch. I'll only be here a few days, I'm afraid. Really I don't want to get well too fast, it is so pleasant here.

But I'm quite homesick for my camp, too. I feel exactly as if I owned it now. Our new Y. M. C. A. hut was nearly finished when I left day before yesterday, and it will probably be done when I get back. Then with this cold cured and with what I've learned about colds, and about what to wear in canteens since I came to France, I needn't get another one, I'm sure. Please commend me for my cleverness and care in coming here; I'm sure I deserve it.

The canteen work doesn't pall at all. It is more interesting all the time. Some of the funniest things have been said to us and we've been given some of the funniest presents. Nearly every boy that gets a box from home shares it with us. I've had everything from a box of Huyler's to three packages of "Lux." A big shy mechanic that I had been giving medicine to presented me with some wonderful fruit-cake that his old mother sent, another brings me buns nearly every day. The day I left, the qm.-sergeant brought me two slices of toast he had made. I have read three diaries and countless letters to and from perfect strangers. Oh! it is a great life. And still never an "insult," father. Never a word to hurt my feelings. When I came up to Paris yesterday, five separate times United States officers came up, saluted, carried my suitcase, got me taxicabs and piloted me out to this place which is rather difficult to find. You see what the Y. M. C. A. uniform does for one travelling alone in France.

A lady was brought into our ward this morning, awfully sick with appendicitis. They operated this afternoon and just now have brought her back and she is coming out of the ether. I know how she feels, poor thing.

I wish you could see how well I'm taken care of. Don't worry a minute.

11

A handful of mail has arrived. I am still luxuriating in the hospital, really having a splendid time. You may think of me lonely, sick, forlorn, homesick and friendless in a foreign city, but *Voila!* By my bedside are two beautiful plants, on my table the most glorious bunch of lilacs (like all outdoors in spring), a bag of real American oranges, and some delicious candy smuggled in by S—— when no one was looking. He comes every afternoon, very gorgeous in his brand new uniform. Tonight he goes to England. But A—— is here, too, and L—— S——, whom I met on the steamer, who have both been good to me. And yesterday, to my great surprise and delight, who should walk in but Miss N—— B—— and Mrs. S. T. M——. If you want to meet old friends, visit France.

I really feel so well I keep forgetting to tell you how I am. The doctor's keeping me on, largely because the weather is so bad; he doesn't want me to go out in it after being softened by this warmth. My voice is much better. I still cough a good deal, but it is beginning to loosen with the cough medicine and the inhaler. You have nothing whatever to worry about. The doctor examined my lungs carefully and I overheard him tell the others, "It is simply bronchitis." I haven't had any fever. It is just the kind of cold that all the canteen people have the first three months or so. There are six or eight of them, men and women, here now. The sensible ones come here and get over it. I'm quite proud of myself.

Mrs. S. T. M—— looks just as ever, and is just as sweet and thoughtful. You know they have just come from Austria. The Austrians are awfully sick of the war, but they don't complain. The food is terrible, however. Lines many blocks long stand in the snow and rain and dark, for hours, waiting for one egg. A great many babies die because there is so little milk. She and her husband lived in the best pension in that great Austrian city of Vienna, and both got fearfully thin, and the starvation affected her eyes to such an extent that she can't do much now. The doctors assure her that she will be all right soon, but she will have to stay in Paris until summer.

You would all be surprised at the amount of food here. I've been almost afraid to tell you for fear you would all stop Hooverizing; but I've had five course luncheons and dinners always at the hotels, both here in Paris and at our camp city. When we buy food, except from the U. S. quartermaster at the camp, who lets us have it at army rates, it is very high, but you can get almost anything—for instance, veal at any time. Sugar really is scarce, except for us at the camp, where we get it from the army quartermaster.

When we want French *patisserie* for the boys we have to supply the sugar to the shops, and now we hear that we shall have to give the sugar to the chocolate factory, if we want any more chocolate bars for the canteen. The French chocolate is just about the same price we would pay for the same amount at home, though perhaps not of the same quality.

We get American tobacco and chewing gum and it is slightly cheaper than at home, twenty-five *centimes* for gum being less than five cents—same with the tobacco. There is some arrangement with the French Government whereby such supplies for the American Expeditionary Forces shall come in duty free, to be sold only to American soldiers, I believe.

It is curious how little we seem to think or talk about the war, at the camp. There isn't much speculation or discussion about it. The big topic is flying, whether so-and-so made a good "hop"—a rise from the ground,—when so-and-so will be brev'ed (brevetted), whether M. T. —— or M. de B —— is the best *Moniteur*, or where Jim went on his second voyage.

Those home letters were certainly welcome. I couldn't have the electric light on when they came because the appendicitis lady was so ill, but the nurse brought me a candle, and I read them just as slowly and as many times as I could before it burned out.

Not one of my letters from home has been censored so far. Send more home pictures, if you can. I love to get them. The packages haven't come. I can hardly wait for them. I wish I had millions of dollars here. Wouldn't I enjoy doing some things, though? I would put up a diet kitchen for the sick ones at the camp, for the first thing.

12

I am honourably discharged from the hospital, but staying in Paris for a week probably, at this small pleasant hotel, with my dear girlhood friend, Mrs, S. T. M——.

The doctor at the hospital said I was perfectly recovered and all right, but if I made the change suddenly from the warm hospital to the cold canteen, I would probably take a new cold right away. He thought the best thing I could do would be to stay in Paris a little while and gradually get hardened a bit. Therefore I am here.

In order to spend the time with something useful to do, I am working in the mailing department at the headquarters, all day.

Of course you got R——'s cable saying that he had seen me and that we were both all right. I was so glad that he sent it, for it would reassure you about me, when later you would hear that I was in the hospital.

By the way, when I tried to pay my bill for ten days of splendid care, good food and complete rest at the hospital, I was told that it was paid by the American Red Cross for all war workers. So here is where some of the bread we have cast upon the waters has come back home.

So soon as I got to the hospital I wrote R—— and he got leave immediately to come to Paris to look after his sick sister, and so without time to notify me of his coming he walked right in. It was perfectly great to see him. He spent parts of two days with me. I've never seen him look so well and he is in such good spirits, too, making the best of his hardships, thoroughly appreciating his blessings and altogether just as you would expect dear old R—— to be. Won't it be great if they send him to our aviation camp for his further training when they get the machines? But almost all the soldiers I have seen are a brave and cheerful and uncomplaining lot.

I am constantly meeting charming people over here. At the hospital I met a Miss R——, a delightful girl, a Red Cross nurse who had come over with a unit of army nurses. We were released from the hospital the same day and came down here and are rooming together. It is an extremely pleasant arrangement for both of us. Our old vacation friend, A—— S——, is now a lieutenant, and for the time in Paris. I saw him the other day and on Sunday we went to church together and had dinner afterwards. Then he wanted my roommate. Miss R——, and me to go to supper with him last night, and it was almost like being at home.

It is astounding how many old friends and schoolmates one sees here. Who should I meet the other day but W—— M—— and Q—— K—— in their uniforms; perfectly delighted to see my familiar face. Mrs. M—— and I had tea with W—— on Saturday. These little surprise meetings and greetings and tea parties of old acquaintances and friends from home in this great strange city in this so unexpected and so amazing war carry one into another world. Are we on another planet? But I am extra glad to have these chance meetings, because truly the boys enjoy them so. You wouldn't believe how happy they are to be with American girls. I have been astonished at the pleasure and even delight some of them show. Of course I am in uniform with the insignia of the Y. M. C. A. and so in a sense a comrade.

Nearly every American soldier I pass salutes my uniform and I bow and smile a response, and several, on the strength of my uniform and service badge, have come up to me on the street and asked if they might talk with me a few minutes. I have recognised the salute of United States soldiers as they passed and they have turned right around and caught up with me and thanked me for "A little piece of home" or "A genuine smile" or "A reminder of someone real." Isn't it pathetic? Not many permissions to Paris are to be given from now on, I learn. This is no place for our nice boys. Everyone says so. Who should I meet on the street yesterday but Miss W—— S——, and it was mighty good to see her and looking so well, too. France is apparently agreeing with her wonderfully.

This letter has occupied itself almost wholly, I see, with my chance meetings with old friends and acquaintances on the streets during this week in Paris. So you see you don't have to think of me as alone, among strangers in a distant land across the sea. I do verily believe I see here and in camp the old friends in greater numbers, specially the scattered college boy acquaintances and the girl friends that I knew at school and, at home, than I would have met in the same length of time had I never come to France. The fact is that a large part, I guess the majority of our acquaintances of my age are "Somewhere in France" or about to come over.

We have a new chief at the canteen, I hear, installed since I left and I met a charming lady today who is going tomorrow to be there to help us. Delightfully as I have spent this week in Paris, I am absolutely homesick to get back to my dirty, cold, little canteen.

13

You see I'm back in the canteen again, perfectly well, and very happy to be here. The experience in the hospital was very interesting and I really enjoyed it, but honestly, I was homesick for the camp. The friends I met in Paris were extremely kind to me. I was out at dinner every night and for most of my luncheons and I very much enjoyed being with Mrs. S. T. M—— and that nice nurse I told you of; but I do love my job here. I'm being spoiled, I'm afraid, by the appreciation these boys show for the touch of home we women give the canteen. I will try to tell some of the pleasant things that happened to us in a single day—yesterday, for illustration. One of the peasants in the kitchen brought us a bunch of violets from her garden. Two cadets each gave us a book. Another brought three new magazines. Another gave us a pretty little wicker basket filled with the most delicious things to eat, gathered from three or four boxes from home. A lieutenant sent us a beautiful basket of flowers that cheer up the whole canteen.

The cooks of the different squadrons seem to be having a competition, with us for judges—and the result is the most delicious food that makes our mess very acceptable. Yesterday we were presented with white biscuits, griddle cakes, doughnuts, apple fritters, a peach shortcake, a mince pie and a big chocolate cake. B—— and three friends of his walked to a little peasant village and brought us a roast chicken, wrapped in a newspaper. So after "lights out" they and Miss H—— and I had a supper party. One of them has just been brevetted, so the party was for him. There are a great many pictures in my mind that I shall never forget.

Our new hut is a memorial from his parents to a boy who was killed in aviation, and we have *carte blanche* to furnish it in the most homelike manner possible. So we are working on it and have ordered wicker chairs (we're sat on nothing but iron camp chairs up to date) and they will seem mighty good. We are to have a big fireplace, and window-seats with cushions and pillows and big heavy tables with polished tops. Won't it be wonderful? I suppose there isn't another such canteen in France. I shall write often to Mr. and Mrs. M——— of New York, and give them descriptions of what goes on, and how their gift is being appreciated. Just now the building is being used for classes by the army, but we expect to get in very soon.

Although it is midwinter our weather lately has been beautiful. We have had regular sunny south days during the past week. I've been out in the sun without coat or hat. I feel so well since my cold has gone, I can hardly stay indoors. Aha! This very hour, while I am writing, a Christmas box came, over a month late, indeed, but it was great fun. It was my first package from anywhere. Everything was there and in good condition. That fig-nut candy makes a great hit. I wish I could get some from time to time. The boys are extremely fond of it and it is nice to have something out of the ordinary to give away. The bulbs mother sent will be a great addition to the new canteen. Don't be sorry the box wasn't on time. I told you what a delightful Christmas I had, and it is really more appreciated coming at this time, for so many of the boys gave us things from their boxes.

I told you that we have two really brilliant pianists here, one very classic, the other the best rag-time man I ever heard. Now we have discovered a gentle-faced, homesick little Southerner, a mechanic, who clogs and does the "buck and wing" in a way to rival the professionals. When he and our rag-time pianist get together in the midst of an enthusiastic mob of soldiers it is a treat. Last night I caught him homesick as anything because he had just received a lot of letters, and made him dance. The applause and admiration cheered him up into another boy and today he brought his girl's picture up to show me.

This morning I went to call on the quartermasters. They have been particularly nice to us. They got out a big cake that had been presented to them by one of the squadrons, took me all over their store house, and showed me their collection of war trophies, I wish so much you could understand how unbelievably kind and thoughtful all these men are. When I told some of the men Y. M. secretaries in Paris that I had never heard a word of profanity and that there had never been the slightest suggestion of unpleasantness, and that no one who had been drinking had ever come into the building, they could hardly believe it. But it is absolutely true. So you see how fortunate I have been in my camp.

I haven't heard from home since you began to get my letters from here, but I do hope you are at last convinced that I did right to come and are really happy about it. I wouldn't change this experience for anything. You know I have only known one sort of people all my life. Now I am becoming acquainted with a good many sorts and am liking them all. The other night I had a long talk with a funny little ex-navy man, his hands covered with tattooing, who delighted in telling the wild experiences that he has been through. This morning an expugilist with the most polished speech, and mild, kindly eyes, and courteous manners, told me of some of his battles in the ring. They love to have a listener while they talk about themselves, bless their hearts. Men won't act really interested in each other, but I listen with breathless interest while they recount their tales of prowess. It isn't put on a bit, either. Every minute of it is like reading an interesting and thoroughly human book.

14

I want to tell you in this letter a few of the excitements which I have kept out of my letters for fear you would worry about me, and to make a few confessions. I went up yesterday in an aeroplane. The most wonderful, indescribable sensation! One of the instructors took me up all done up in leather coats, helmets and goggles. We went up four thousand meters; higher, I think, than any of the boys have been. Oh! it was great! There was not the slightest suggestion of fear; just a tremendous exhilaration. Never in my life have I so enjoyed anything. All the time I was up I wanted to shout and sing. I looked down at the camp and felt as though we could plough right through all the buildings and never hurt a wing tip.

Such is the sensation of irresistible power imparted by the machine. From the standpoint of the ground I've always thought one must feel in an aeroplane like a mere atom. On the contrary, I felt as though our machine was the centre of the universe, the master of the elements, and that we could play with that world down there and its forces as we play with the air and the clouds. Our big, wide, straight road was a thread, below, and the river a dark little ribbon. I'm so glad I went up. I shan't again, so you needn't worry. But this one trip I will never forget, you may be sure.

My other adventure was a delightful moonlight ride in a motorcycle side-car, with an ex-national racer driving. Maybe that wasn't fun, too! He is one of the nicest fellows in camp; very mild and quiet, with really charming manners. He has raced under an assumed name. His family have never known about it. I don't think he is much over twenty, but the minute I heard his story of racing I remembered that I had seen his picture on the sporting page and his assumed name. He drove as carefully as if I were a basket of eggs and never let out over twenty-five miles an hour, I should guess, but it was great fun. No windshield and being so close to the ground made it seem entirely different from an automobile.

Another tardy confession is that I have been having a little touch of water-on-the-knee, that dear old friend of mine and of the family. I got a splendid rubber bandage and also a crepe one and bound it up, and used a cane the last few days I was in Paris, and it steadily improved. Then when I got back one of the army doctors fixed it and it got well immediately. He is a wizard with adhesive plaster. He put on a strapping that was twice as comfortable and just as firm as a plaster cast. Today the bandaging is all off and the knee is perfectly well. I really haven't minded it at all, as it was only for a couple of weeks, and only enough for the use of a cane anyway. I only speak of it for fear you will hear somehow that I have been hobbling and would think I was concealing something serious.

Now don't worry about me! I wouldn't have told you these things except that I thought they would interest you and knew that if my letters went on too placidly you would get suspicious. Don't you wish you were having some of these excitements? It 's a great life.

The officers are extremely nice to us and it helps us to feel that we are really useful here. They are particularly helpful about the new hut, and are arranging for a special electric line that will give us lights all night, and a long distance telephone, and all sorts of thoughtful extras.

A French officer just came in and said he had two large pictures of his home in Biarritz, which he would be happy to present to us. Wasn't that nice of him? It will help in the decoration.

We've just added apple pie to our menu and you ought to see the boys eat it. We have to furnish the sugar, lard, flour and apples to the baker. And it was a struggle to teach these French cooks how to make American pie-crust. But it is worth the trouble. The boys eat a hundred pies—four hundred pieces (and only one piece is allowed per man) in an astonishingly short time. It is a joy to see the room crowded with men, each with a piece of pie and a cup of chocolate, munching contentedly and happier and more comfortable than at any other time of the day. This job has its satisfactions, you see.

15

Such a fat handful of letters have come in each day for three days that I have had a great treat.

And now a trusty young lieutenant has offered to censor my letters, so I shall be a little more free in what I tell you, for I have been a little hesitant about detailing some of the interesting things that have happened for fear that somehow my stories might get back to the boys.

Everything goes on swimmingly and I am busy and happy all the time. This afternoon Dr. Anson Phelps Stokes was here for a short time and promised that he would tell you how well I am and how nicely I am situated. He is to return soon and will probably see father in six or seven weeks.

I'm wondering how you liked the letter full of adventures—my last it was. Just after it had gone I received several home letters, all breathing a spirit of thankfulness that I at least, of our four in the war, was having a quiet, safe time, and no one need worry about me. And now I am afraid you will all be up in the air. But I hope you'll trust my good judgment as well as my good luck and a kind Providence which takes special care of children and—such as me. I promise you I will never transgress again. For I am not working up another adventure. My wildest dissipation lately has been a motorcycle ride or two with the ex-racer, who is one of the nicest lads I ever met. He reminds me very much of our P——. The same quiet, considerate manner and a lot of fire under a calm exterior; about the same age, too, I imagine—hardly over twenty. The trips are really a fine out-of-door recreation, and as he is much interested in looking up historic places, I anticipate some rare trips when the weather gets settled.

It is much warmer now and I am able to wear normal clothing again. For in cold weather I have been obliged to wear all my heaviest clothes, with a sweater, and that long leather coat, and the heavy wool and fur coat besides. Then I had to wear over my shoes, aviation boots, leather, fur-lined affairs that make one feel just like Charlie Chaplin. Though the mercury does not go very low in mid-winter here, the cold is damp and penetrating and it seemed impossible to get thoroughly warm. But we are very comfortable now.

An unusual party happened on last Saturday night. Miss H—— and I were invited to a *"Petite Soirée,"* in a French home. It was kind of them to do this honour to the American strangers; and a gentleman who had been active in it had been very helpful to the Y. M. C. A.; so we accepted, of course. It was in the tiny home of a French soldier (*blessé*, he has lost a leg) and is living all alone in the littlest, cunningest house I think I ever saw. The walls on all sides were decorated with old fire arms, and battle axes and sabres and other relics, some from the time of Henry of Navarre. He had a big red leather shield in the hall with the arms he carried in this war.

I can understand enough French now to follow ordinary conversation fairly well, and he had some wonderful tales, both legends of his relics and stories of his own adventures. He was really charming, all dressed up in his finest uniform and bearing all his medals, and so pleased to be entertaining Americans that it was quite touching. There were several other French people there, among them a refugee girl from Lille who spoke English. We sat about a table and ate big ham sandwiches, prepared with much forethought as a special American dainty, and delicious, rich cake. The others drank wine, but when I declined they were very tactful and sent immediately for some water, concealing their wonder at my strange foreign ways very sucessfully.

Some of the mechanics here say the most delightful things. The other day I sat in the neighbourhood of a big husk with the skin off his nose and both eyes black. I asked if he had been in a wreck. He said "No, it was just a fight." After describing it in detail, he relapsed into an embarrassed silence, but I could see him struggling to think up a topic of conversation. At last he said, with his eyes on that still visible scar on my neck, "And what happened to you, ma'am? Was you tryin' to commit suicide?"

Another one, a jolly, round-faced, loud-voiced cook, announced that it was all right for the cook of a rival squadron to give us griddle-cakes if we could manage to swallow the things, but when it came to "stealin' his girl" (I being the girl) away from him, that was more than he could stand.

One came up with great seriousness the other night and said he would be mighty obliged if I would do a little errand for him in Paris, and when I asked what it might be, he opened his fist and displayed a tooth which he had broken off and wished me to match. A thousand times I have wished my merry friend C—— were here, but she would have died of laughter long since.

They give us such subtle compliments! Like this: "Which is the nut choc'lits, ma'am?"

"This in the blue wrapper. Do you like that kind?"

"Yas'm, I like blue wrappers and I like blue eyes, too!"

Then embarrassment and blushes for fear he has said the wrong thing. Oh! I tell you, men are rich!

We haven't moved into the new canteen yet, but I've been down to inspect my own room and I'm going to love it. It looks about two sizes smaller than my bathroom at home and it's going to take careful planning to get in it with my luggage. One of the cadets who is in the room as I write this, and who has been kind to us, has offered to make some shelves and so arrange things that with my impedimenta packed in the most military precision, I can still get in the door and perhaps even turn around. It will be necessary to keep every smallest article in its own particular place all the time. My good friend and I were down there planning most of Sunday afternoon and it is going to be fun to settle things. Do you remember that summer at K—— when L—— and G—— and I each fixed up a box-stall in the barn as a little room and invited each other to tea every day? This reminds me of that.

The moving picture machine has been set up today and we think we'll stage a show tonight, though the place is littered with debris from the carpenters and there is a big hole where the fireplace is to be. The new stove will be a joy and the ovens with fire boxes underneath will lessen our present work greatly. We are cooking now on two rows of brick with a piece of sheet iron across the top and the wood smoke is pretty bad. It is in the kitchen; we don't have to be out there much, though.

I'll have to close. My letters do string out indefinitely, don't they? Usually they take six or eight sittings before they are finished, as I am constantly interrupted. Tell L—— I have the most miserable job of knitting ahead I've ever tried. One of the boys broke his shoulder and the doctor cut his perfectly good new sweater off and I have the job of mending the sweater, almost a hopeless thing, I'm afraid. I have just sewed one of the boys' wristwatch on and am now wondering what he will do in the event of a bath.

This is truly the end. Oh! do send me one of those big boxes of marshmallows now and then! Wouldn't they give the final homelike touch to our fireplace, though? And there isn't such a thing in France. Everything comes better in tin, by the way, especially nut candy.

16

I have postponed writing for a day or two beyond the usual time, partly because we have been even busier than usual and partly because I've had a little touch of indigestion and wanted to be able to tell you when I wrote that I am absolutely well, as I now am. F——'s mixture of soda, bismuth and magnesia effected the cure. By the way, I wish I might have a lot more of the stuff, because I give a dose of it to every boy who comes by with the tummy-ache.[1]

Things go on like a breeze. The canteen is crowded almost all the time and the boys are appreciative of the tiniest little things we do for them. Why, when we just give one a cup of hot milk when he feels a little under the weather, he remembers it for weeks and tells his friends, and even writes home about it. That happens over and over again. That sort of thing grips one's imagination, you know, and you can't let a single chance slip.

One thing that has been quite touching is the delight of some of the boys when I have "trusted" them for little purchases when they were "broke." Some of them can hardly believe it when I tell them to pay me when they can. I always slip the money into the box myself, as it isn't fair to the Y. M. to take a chance, but I wish you could have seen the number that came straight from the paymaster to me the other day and gave me the shiniest *francs* they had, reminding me of the time I gave them some cigarettes or chocolate weeks before. Honestly, I believe I got back a lot more money than I loaned out, and every one of them seemed to be so pleased that I had been willing to trust him. What tiny little things count.

Presents come in to us every day. These are the most generous

---

1. This stomach powder is composed of one part of sodium bicarbonate, one part of bismuth subnitrate and two parts of magnesium oxide by weight. Dose: half teaspoonful to a teaspoonful in water; for sour stomach, heartburn and indigestion, etc.

boys in the world. They really embarrass us with gifts. Last night a boy whom I know quite well gave me a newspaper parcel, saying it was a present that another chap had received from his sister. It was no use to him (I think myself it was sent by mistake) and he wanted to give it to me but was too shy to do it himself. When I opened it, I discovered a really lovely silky lace muffler affair, the sort of thing to put over one's head in an automobile in the evening. Now, I don't know that lad at all, but he told his friend that I gave him a cup of water one day when he was on guard. Isn't it touching? Mother, aren't you a little glad that I came?

L——'s letter saying she had a big box of Page & Shaw's on her desk that she wished she could share with me came at a psychological time. At that very moment I was opening the most wonderful tapestry-covered box of candy I ever saw—a present from a lieutenant who was stationed here, and hadn't seen another American girl for months.

This morning a boy came in with his pockets bulging and fished out the greatest collection of stuff,—Washington coffee, some bacon, candy, sugar and sterno, saying he thought I could use it better than he.

A lovely long letter came from mother yesterday, just when I was feeling depressed over the rumour that thirty thousand sacks of mail went down in the Tuscania. If you get a chance, assure L—— H—— that whoever told her not to come here for the purpose of singing was just right. It would more than probably be the ruin of her voice to try to sing here in the cold and damp of the canteen and the altogether different climate. I haven't told you this before, because I know F—— was particularly anxious for me to sing. But I haven't sung a note since I came. The climate and the circumstances of our daily life are really very trying on the vocal chords. My speaking voice is only now getting natural after these months and I know that the only way to save my alleged voice is to lock it up and leave it until summer, or perhaps until I get home. It is too bad, because most of the time I am so happy, and feel so well, I want to burst out singing, just as I used to at home, but I have held in so far.

It was a coincidence for mother to mention that L—— was visiting at the H——'s for a few days, for I looked up from the letter and smiled across the room to their boy C—— H—— drinking coffee and eating ginger cookies at a little table in the corner. Do tell his family that he is here, well and cheerful, and making the best of everything, just as all the real men do, and that I'll take the best care of him I can. Isn't it pleasant to meet old friends this way? C—— H—— is such a cheerful soul and sees the humorous side of things so refreshingly, I am especially glad I can see him here every day.

And you'll be glad to hear that Dr. Harry Emerson Fosdick is to lecture for us tonight. It will be great to see him. I'm hoping he doesn't know I'm here, it would be such fun to surprise him.

17

Several packages have come all at once and in good condition.

There is one thing I wish you'd send: Quite a supply of American adhesive tape, surgeon's plaster, you know. The French tape is poor. I need tape every day on all sorts of cuts and sores I try my first aid on. My greatest surgical triumph is the successful treatment of the thumb of one of the secretaries. He cut the end of it off in the bread cutter and I fixed it with bichloride of mercury and the most scientific bandage I could make. He took it to the doctor, who sent him back to me to complete the cure—*Bon!*

These boys are simply delightful. One who has a talent for caricature and writes clever little rhymes, cheers us up almost every day with a funny sketch and a poem *apropos* of some situation that has arisen in camp. I'm saving some of them to show you. And I am so pleased with the way they confide in us. I went walking with one the other day, a boy I've known very well here, and who has been among the most thoughtful, cheerful and helpful of our friends. On this walk he told me the story of his life. It wrung my heart. It was more tragic than anything I've ever read in my life. Such things are not fair. Oh, how I wanted to give him some of the fun and love and happy memories I've been simply smothered in all my life. He deserves them far more than I. Why should his life have been so hard that it would simply have wrecked any one with a character less strong? How I honour that man!

By the way, there are girls in the United States and not a few, whom I could almost kill, I do believe. If they could know what it is like for these trusting boys to come over here and long and long for letters that don't come, or when they do are such a disappointment, perhaps they would have a heart. I know no less than seven men here who were definitely engaged when they left home and who have heard since that their girls were either engaged to someone else or married. If I know seven such, how many are there in all? Fortunately most of them have sense enough to consider it a lucky escape; but it certainly enrages me when they tell me about it over here. I know what it means from this end, what the life here is and what these boys have to look forward to, and I cannot bear to see them treated cruelly by their most loved and trusted ones at home, for whom they are surrendering life itself.

Do you remember that I spoke of our housekeeper's husband who is a cook at the front? He is back for a ten days' leave and is fearfully worn, poor man. On his way back the other night the Boche dropped a bomb on his train and killed seventeen men in the car just ahead of him. That seemed a trifling incident to him, so you can imagine what he has been through.

We are having wondrously beautiful moonlight nights lately, but those that know shudder at the terrible "*les nuits blancs*" and think what it means somewhere, and hope for a merciful cloud.

While I was laid up (just a part of two days) one of the cadets, who is an architect, sent me a lot of model alphabets so that I could practice lettering and printing free hand. It is really interesting. When I get a little more expert I'll send you a sample.

We wear uniforms in the canteen now—long blue overall aprons and white Dutch caps. It's a great saving in clothes and will be very suitable in summer.

18

There is a lull for an hour or so and I'll talk to you. Despite the rumour of a great loss of mail on the Tuscania I have received quite a handful of letters this week, including two from G——, containing pictures, and a package of fig loaf from L——.

Thanks a lot for that. I dole it out to the gloomiest looking ones I see, and always the little personal attention and "something from home" brings a sincere response and they are likely to speak of it for days afterward.

And the pictures were more welcome than I can possibly tell you. The one of G—— on the veranda down South and of P—— in his uniform outside the dining room door, when home on his leave, I simply adore. I have carried them about in my apron pocket for three days, showing them proudly to all my best friends, and I actually have lit my bedside candle several times in the night to look at them. Do enclose snapshots of the other members of the family as often as you can. None of my mail from home is censored and I look eagerly in every letter for a possible picture of some dear person or thing.

I sewed J—— R——'s wings on his new uniform yesterday and today he has left for the acrobatic school. He has made a fine record here, but I was very sorry to see him go.

Last night Miss H—— and I went to the opera with Col. ——, the commandant of the school and a charming humorous captain. The opera was *Herodiade* (very well done, too) and that "*Il est doux, il est bon*" aria that I sang for months, from this little opera (father will remember it as the acrobatic one he liked), brought the dear music room back to me with some of you over on the window seat while I sang at the piano. By the way, the captain firmly and consistently denied ever having heard of John the Baptist. Don't you love that?

The colonel is a peach and I think he is going to try to have

R—— transferred here. He asked me all about him and took his name, so I'm hoping hard, but I'm like father about not trying to steer another's destiny, and anyhow I just couldn't make the direct request. Anyway, it isn't fair to bother these busy army people with personal matters. But it may come about and then wouldn't I be glad?

The other day a boy whom I have noticed in passing and had seen sitting about a good deal, came up and said he'd like to speak with me alone. I'd never talked with him before. He said that when he came here he hadn't written home for nine years, but he had been looking and looking at me and at last had written home. The very day before he had received a beautiful answer from his sister, enclosing a photograph of herself (a very sweet-looking girl) and had heard the news for the first time that his mother was dead. And it seems that the reason he had written in the first place was, that I look so much like his mother of the years ago! Wasn't it dear of him to tell me? It is the first time in my life I've ever been grateful for looking like this, but I'm glad I do, if it helped him. He has had his picture taken and came up this morning to show it to me and to say that he is going to do everything he possibly can to make up to them for what he has caused them of sorrow. He asked me to write to his sister and tell her about him, and I'm going to do it. He wants to tell me the whole tale as soon as he has time enough to give me the whole story at once.

19

I'm often asked to write and give assurances to anxious parents. Here is something I wish mother would do for me. There is a lad here, one of the squadron cooks, who has been particularly thoughtful of us, bringing in hot biscuits and pie and griddle cakes and cooking little extras for us. He hasn't been very well and was detailed to kitchen work and he certainly is a great cook. He has been a real spot of sunshine for us and has been so cordial and pleasant and has seemed so glad to give us little attentions, that it has added to the pleasure of receiving them. He told me today that his mother is very anxious to know where he is, but of course he hasn't been able to get the location through the censorship. I suppose they are afraid the letters might fall into the hands of the Germans. So I said my mother could make a pretty close guess as to where we are, because our early letters were plainly postmarked from here, as I found out from the answers and I was sure you would be glad to write his mother.

His name is C—— and his mother's address is Mrs. —— of ——, Arizona. So please write and tell her that he is here and quite well again, and has been helpful to your grateful daughter. He expected to be sent home and came in one day to get your address, saying he wanted to write a note to you when he arrived in America, and tell you about me, but since his health has improved so much he isn't to go. I told him to go and see you. He is a rough diamond, but a thoroughly dear boy. If any such appear, just be good to them for me, won't you, for if I send them to you it will mean that they have been kind to me. Bless them!

Our movie machine is working now and we have shows twice a week. Mr. and Mrs. Sidney Drew and all sorts of familiar scenes, for all are American pictures. With H—— R—— at the piano, the soldier-artist that I told you about, and the big hut crowded with enthusiastic boys, making killingly funny remarks, the movies have a charm here that you don't know at home.

I saw Dr. Harry Emerson Fosdick on Thursday and he gave us a surpassingly fine and charmingly appropriate lecture, precisely adapted from beginning to end. He said he'd write father about me and I am very glad, for he can't help saying I 'm very strong and well and very happy.

Oh! Don't you love this? There is a curious man here, a sailor from childhood, who has been all over the world and tells us tales by the hour. He says he has sixty pictures tattooed on himself. On his forearm there is a head of Christ with the Crown of Thorns. I asked him yesterday to show it to our solemnest and most pious Y. M. C. A. secretary. The secretary said in a somewhat pained voice: "Why, that is the Head of Christ, isn't it?"

And my friend replied, cheerily, "Yep, that's the ol' boy himself." He told me he had a couple of spaces left that were to be filled with the "Ascension," and "Hunting in the Jungle." He also has two brothers, but as he has never seen them he "don't take much interest in 'em."

20

I haven't written you, I know, for a longish time, but R——'s cable will reassure you and I've been so busy that if I'd even taken time to write I would have felt that I was not on my job . . . later: I got that far in two and a half hours, writing a word every time I got a chance. Now I 'm hiding behind the piano and hope to accomplish something.

We've moved! That sounds like nothing but means a great deal. Miss H—— went away for two weeks and I was alone to serve. The weather took the opportunity to be terribly bad so that flying was impossible, and the little old canteen was jammed to the doors every minute. Last Saturday and Sunday I poured one hundred and sixty-five gallons of coffee and chocolate each day, sixteen cups to the gallon, which means twenty-six hundred and forty cups. I leave to you to figure out the amount of elbow-grease expended. But the boys need and appreciate these refreshments. It is well worth an "after-the-ball backache" and I sleep so well I am completely restored the next morning.

We took four days to move, all of them in terrible weather, too. I moved into my little room. At five p. m. it didn't have either window panes or a door and had cracks all over it big enough to view the scenery through. Somebody dumped my bed and suitcase on the floor. Then I was called away—purposely as I now know. When I went back I felt just like Sara Crewe in *The Little Princess*. My bed was up, my sleeping bag all fixed, two extra blankets on the top, the suitcases on saw horses, a work bench fitted up like a dressing table, with a trench mirror above it, a pail of nice hot water, the windows fixed and the door hung; a little kerosene stove warming it up cosily, some red curtains nailed over the windows, a chair from somewhere, three or four lighted candles, most of the cracks, stuffed up with newspaper, and a plate of good hot dinner on top of my stove. Bless the boy or boys that did it! I am suspecting J—— L—— of it.

I made thirty curtains for the new hut, and to hang them was a job. But every boy that helped me wrote his name above the window that he fixed and so we have fifteen memorial windows, some with sketches besides the names. One man did two and named one after me, so I have one, too. There was a long line clamouring for windows when they were all done. I let two men fix the curtains in my own room, so they are memorial also. Yesterday I was starting to cut some more curtains. They were for my washstand and wardrobe. But some boys came along and insisted not only on cutting them, but on pinning and hemming them, too, while a crowd stood around and commented.

We opened the new canteen to a hungry, cold mob that had been chocolateless and tobaccoless and bread-and-jamless for four days, and they rushed in to find a blazing fire in the fireplace and the big window seats (so wide that my feet don't come to the edge) piled up with pillows, a new Victor, a fine billiard table, a piano, and five or six hundred books; good books, too. I haven't a doubt but this new hut is by far the best and most attractive in France. The boys simply love it and are here every minute they are off duty. I've been down to the city several times lately, and it is full of American soldiers, but not *our* boys. They are all up at our Y. M. My! I am glad.

And they are so thoughtful of us! Yesterday morning the cadets had doughnuts, for breakfast for the first time in the history of the camp and *fourteen* of them saved their doughnuts for me. Almost every time I go to my room I find that someone has opened the door and slipped something in. Today I found a book, a box of chocolates, two magazines, four very pretty pictures for my walls and a big pumpkin pie.

Two splendid packages have come lately: fig loaf and fruit cake and L——'s chocolates. Oh, delicious! I have the best of luck with my mail. Anything edible that is sent in tin is perfect when it gets here. Don't forget to send me a big box of marshmallows every now and then. Can you imagine how the boys will love to toast them around the open fire?

21

My room is a peach.—the best little room in camp, I know. I bought a bureau and a mirror and a rug and an easy chair, and with a dozen metres of pink cretonne and some help in shelves from the boys, it's turning into a cosy little place. I have a shelf for a wardrobe, with another shelf above for hats, cretonne curtains covering the whole, a shelf for a washstand, with another below for soap, sterno, etc., with cretonne over that, too, and a long window with four panes and a convenient little ledge beneath it. I have tan-coloured net curtains at the middle panes and pink and tan cretonne ones at the sides and mother's bulbs growing on the ledge, with a *carafe* of water on one end and a box of candy on the other. Oh, I'm in real luxury now! I do so wish you might be here even for fifteen minutes, so I could conduct you about as I have just done for some Y. M. C. A. inspectors.

A great many of the flying cadets are being brevetted now. I sew on the wings of nearly all of them and am getting an almost uncomfortable reputation as a mender of sweaters and uniforms and cuts and colds.

We are having quite warm weather now and are serving about as much cold milk as hot chocolate. I have worked out a plan for a little Italian garden. The new secretary in charge is a peach of a man, by the way, the best Y. M. C. A. secretary I've ever seen. Perhaps it's because he lets me do pretty much as I like. So I think I'll get the Italian garden. The new hut is very complete and convenient. I'm going to plant a lot of morning glories at the front tomorrow, and the secretary agrees with me that we can make the whole front yard, consisting of several hundred square feet, into a nice place to sit all summer. We are to have cinder and awnings and chairs and tables. The little court in the back will make a very perfect little garden—a pergola on top, some box trees, some plants and green garden tables and chairs. Oh, you wait!

It's the most fun you ever imagined, planning and fixing comfortable things and even unheard-of luxuries for these dear boys.

22

I'm trying to get another letter in sideways. If you knew how interrupted my attempts are, how I can only write a few words at a time, often keeping a letter going for days, you would pardon the incoherence, I know.

Miss H―― has come back, so I am not quite so rushed as I have been for the last two or three weeks. I actually had an hour's nap yesterday for the first time in two months. I am really amazed at the way my health keeps up and I laugh when I think of all the worry before I started, about my insomnia. I sleep right through reveille now and have had to train myself carefully to wake up in time for business.

This new hut is a perfect joy and the two new men secretaries are delightful, so all goes even better than usual. We are to have another lady here and I am trying hard to engineer it so that E―― D―― may be the one. She would love it here, I know. I am certain that she could stand the work. I wish you would reassure her mother about the whole thing, for I know how she hates to have her daughter come, but from all these months of experience I do not hesitate to say it will be a great thing for her in every way. I am mighty glad to hear that she is on her way and hope she will be assigned to this camp.

On Sunday I looked up to find Q―― K―― and J―― A―― standing in front of me, both wreathed in broad smiles. I wish you would let their families know that they are here and looking husky and cheerful.

Someone or rather some "United Fruit Growers," I believe, sent hundreds of boxes of delicious apples to the Y. M. C. A. to be distributed to the boys. You've no idea how good they taste, after these insipid French apples, and the boys have all been chewing steadily for two days. The floor gets so covered with cores we have to sweep it out every little while. Wasn't it mighty nice of those people to send them? I don't know of any gift that has been so appreciated, not even free tobacco.

My little room that I have described is done now and is very cosy and homelike. It is pathetic to see how the boys love to stand in the doorway or look in at the window, and just gaze at a place that looks like home. Their barracks are so bare, you know, and this little cretonny room with its pictures is a great contrast.

We have been having perfectly glorious weather for two weeks, ideal for aviation, and many of the flying cadets have been making fine progress. But not all our weather is good. Last night we had a most terrific combination of wind, thunder and hail storm, if you can imagine all those things together. I thought the hut would flatten down to the ground or else bowl up the road, but we survived with no greater damage than the discovery of a number of leaks in our new roof. Today it is blowing too much for flying and the French housekeeper says that March is always like this. So the business of the *Ecole d'Aviation* will languish and the Y. M. C. A. will flourish for some time. This morning we had a long line winding about the room and out of the door waiting for coffee and the line kept up for hours. My coffee pouring arm is getting to be a strong one.

23

Two of the boys I know the best have just had their tonsils out and I promised that I would go to see them in the hospital. So I managed to break away on Sunday and got to the hospital about six, only to be told that ladies were allowed to call only between two and four. It is a big hospital full of Americans, built on three sides of a large court yard, with hundreds of windows. Some lad that knew me saw me there in the court yard and pretty soon the windows were full of heads in all stages of convalescence, some in pyjamas and some in bath robes, with the nurses and orderlies trying to get them back to bed from behind, and all talking and whistling and sending messages, and letting down strings so that I could tie the flowers I had brought on them. I had a big bunch of jonquils that went up in a minute. My, but it was funny! Pretty soon a few doctors came along and decided to let me in to see my friends in order to stop the general riot.

Our new head secretary insists upon a day off a week for each of us, so I will be able to write regularly at last. I hope to see some of the interesting places in this vicinity. This is one of the most historic and unique places in the world. We must all come here after the war is over and I will show you about. The other day I took a ride along the bank of the river to see the curious caves. There are great chalky cliffs for miles, and the people have hollowed out caves and live in them, regular cliff dwellers. You see doors and windows and steps fifty or sixty feet up in the side of an almost sheer cliff, with chimneys coming out in the meadows above. I don't know whether they have skylights in the ground, but if so, I should think an occasional cow might fall through. Then they have great wine caves, too. J—— L—— explored an interesting looking tunnel the other day and walked right into the kitchen of an astonished French woman. I wish I could tell you more about the neighbourhood, but am afraid that even what I have written will be "*defendu*."

I think of our dear flyer P—— almost all the time and wonder if all goes well in his American flying field. We have lots of smashes here, but no one seems to be seriously hurt. There has been only one flying fatality since I came and that did not happen on the school field. The war is coming close, though. One of the best friends I have had here was killed at the acrobatic school the other day. It has made me feel pretty badly. Almost everywhere I look I am reminded of him. He gave us so many things, books and pictures, the Lux, even, that I wash my handkerchiefs in. Such is war.

We are giving the boys nice fresh milk now in the afternoons, and they simply love it. The French people about here seem not to have mastered the art of cream separating, and the whole milk is quite like our rich Jersey milk on the farm down South.

Tell L—— that I can't imagine anything more delicious than a tin box of nut fudge. This French candy hasn't an honest-to-goodness taste at all. And oh! do try to send some peanut brittle some time. Isn't it funny what we crave when we can't get it? I never thought anything of peanut brittle at home,—and don't forget the caramels.

Father asked why they took away my passport at the Y. M. C. A. in Paris. It is because being a member of the United States Army I have to have a military movement order card, signed by the general's adjutant, to enable me to be in the camp, to travel at military rates, etc. My original passport is filed at the Y. M. C. A. Headquarters and I can get it when I go home.

24

Yesterday was Easter, with terrific thunder showers and glorious sunshine. The showers disclosed a lot of leaks in my ceiling, I kept busy moving the table out from under and changing the position of my bed until there were so many that I put everything portable away and let her rain.

We had our regular morning siege of coffee pouring. There are two or three thousand soldiers here now and our line twines all about the main room and out into the billiard and reading room for most of our three hours' serving time. They drink hundreds of gallons of coffee every day, besides the nice cold milk and the hot chocolate.

I thought it would be homelike to have some Easter eggs, and so boiled some pieces of pink cretonne for a time, trying to make pink dye, but it wouldn't work. So I made some dull green and deep orange eggs with a curious weed that grows here and some onion skins. The secretaries were duly surprised. They think I am awfully kiddish, I know, but I love to do things like that and can't stop now so they are getting used to me.

In the evening (I'm still talking about Easter) we had a service, with a very fine little bit of a sermon and lots of singing. It is odd to go to a Sunday service and sing "Love's Old Sweet Song," and "Annie Laurie," and "Keep the Home Fires Burning," and even "The End of a Perfect Day," instead of hymns, but they seem to go better and we do sing two hymns anyhow. After the service we distributed four hundred boxes of candy, sent over by the American W. C. T. U. Wasn't it funny, after church on Easter? But why not?

I had another cold early in the week and this time I managed differently. Instead of letting it get a tight clutch as the last one did, I stayed in bed two days,—very discouraging to the cold, which has become much weakened and will probably soon die. It sounds like an awful bore to stay in bed here, but honestly, it was a good time. I sewed on a lot of R. M. A.'s, read five books and made several hundred cards for our Library Catalogue. I wish you could have seen the things the boys sent to interest and amuse me, the dear things! Flowers galore from glorious azalea plants to little bunches of weak white violets, with short stems and no green leaves about them, that they had picked themselves; oranges, dates, figs, pounds of candy, enough books and magazines to start a small shop, lots of pictures, any number of jokes clipped from magazines, countless notes, a jar of guava jelly and even two or three kinds of medicine. You see it's so long since they have had a chance to do anything like that, they shower everything on me.

Will mother or L—— or someone please write a note to Miss L—— T—— of B—— in M—— and tell her that her brother A—— is here and is very well and cheerful. He is a nice fellow who wants his family to know how he is, from some disinterested viewpoint. He will probably be here several months.

25

I wish you could see the scene about me and hear the noise in which I'm trying to concentrate my thoughts as I write. I am sitting at a wobbly wooden table, on a wobbly wooden bench, with six boys eating bread and jam, with coffee, at the same table. The room is simply jammed and is full of voices and laughter and tramping feet and the crashing and clinking of dishes and cups. The piano is going and a splendid voice is singing "Mother Machree" in one corner, the Victor is doing "The Hunt in the Black Forest," four men are giving an exhibition match of billiards, every seat is taken at the writing benches. I have to keep my eyes down on my paper every second, for if I look up and catch someone's eye he will almost invariably come straight over to talk.

A six-year-old Belgian boy that we seem to have adopted (he says his mother is dead and his father is fighting and he doesn't know why he is here) is tugging at my arm, hoping I will admire a curious picture that might be intended for an aeroplane that he has drawn. A soldier has just shown me a poem (awful rhythm) that a friend of his wrote and which was just published in the *Wheatville Chronicle*. Oh! this is a great life! Ah! Another wishes me to read four or five letters from his girl and see if I can make out what's the matter; he "didn't know he'd done nothing," and do I think she's really peeved or "just kiddin' him along"?

Our program is going on well: Movies twice a week with a most terrific jam every time,—humanity clinging to all the rafters and crowding the windows, one or two circuit concerts, or shows, or lectures sent down from headquarters. One night is reserved for home talent and one quiet one for writing letters especially, and the Sunday evening service.

Dear old P——, I wish you were here in my camp for your flying.

You'll never know how many things your sister has tried to do for stranger boys just because somehow they reminded me of you—age, or size, or eyes, or hair, or expression, or some vague resemblance that I can't analyse.

26

This is a most dismal, rainy, windy Sunday afternoon. We had just made up our minds to close the canteen on Sunday afternoons, so that our well-meaning, hard-working staff might have some time off, and were all looking forward to *château-ing* and possibly even picnic-ing when this awful day dampened our plans. And as I've told you, the boys flock to the canteen in crowds when the weather forbids flying; so we've decided, of course, not to close today, but give the cold, hungry, melancholy boys their chocolate just the same.

And besides, I did have a day off this week, the first regular one I've ever had, although it is a rule of the Association that everyone shall have one each week. Our staff has never been large enough to admit of it before, but we hope we can manage it from now on. My first was inglorious—a few errands in town, a hot bath, Oh! delicious, and a long sleep in a real bed with sheets! It doesn't sound like much of a party, does it? But I know now how to enjoy such luxuries.

My days go rushing by as full of interest and work and fun as usual. We have a new lady with us, making three in all, at this canteen. She is a Miss J—— A—— of N——. I like her very much. She is great fun, a good sport and a hard worker.

I have had other Christmas boxes, but mother's, sent on the scheduled time and delayed nearly four months, came yesterday. How I laughed when I unpacked the things for Christmas only. We'll save them for next Christmas. The wool I asked for is most welcome and I've already started a sweater with it. My own blue sweater with the grey, furry collar, is the most homelike thing I've seen for months. The pictures of myself that you sent me, taken at the time of starting, are out of date. I don't look like that any more. No, I don't mean that I've lost an eye or gone bald or anything, and have been concealing it from you. I've just changed quite a lot inside and out. But it was to be expected, wasn't it?

They are so kind to me here that they sometimes overdo it. I must tell you about the lights in my room. You know it isn't large, perhaps a quarter the size of my blue room at home. One day the head electrician called me in and there were five under electricians, all beaming broadly and waiting to see how I liked my room. They had put a light over my bureau and had bought a sort of holder for it in the shape of a glass rose, and had put a hanging reading lamp over the head of my bed, both brilliant Mazda lamps. The illumination nearly blinds me. And then yesterday they came around again, this time with a table light they had made out of a broken aeroplane propeller—a cute little holder, but it had a Mazda lamp, too. Now my room looks like the Great White Way itself. Of course I can't ever have them on all at once. It gives me a headache. But I do appreciate their desire to meet every possible need.

We have received orders that we must all wear identity tags, two around our necks and one on the wrist as, a bracelet, and as an ingenious boy is making me a ring out of a two *franc* silver piece, I shall soon be feeling with all my decorations like a Zulu princess, though I carefully left all such encumbrances at home.

A humorous incident with a pathetic side happened last night. One of the squadrons was suddenly ordered away and two of the boys came down with a wooden box and gave it to us. What do you suppose it was? Two live rabbits! It seems they were pets of the squadron and had been hopping around the barracks for months and the boys all loved them. So, when they were ordered away they brought them to me and said they "didn't mind goin' to the front just so long as you'll take care of our rabbits, ma'am." Goodness knows what I'll do with them. The general consensus of opinion favours rabbit pie, but they'll have to have it on my day off, that I know. When I think of what these boys are up against at the front, it wrings my heart and lends pathos to their every action.

27

There are a lot of Chinese French Colonials here, ditch diggers, etc. Some of them from Anam. They are about the lowest down people in the world, I think, especially the Anamites, who are a grade lower than the "Chinois." The boys call them "Dynamites" and "Carbides," the latter from the odour in their vicinity. They seem almost like mere animals, far less human and with much less personality than the most degraded blacks. They come into the canteen to try to buy tobacco and we aren't allowed to sell them a thing. They drop their money on the counter, grab the cigarettes and dash for the door, pursued by Americans, who lead them back, return the cigarettes, give them back their money and turn them out. They make believe they can't understand English, French or even head shakings and pointings at the door. So in self-defence we've had to learn three words of Chinese, "*Hanga cahai finili,*" which are entirely effective. I have no idea what it means. The boys declare that it is probably frightful swearing. But when the Chinese hear it, they go right out.

My cold is gone and I am feeling perfectly well again. The bulbs mother sent have bloomed. All day today I have had a charming little spray of narcissus. I do believe a hundred men have smelled of it and said it reminded them of a certain garden, or a certain person, or some dance or just "home."

I must write now to the mother of my friend, the mechanic with a broken hand. He broke the bones by getting it too near a revolving propeller. You know those propellers, going with frightful velocity, twenty revolutions per second or more, will draw anything in front right into them. I started out wrong with this lad, for in the first letter to his mother I added a P. S. to the effect that I would be sure to let her know each week how he is, and now seven or eight weeks have gone by. His hand is still bound up and I have no way of knowing whether there is anything wrong underneath the bandage; and now he even refuses to dictate. He just sits there and says: "Oh, you know how to say it better than I do. Tell her I'm all right and about the show and everything and ask about Helen and thank her for the package. You know—you can do it fine. I can't tell you the right words. You know how. Oh, please!" And the end of it is that his mother gets a letter per week from a perfect stranger, couched in un-son-like language which she probably hates. The chocolate boileth.

28

So, dear old P—— has got his wings, bless him! I knew he would make good in flying. I'm an expert aviator picker. Honestly, I know the earmarks. It amused me to have father describe and even draw P——'s wings. I've sewed on sixty or seventy of those things. The boys get awfully superstitious over here, and as it has happened that none of "my" aviators have been hurt, they all come to me for good luck. Yes, I'm keeping a list of the names. When is P—— likely to come over? Wouldn't it be perfect to have him and R—— here together? F—— suggested in a letter that the very worst that could befall the family would be to have them both flying here and for P—— and R—— to have a collision in midair and fall on me.

By the way, you wouldn't worry half so much about your aviator sons if you could live in an aviation school for a few weeks. Why, just this morning there was an awful "*zum-ming*" and sudden starting and stopping of an engine almost over the hut. My heart stopped, for I knew it meant a wreck in five seconds. The crash came and everyone rushed out but me,—I can't look until I know they are all right. The machine was just smashed to flinders, and the two aviators climbed out and laughed. You see? That aeroplane was in such small pieces that I could almost have carried away the biggest of them myself, and yet the men were barely scratched. As aviation is practised in this camp it isn't so dangerous after all. One of the aviators explained why. He says the machine they use here for instruction is probably the safest flying machine made. They have a very large wing area for their weight, and as a result can support themselves at very low speed, allowing one to land at reasonable velocity.

The passengers are strapped in the fuselage, which is in the centre of a network of spars, brace rods and wires. These are a great protection and the machine can be smashed to bits without seriously hurting the occupants. Besides, the planes are of tractor type; that is, with the motor in front, so that in case of a fall the motor strikes the ground first, instead of falling on the pilot, as might be the case with a pusher. Then, too, there are in a great camp like this a large number of spare planes and extensive repair shops, so there is no temptation to put the flyer into a doubtful machine. Perhaps these are some of the reasons why we have so few accidents here and practically no fatalities. My friend adds that he feels just as safe in his plane as in an automobile and he believes his chances of being injured in the plane are actually less.

We've had a busy two days—pay days. That always means an awful rush. The line winding round and round the canteen has never shortened. In half the allotted time they drink every bit of coffee and milk and chocolate that we can possibly prepare.

Tell dear G—— not to worry about that noble *fiancé* of hers. So far as the actual fighting and falling goes one must turn into a fatalist. It's the only way. But let her thank heaven that she doesn't have to worry about her soldier lover in any other way. And she is a mighty lucky girl. It's hard for these boys over here and I am learning considerateness and charity. You know that my ideals are just the same high ones that I learned, mother dear, in our sweet home life. But I pity these boys and forgive them and try to help them even when they are not behaving. Just let me tell you the story of one lad. He flunked out of college and joined the ambulance because he couldn't stop drinking. Then he transferred to the flying and fortunately got in with a group of fine boys, who pulled him out of it and he absolutely stopped for several months. Then these friends went on and some of the other sort got hold of him and he fell in further than ever.

He didn't come to the hut for weeks. Then one day he wandered in alone and I could see that he was wondering if I knew. I turned over my counter job to someone else and talked with him an hour—just about anything. Since that day he has spent every spare minute in the canteen. He is here every evening without fail and I've hardly had time to talk with him, either. I just tried to save good books or magazines that came my way for him and once or twice had given him some medicine or fixed a cut finger. Yesterday he finished, and when he went he said, "Goodbye, Miss ——. You've done one piece of work here that you don't imagine and that I would have said couldn't be done. I'll thank you all my life for it and someone in the States would bless you if she knew." Jingo! isn't it great to be a reminder? I didn't do a thing; it was just that he was given a chance to think about "her," whoever she is, at home.

29

Father wanted me to tell the story of the boy who had had such a hard life. I can't write that even to you, for it was told me in confidence. And so was another, nearly as tragic, that I got the other day from one of the oldest and most reserved men in the camp. I would have said he never broke out of his shell, but every one of them seems to be bursting to tell something to someone who cares.

F——'s timely package of stomach powder and adhesive plaster arrived at the moment when twelve cadets had eaten some perfectly indigestible thing and three of our French peasant maids had cut their fingers experimenting with a new bread cutter. So the whole sixteen of us send thanks.

Do you remember how before I came away you teased me, advising me, anent my insomnia, to practice sleeping in the garage and I said I was sure I could sleep in a garage without practice, if necessary? Well, I spent last night in a stable and thoroughly enjoyed it. So there! You see we are getting our day per week off now (it certainly is a life saver) and yesterday my motorcycle friend took me to town for my rest. He took me to three hotels, all of which were jammed. Then he said he wouldn't allow me to go anywhere else except to the Y. W. C. A. Hostess House. (You would be amused to see the pleasure these boys take in bossing me, telling me what I can and cannot do; it is delightful.) So he deposited me there and the only room they had was in the stable. I took it and slept *eighteen hours* in a regular bed with sheets. When I left the bill was two *francs*. Imagine it, just about thirty cents. And now after that rest I am feeling like dear old Bess in her younger days when she used to meet a steam roller.

Miss H—— and I don't go to the counter in the evening and as we have some sort of entertainment nearly every night, it is a real relaxation after dinner.

Dr. Vincent of the Rockefeller Foundation gave us a glorious speech the other night. It certainly was great! The boys simply loved it and have been talking about it enthusiastically ever since. He "put over" some specially fine and pointed ideas, clothed in humour and *"beaucoup"* language that made the boys roar with laughter, and yet carry away a lot to think about afterwards. I could have hugged him just for making the boys laugh that way, even if there hadn't been a splendid, deep meaning beneath it. They hadn't really laughed spontaneously and continuously and with such boyish chuckles since they left home.

30

I get letters nearly every day from the boys who have gone on to the acrobatic school, and only wish I had time to write to the whole blessed lot of them once in a while. Several of my oldest friends have come back here to be instructors and it's mighty nice to have them. That original crowd, the ones who were here when I came, and who went through all the dark, cold, bleak, non-flying, muddy, uncomfortable weeks, when most of us were sick and all of us were blue, and we had to pitch in and help each other all the time to keep from getting too awfully homesick and discouraged—*we* are real friends now, held together by a peculiar bond that isn't often welded.

Nearly every one of those old boys is brevetted now, and the new cadets skip through in a few weeks of this fine summer weather, so that we don't learn to know them so well. The old crowd had nothing on earth to do for three months but sit around the fire in the little old canteen and play checkers and dominoes and listen to H—— R—— cheering the whole bunch of us with his wonderful piano playing. *There* is a cadet who has done an awfully fine bit over here. He played last winter literally for hundreds of hours, always with a cheerful willingness and generosity, that added to the charm of his music. He played during every meal at the cadet mess, too, eating a few bites and playing between times. Isn't it a fine spirit?

We are going to have a big addition on the hut, 30 ft. x 40 ft. on the canteen room, a new auditorium 40 x 100, with a fine stage, more room for kitchen pantries and laundry, and a barber shop on behind. Also they are planning an entirely new hut as an officers' club. Some of us may be shifted to it, we don't know which of us, and don't much care. We find we get on beautifully with the mechanics, as well as with the cadets.

One of the boys, the only one we have from Vermont so far as I know, gave me some maple sugar yesterday and I've been having great fun giving it out and watching their delight when they taste it. I hadn't realised before what a distinctively American product maple sugar is. I proudly gave some to two French Monitors, who were highly enthusiastic and declare they are going straight to the United States after the war, if for no other reason than to have an orgy of maple sugar and fig newtons.

I'm sure it will be no surprise to you to learn that I am hoping to stay right on after my eight months are up. I could not drop this work now and feel right about it, especially as I have no excuse so far as health is concerned. I *love* my job and so long as all goes well at home you really don't want me to leave it, do you, way down in your hearts? I know you don't. I probably shall not "sign up" for any definite period, or for the duration, but I'll just stay on as long as there is a place for me to help a little. While there is a bit for me to do, I *have* to stay with it.

31

Nearly another week has gone. I wish they might pass as rapidly for you as they do for me—we would be home with the war cleaned up behind us before you'd hardly have time to miss us.

This is my day off again and I'm spending part of it in the garden of a Y.W.C.A. Hostess House in town, writing on a little green table beneath a big green tree with lots of chirping birds in it. The tree and the birds are a special treat to me, because trees are discouraged at aviation fields, and therefore the birds don't care much for us. Inexperienced and nervous aviators are prone to pick out trees as landing platforms. So the trees have been nearly all cut down, except that wonderful avenue of poplars which I shall show you some day after the war when I conduct you about and say "this is where" and "that is the exact spot where . . ."

Everything "marches" beautifully. A number of new cadets are coming in a few days and that will settle the great question of whether or not R—— will receive his training here. The last few hundreds at his camp are to be distributed at once, some going to England, some to another school in France, and the rest here. We shall probably cable if he arrives, but don't conclude that he didn't come if you haven't received a cable before you get this, for it is becoming every day increasingly difficult to cable. I've been trying to get one off for some time and it's quite a job. I don't need to recall the five that I've sent that you never received. And don't feel too disappointed if he is assigned to another school. It would be wonderful to have him here; but if it doesn't happen, I shall console myself with the thought that I would have had difficulty in keeping my mind on my job when I knew he was in the air.

I would have gone faint when I saw or heard a crash in the distance, and the boys didn't know yet whether he was hurt or who it was. I have heard that no one at all with a husband, or like me with brothers in the service or indeed any near relative, is being accepted in the Y. M. C. A. service now, so I'm lucky to have come when I did and I don't dare to make a move to get dear old E——— here. They say that several anxious mothers who came over for the Y. M. C. A. ostensibly, have been so pestiferous in making applications to be constantly shifted near their sons they've had to be sent home. I guess I can help some one else's brother—anyway my own does not need me as some of them do, bless his dear old heart!

(Next morning,) I was stopped at that point and I now have something else to tell you. The maid waked me out of a sound sleep to give me a note from my motorcycle friend, saying he must see me at once, something very important. I thought the camp had burned down or that he was in some dire trouble or perhaps the war was suddenly over. I dressed like a streak and rushed downstairs. There stood my cyclist looking very sober. I suggested that we go and talk in the garden, but he conducted me into the living room and there was a figure in uniform with a yellow pillow up in front of his face. Of course I guessed in an instant and grabbed the would-be ostrich, pillow and all. Yes, R——— is here; here to stay for his training this time, and his friend S——— is here, too. They arrived at two o'clock this morning and R——— went and pounded on my window at the canteen and the guard asked him why he was tearing the Y. M. C. A. hut down. R——— said he had a sister in there and the guard thought he was drunk and denied that Miss ——— had a brother.

But when he had closely examined R———'s features with a lantern, he decided that she might have a brother after all. So in the morning my friend the cyclist brought him here and my! but we're happy to be together. He probably won't fly for some time yet. New cadets always have to wait and do guard work and K. P. (kitchen police) and be orderlies and drive trucks for a while. But our "Somewhere in France" is just the very best spot on this side of the ocean now.

He looks wonderfully, just as heavy as when you saw him last, with splendid colour and all the marks of a 100 *per cent* perfect physical specimen. And he is wild with joy to be here, as you will be to know it.

I've been telling the boys for weeks that my brothers don't smoke those miserable cigarettes and that they never played craps. But they'd just laugh and laugh and say that if he came they'd get him out behind the barn and see how much his sister knew about him. All right! He's here now and they can look him over.

32

Elsie Janis has been in town for three days giving fascinating entertainments for the American soldiers. We went down to see and hear her on Monday night. Miss H—— and I were about the only ladies present in the huge opera house, jammed to the doors and roof with yelling "American Expeditionary Forces." They acted like regular college boys, singing and stamping, and when one of the military police, usually abhorred by the rest of the army, stalked majestically across the front of the stage, you ought to have heard the mighty roar they gave.

And Elsie was captivating. I've never seen a cleverer entertainment, cute songs, beautiful dancing, stories really new and really funny and perfect impersonations.

I must tell you about our new secretary, Mr. B—— R—— of N——, who has come to take charge of the athletics of the camp. He is a great reinforcement to our staff, and it adds not a little to the zeal of our little personnel to have him here. He has a delightful sense of humour, a quality sometimes lacking in men secretaries, and a charm of manner that captures the boys. Dozens of them have spoken to me about him, though he has been here only a short time. Already he has managed to get them to playing games, baseball and volley ball and football kicking and making tennis courts. All winter I've been wondering why the boys didn't spunk up and play a little. Now I see it was only for lack of a leader. He has already done a lot of fine work and started the enthusiasm, which I've been hoping for.

I am sorry to say that we had a bad accident the other day—a double fatality—the first deaths on the field that have occurred since I came. I happened not to know either of the men and the boys kept me from going out to see the wreck. We have so many smashes with no one hurt that it has become the custom to go out to look over the splinters, but the boys remembered me in the midst of the excitement and hurried back to stop me.

The next day we had the funeral, with full military honours. It was the most impressive thing I ever witnessed. The exercises were held in the central flying field near the spot where the boys fell. Every man at the post was drawn up at attention and salute while the two flag-draped coffins were placed in front where the chaplain stood, and a wonderful military band played "Lead Kindly Light" and "Rock of Ages." There was a short service and then we all followed the hearse to the cemetery, perhaps four kilometres down the road. One of the staff cars picked up Miss H—— and me, so we didn't have a long walk, but we would have gone anyhow. I couldn't have borne it not to go. It seems somehow as though there should be some *women* at such a funeral. Don't you think so?

All the time that the service was going on and all during the long slow march and at the graves, three aeroplanes circled above in graceful formation-flying, and while the coffins were being lowered into the graves each one swooped down low, just a few score feet above our heads, and dropped flowers. It was a beautiful and never-to-be-forgotten sight. I did so wish the poor parents might have felt the thrill and seen the glory of it. It might have helped to soften just a little the hard blow and alleviate the bitterness of their sorrow, even though for but an hour.

33

My letter of yesterday was interrupted by one of the boys. He had just bad two teeth pulled, and was a most forlorn, swollen-faced, homesick sight. I got him some hot salt water to stop the bleeding, gave him some of P———'s stomach medicine, a cup of black coffee, a hot water bottle, a thermos bottle of gargle, and two codeine tablets, and sent him home to bed. My treatment worked all right, for he came beaming in this morning after *seventeen hours' sleep*, and didn't have to take the codeine either.

Yesterday two boys were slying around the kitchen every time I went out there, and refused to tell me what they were doing, putting on a great air of mystery. At dinner we discovered what it was—strawberry ice cream! There wasn't any freezer and they had put the ice and salt in a bucket and the cream in a smaller pail, and twirled the pail around by hand for uncounted hours. I tell you we appreciated ice cream under those circumstances. It was the first *real* stuff we've had since we came. It has been served a few times, but always sweetened with honey, and tasted very strange—something like sour cream. This is Memorial Day, and the boys are having a holiday. Most of them have to be in a parade this afternoon and almost all the others have skipped out of camp. So we decided to take a half holiday ourselves. I never appreciated longed-for Saturdays in grammar school as I do an unexpected afternoon like this, or my day off. I don't mean I'm the least bit tired of my job, but a short change to quiet is a great rest, and I always go back to the canteen afterwards with the same enthusiasm I've always felt.

We had two hundred and fifty new men come in last night and I had a busy morning trying to say a word of greeting to the strangers. For some of the old boys have confided to me that it was such an unexpected and flattering sensation to be recognised as a newcomer, and told they had come to a nice camp and that they were particularly welcome at the Y. M. C. A. Most of the newcomers of today hadn't seen an American woman for months and months.

The quartermaster got a shipment of chocolates the other day. They were tin boxes of "Maillard's," and we had a "sale" for one hour in the evening. There were only about four hundred pounds of it. We set up a special counter, a couple of the boys helped us, and you should have seen it go! The line twisted all round the canteen and out to the road. Everyone in camp munched for about three hours and in the morning there was nothing left but hundreds of empty tins and the memory of something "Just like home." The French candy is very poor, made of substitutes mostly. I have never figured out what it does taste like.

I wish you might all be here for a short time, just long enough to get the *feel* of the war as I have. It is simply indescribable. Perhaps it's fatalism, perhaps it's patriotism, perhaps it's just becoming accustomed, only. But we simply don't worry any more, even when we are aware that many of our best friends are in constant danger. It is the salvation of us all, over here, that we come to that frame of mind.

34

What a time we've had these last two or three days! If you could have seen us you couldn't blame me for not writing as promptly as usual. Pay day; that was our trouble. It was yesterday afternoon, and in the evening we took in four thousand two hundred *francs* in one hour. The quartermaster furnished us with a lot of splendid stuff to sell—combs and razors and soap and brushes and tobacco and delicious candy (American Lowney's) in tin boxes. I set up a little special candy stand in the evening, making change with chewing gum and matches, and in less than an hour took in about a thousand *francs*. No one was allowed to buy more than three and one-half *francs'* worth. It was an awful rush.

We had a splendid " movie" the other night, an extremely well done staging of Mrs. Andrews' story, *The Courage of the Commonplace*. It was taken at Yale—President Hadley and all—and was very fine. . . . (Interruption lasting two days.) Yesterday was the hardest day I ever had here. I sat at the counter just crooked enough to twist my back into an ache and added, added, added, and made change for nine and a half hours. The line never stopped one instant. Miss H—— was having a day off, and the boys still had their pay, and there was a lot of new stock. I figured in my sleep all night. Today (I'm wedging this in at lunch time) is nearly as bad, but surely by now most of them must be stocked up. There will be one more big rush this afternoon and evening, when another thousand pounds of chocolates is to go on sale.

It is just the middle of the fruit and flower season, and it does seem as though half the boys that go to town bring us either one or the other. My room looks like a flower and fruit store. Every night just about closing time we invite the last lingering four or five out into the kitchen and eat the day's harvest of fruit. Everyone has a plate with some sugar on it and a little white bowl of water. Then the boxes of strawberries, cherries, apricots and oranges are lined up in the middle of the table and each one helps himself, washing off his fruit in his own particular bowl.

We are having to enlarge the hut. There is being added a big store room, a refrigerator room, twice as much kitchen space and a barber shop. The barber is already barbering in a little shack outside the kitchen. . . . Two days later. I just wanted to tell you that I'm having my day off. I am writing in bed and think I'll stay in bed until evening. The crown and climax of the four days' rush after pay day was two and a half hours at the close of yesterday. A great lot of crates of candy came. The boys built up a sort of fort with high ramparts. I stood in the middle and could just see over the top at first. In this fortress with me, opening the crates and handing me the one pound tin boxes of candy, were S—— and a nice little prizefighter.

There are many highly trained boxers here and some of them have been in the professional ring. All the boxers are pals of mine. I sold the boxes of candy at three and a quarter *francs* each, about sixty-five cents. If a man had not the change within five cents, he had to take it in chewing gum to save time, or Sweet Caporal cigarettes, or Bull Durham. You would be astonished to see the number that said they didn't smoke at all themselves but they'd give it away. Gradually the rampart of boxes was demolished and we became exposed to public view. In two and a half hours the last box went and we had sold over one thousand in all.

I know mother is wondering and the rest of you are laughing about my prizefighter friends. Really, it seems to me that they are quite high-class chaps. You know that both R—— and P—— have taken boxing lessons and had a good many amateur fights, and P—— even taught boxing in one of the camps. The fact is these boxers keep themselves in fine condition, allow themselves no bad habits at all, and they are fine sports. They hang around the Y. M. C. A. more than almost any of the boys. This particular little flat-faced, cauliflower-eared, midget fighter, that I just now spoke about, is always on the job to hand us cans of fruit and open new boxes of cigars, so we don't have to jump down from our cashier's stool, and it helps a lot.

I've meant to tell you—on Wednesday evenings a fine public spirited officer, a Captain S——, comes to our hut. He is stationed at this post and is in charge of one of the aero squadrons. On these evenings he teaches the boys songs. They simply love it. He always has three or four new ones—trench songs and those that have just come over from home. And then we sing the old ones over and raise the roof. After three-quarters of an hour of it we have " movies."

Captain S—— is doing more than he knows to keep the boys cheerful. I hear a carpenter working near, whistling one of his songs this minute. An hour ago twenty boys stopped playing volley ball and the victorious team marched off singing another. I wish there were more officers to volunteer their services in this pleasant, unselfish way in things they can do well. We all appreciate this unofficial service very much.

35

In my last letter I said something about my admired friends, the prize boxers. We have had a big bout and I must tell you about it. No! mother, let me relieve your mind at the outset, I did *not* go. We really have some famous battlers here in the camp and they decided to give a tremendous fight. They arranged six big matches, with an admission fee, which was to pay the cost of improving the enlisted men's mess. By the way, when a new squadron came in the other day and some of the men heard that I was from the State of —— they said to me: "Oh, gee, we've got a feller with us you sure must know. It's S—— H——, the big fighter. He's from your State."

The best fighter in camp is a great friend of mine. He couldn't fight because he is just getting over a broken arm. So they made him manager and referee. He was keen for Miss H—— and me to go and asked us about it so often that it began to be embarrassing. We said we thought the boys would rather we wouldn't. But the next day he came round and said he had just put it up to the fighters and they all wanted us and we were sure "gonna git to go." Then I said I knew it would be a great dampener on the spirits of the crowd if two ladies sat in the front row and he said: "Well, my goodness, if a man can't be a gentleman at a *prize fight* where on earth *can* he be a gentleman!" I couldn't answer that question.

Anyway, we didn't go. Of course it would have been poor of us to do it. It was a wonderful success. The hangar was simply jammed and the noise came across to my room in great waves. I forgot to tell you that my friend said "I shouldn't be talkin' as referee, but you're a good friend of mine, and I'm gonna give you a little tip, don't put your money on ——." No doubt he pictured Miss H—— and me betting heavily between ourselves!

I am feeling quite delighted with myself this morning. Last night

I was sure I was getting the "Wop fever," a sort of grippy malaria, that was brought here by a lot of cadets who came up from Italy. Two days after they arrived forty-seven out of fifty-eight of them were ill with it. A good many of the old cadets took it, and the lot of them have been going about with languid steps, bloodshot eyes and drooping spirits. Most of my time off the counter has been spent in fixing "oyster soup," made of hot milk, with butter, salt and pepper in it. Try it and see if it isn't like oyster broth, without the oysters. This, with toast and quinine and cough medicine, I give or send to the sickest ones. I wish I had counted the number of times men have said that they "hated to bother" me, but there was a fellow in their barracks who hadn't eaten a thing for two days and he just lies there and coughs and "honest, he's getting on my nerves. I don't even know his name."

So I fix him something, and a couple of days later some aviator comes in and says, "Say, you know I was the one you sent that stuff to? It was just fine. I'm all right now and I certainly want to thank you." And I have to make believe I remember which particular one he was, and also try to register his face in my mind so I can ask him a few times in the next week if he is really all well now, and wouldn't he like a cup of milk at night or something. They almost never take it—lucky thing, as there is rarely any left. How pleased we all are to be babied a little. Most of the patients are well now. But as I started to say, last night I thought I was getting it myself, and I certainly was disgusted. I took a big dose of quinine and went angrily to bed about half-past seven, and here I've just awakened after about fourteen solid hours of sleep. It's my day off, and am perfectly well! Ha! some doctor!

I am living in even greater luxury than usual, for one of the boys gave me some sheets for my bed. Not a very conventional present, is it? But I certainly appreciate it. The quartermaster issued some to a few of them and this boy "won" some for me. He said he couldn't bear to have sheets himself if I didn't have any. Bless his heart!

How strange it seems to be in France! Sometimes after all these months I can't realise that it is true. I will have, for instance, a long vivid dream about home, and when I hear a bugle outside my window and awaken and see D———'s little silk flag at the foot of my bed, and feel the heavy grey Canadian blanket mother made me bring, and that I have used every night since I came, I get a very real jolt. And yet it's all so natural now, too—pouring the coffee and taking the change and walking about, often the only woman in sight, and telling the boys not to inhale their cigarettes, and going to the "movies" in the midst of a khaki crowd of men, and going over to the guardhouse to visit the prisoners and guards, and taking bread and milk over to the garage for the cunningest, tiniest, white woolly dog I ever saw, and helping Marie hunt through masses of bundles for the laundry of some worried soldier, and showing a squad of jovial carpenters that I can hit a nail on the head, and going out to say goodbye to a truck load of departing cadets, and sliding chocolates to the guard when no one is looking—why, such things are so much a part of my every day life that I wonder sometimes what I was like at home.

36

Last Sunday for the first time we closed the canteen all day long—the counter, I mean, not the hut. There was the regular Catholic mass at eight, always well attended, and we had a Protestant service at eleven, I have told you about our secretary of athletics and the necessity and value of his leadership in organisation. Nothing is more healing and inspiriting to these too often homesick and low spirited boys. So there has been formed a regular baseball league between the different squadrons of the camp and the excitement runs high. Last night I went to the final game of the present series. Our pitcher used to be on the New York Giants not so long ago and he made twenty-one strikeouts. The other team had a second baseman from the Red Sox and a catcher from the Phillies. Our third baseman was one of Yale's latest captains.

They had terrific bands, with instruments composed of galvanised iron cans, pieces of wrecked aeroplanes, automobile horns, alarm clocks, organised cheers and miscellaneous yells. To add to the excitement the evening flying class was just "taking off" only a few hundred yards from us, starting right in our direction. So there was a constant thrill that one of them would not get off the ground in time to miss the baseball crowd. Lots of them skimmed just a few feet over our heads, and some few practical jokers dived down at us and tried to make us lie down. Then the mascot goat of one of the teams cavorted out into the diamond just in time to almost, but not quite, ruin a home run. It was a great time for everybody, and we won 7-6.

Speaking of birthdays, I must tell you a touching little tale of one that happened a couple of days ago. I was conscious of someone hanging about the end of the counter for quite a while and at last when the line ended he came up and began a conversation. He was awfully young, just a little kid, really, and with such a boyish, almost infantile face, it made me sick to think of his being here.

Finally, after a little pause, he said, "You know"—and swallowed, and then—"You know," and blushed, and at last got it out; "You know, day after tomorrow is my birthday; I'll be seventeen."

Poor kid, he just wanted someone to share his birthday a little. So I put his initials on a couple of bath towels and wrapped them around some chocolate and told him to be sure to come to the "movies" that night to get his birthday present. But he never showed up, though I looked carefully for him. The next day we found it all out. Somebody had been feeding that child liquor and the boy had managed to escape arrest with difficulty. That night he came down to the canteen. I saw him waiting for me, biting his lip and watching to see if I'd speak to him. When I went up he burst out: "Miss ———, I just don't feel like I could take it; *I just don't feel like I could take it.*"

I was terribly afraid he would cry right there in the crowd. But we had a nice little talk and he went off declaring that if he ever got home his little brother wasn't ever going even to *smoke*; no, not even a cornsilk cigarette; not if *he* caught him at it.

I've told you often before these men are just little boys inside, homesick and longing for a bit of petting. It is almost ludicrous to see how they respond to it; that is, it would be ludicrous if it were not so pathetic. You should see how grateful some six-foot-four mountaineer is to have his cut finger bandaged (with a nice clean one for Sunday) and how the toughest East-sider you ever saw will almost have tears in his eyes as he thanks us for a hot water bottle when he has a toothache. But aren't we all that way, the oldest and strongest of us, and at home hardly less than abroad? . . .

Dear me, a lapse of ten whole days. The first three because I couldn't get a minute to finish this letter, the last seven because I forgot it and nearly everything else. I came down with Oh! such a case of miserable "Wop fever." I thought I had managed to avoid it, though half the camp was ill with it a couple of weeks ago. It is reported to be all over France and England, and particularly prevalent among the German troops. Poor things! I am sorry even for them. I have only just recovered enough pep to lean on one elbow and write a little at a time now. For three days and nights I had a fever of one hundred and three. Unfortunately they happened to be the three hottest, most breathless, blazing days we've had. I thought I should burn up. It has taken me four days more to get rid of the fever, which persisted in hanging around one hundred and one, no matter what I did; but, thank goodness! It's gone today. I feel like a burned out lamp, but oh! so much better.

And I'm actually almost hungry. For five days I couldn't eat a thing but a little orange juice. By the time you get this I'll be working around just as lively as ever. Miss H—— has been wonderfully good to me, doing all she could to make things easier. One of the boys has gone down to try to get me a room in the Y.W.C.A. Hostess House for a few days, and while there I'll just lie about and sit in the garden, and read and knit and write letters and recuperate. Bless these Hostess Houses! I wouldn't have told you all this about my illness if I did not remember that the one actual promise I made you before I left home was that I would report with absolute honesty any and all illnesses. So I've done it. Now it is up to you not to let it worry you. One of the most miserable parts of this sickness is the awful racking cough that comes along extra. At one time I coughed for nearly two hours with scarcely a moment's let up. There is a man in one of the nearby barracks with a cough just like mine, and we have had a sort of dialogue, or duet, or is it a competition, night after night. If we had arranged signals, or a code, we could have conversed in coughs by the hour.

I'm so glad you are at last satisfied and reconciled about my work, and about my staying, too. I was a little afraid you were counting the months and weeks until my enlistment expires and were expecting me back at that time. I don't see how I can stop this side of the end of the war, and ever look myself in the face again. I *know* that American women are needed here. I know that even I, personally, have done a little, thank Heaven! to help. I should like to stay here for the duration. I've got my place. I know the men, I know many of them by name. They are coming to me with their confidences increasingly every day, sometimes funny, but often tragic. I cannot leave this service.

Betty Stevenson, Y.M.C.A.

Betty

To them that knew her, there is living flame
In these the simple letters of her name.
To them that knew her not, be it but said:
So strong a spirit is not of the dead.

G. Meredith.

Contents

Preface	197
Before the War	199
Belgian Refugees	207
Kessingland	211
The Two Ships	215
A Story of Christmas	219
St Denis	223
Her Mother Joins Her	232
Her Mother's Journal	237
Étaples	243
Anzac Day	248
The Day's Work	251
Mumps, and Stories of the Day's Work	255
More Reminiscences from Maison Mumps	263
At Work Again	272
Coming-of-Age Leave	279
Winter, 1917	281
Christmas Time	293
The Bridge	296

Flying Fox	299
Last Leave	307
May, 1918	312
30th May (Corpus Christi Day)	316
Memories	322
Letters	327
More Letters	335

Because of you we will be glad and gay,
Remembering you, we will be brave and strong.
And hail the advent of each dangerous day.
And meet the great adventure with a song.
And as you proudly gave your jewelled gift.
We'll give our lesser offering with a smile.
Nor falter on that path, where, all too swift.
You led the way and leapt the golden stile.
Whether you seek new seas or heights unclimbed,
Or gallop in unfooted asphodel,
We know you know we shall not lag behind.
Nor halt to waste a moment on a tear;
And you will speed us onward with a cheer,
And wave beyond the stars that all is well.

The Times, June 1915.

Portrait as a child

Preface

This story of Betty's twenty-one years has been printed, first because she was one of a big family of friends who loved her dearly, and who wanted to have a record of her life and death which another generation might still remember, when our stories and memories are silent. And secondly, because it seemed to us, who knew and loved Betty best of all, that, although she never thought of it herself, she had a message to give the world.

During the testing years of war, the spirit of England has been kept alive and strengthened by the gallant devotion of those who fought and died for her, and whose motto, whether they knew it or not, was the vow of Blake:—

> *I will not cease from mental fight,*
> *Nor shall my sword sleep in my hand,*
> *Till we have built Jerusalem*
> *In England's green and pleasant land.*

Devotion and self-sacrifice must draw the picture, but, none the less, joyousness and gay adventure may colour it. It was so that our Happy Warrior set out, and so she did her war work to the end.

She could say with Antigone:—

οὔτοι συνέχθειν, ἀλλὰ συμφιλεῖν ἔφυν.

"I was not born to join in hate, but love."

And it seems to us that, in the building up of the new England that is to come, the world needs this message of hers: a message of youth, of sympathy, of duty happily and cheerfully done, of joy in everything she did.

This is not a formal biography. Except for the time during which her mother was with her, we have just put together extracts from her letters and diaries, and left them to tell their own story of what she thought and saw and did. We have filled in some names of places which were only indicated by initials in her letters. Betty was always a great letter writer, from the first, written with baby fingers, to the latest written on what was her last night on earth, full of love and concern for us at home, with not one word of the peril, weariness, and strain through which Étaples was passing.

We have added a little poem, *The Two Ships*, and a little Christmas story, both of which she wrote in 1915. We are grateful to Betty's many friends who have allowed us to print their letters. Each adds something to the picture of Betty.

C. G. R. S.
A. G. S.

1919.

BETTY
1898

1

My little Maid, my Betty,
My little blue-eyed Maid,
What sweet gay thoughts lie hid in you,
Behind your eyes, your eyes so blue?

2

My little Maid, my Betty,
My little gold-haired Maid,
What do you say to the breeze so bold
That lifts your curls, your curls of gold?

3

My little Maid, my Betty,
My sleepy, sleeping Maid,
What gay little dream do you dream in your bed,
That parts your lips, so soft and red?

4

My little Maid, my Betty,
My little softling Maid,
What do you hold, that I cannot see
In your strong small hand, flung out to me?

1898.   C. G. R. S.

Chapter 1

Before the War

Looking back on Betty's childhood, one sees more clearly the beginnings of all the qualities which inspired her work later on. Born on 3rd September 1896, she was very happy from babyhood, keen and eager-hearted in everything she did. Like Browning's little Duchess,

She liked what e'er
She looked on, and her looks went everywhere.

From the beginning she had a great love for "*all things both great and small*."

"Tell me how snakes cry and squeak, please," she writes, at 4, and a few years later: "I have found a flower called Vipers Bugloss. It had been the dream of my life to find it, and now I've found it. Hurrah."

When she was quite a little child we found her indignantly picking the flies off the flycatchers, and washing their legs. Then there was an old rheumy-eyed horse which used to put its head over into the garden at East Garth, and Betty felt she had to wipe its eyes and make it comfortable. But it was a pity that one of her mother's best lace handkerchiefs was the first thing that came to her hand! She was very fond of mice, and used to make friends with wild ones, which let themselves be caught, and added to her Mousery. When she was quite small, she went in for an Essay Competition about Mouse-keeping, and amused herself greatly by writing it to suit the style of "The Fancy," who wrote in the paper. The prize, a box full of some special breed of mice, multiplied alarmingly.

She always had dogs, from Kelpie, a little Aberdeenshire, to Grim, the Samoyede; and just at the end, in France, she befriended two little dogs, one of which died in an air raid the day after Betty left us, while the other is kept and loved by one of her colleagues in memory of her.

One of her great delights was hunting with the Bramham Moor and York and Ainsty Hounds. She began before she was nine, and hunted regularly on Fanny, her beloved pony, till she went to school.

She loved birds, and used to stalk them by the hour, with a field glass, studying every detail of what they did and how they looked. She used to make innumerable notes of bird life. One essay describes their beaks and feet, and how these were adapted to their various needs; and another tells all about the size, shape, and marking of their eggs.

In September 1910, at fourteen, Betty went to a boarding school at St George's Wood, Haslemere. Her first letter home begins characteristically, "It's perfectly lovely here." Betty was always a great letter-writer, and from this time on she used to send home enormous letters every week, telling of all she saw and did and thought. She found romance in all the little details of her school life, and made the best of everything.

> Everybody has a duty. The first week me and Betty Renwick had the boot-hole (it is really a room); it was lovely, we had to keep it tidy, and we were allowed to (or rather had to) confiscate anybody's clean boots or shoes that were left out. It was simply heavenly. The feeling of confiscating other people's boots till they paid ½d. each for them: it was too lovely for words!! When I was on the way down to tidy it, people would rush in and throw their boots into any hole they could find, so they wouldn't be left out; it was lovely. Last week I had to see to the flowers in the Fifth Classroom, and this week I have to mark the Hockey Lawn. . . .
>
> . . . It is so funny, every now and then little things happen or are said, not to me, but to anybody, that make me feel terribly homesick. I don't know what it is. Only every now and then. In church this morning in one of the Lessons came something about '*Be not weary of well doing*,' and I remembered you putting that in *Flowers of the Field* that I won for exams., and for a moment I felt horribly homesick; then I forgot, and felt quite all right. Wasn't it funny? I wish you'd come and see me.

From the beginning, Betty saw life with very clear and fearless eyes. She always got outside her troubles. Behind her fun, and joy of life and spontaneity, she had a fine sense of duty and the meaning of life. The little school essay which follows was written in her fifteenth year.

What is a Vocation?
25 .6. 11 .   Betty Stevenson.

A vocation, in other words, means a calling, a calling from God. Nearly everyone's work can be a calling, but not everyone knows it. It makes a great difference to your life, if you have a vocation or not. If you have, it makes you feel as though you had some real object or aim in your life and work. I think any kind of charitable work must be an especial calling from God.

I am sure that God has special work for each individual person to do, and it is for that person to find out what his or her special work is, which is impossible for one who has not had a vocation, and has not the divine knowledge and understanding of God as He is. No two persons' work can be alike.

Any work, however dull or hard, becomes interesting and easy if you feel you are doing it for God, not merely for yourself. There is *no* work which is too hard to be done. God gives us our work, and He would not give it to us, if it was too hard to be done. Take for instance, as an example, the life of Our Lord. His life was from beginning to end a vocation. He gave up the whole of his life and thought to his work. Nothing is too hard for God, and man is God's image. Therefore, nothing should be too hard for man, and nothing is, or would be too hard, if man would only understand this.

Man cannot live without God. Those who care not for God are not really alive. They are dead, and it is the business of those who *do* know, and do love and care for God, to teach those who do not know God, for God made man to teach man.

If one believes that one really has a vocation, it makes life a totally different thing. If everyone believed they had a calling, and were trying their utmost to obey it, there would be no discord, and all would be harmonious. There would be nothing ugly; all would be beautiful. God only made beautiful things. Everything that we see around us that is beautiful is a thought or an idea of God. To really obey and understand one's calling, one must understand God; not merely believe, but understand. When a man really understands God there is nothing more to fear, for he is living in God.

In September 1913 she went to Brussels, to study music under M. Sevenants. She had always been a lover of music, and had always worked thoroughly and steadily, and she was delighted at the idea of studying in a Conservatorium.

18 Rue Dautzenberg,
Brussels, 8th October 1913.

My Darlingest Mother,—... It is so lovely to be able to do, to a certain extent, exactly what you like, and not to have someone always making up your mind for you. Of course, I am not talking about home, but School! (x).

I have to do three hours a day practising, but then I can do it when I like, only I mustn't do more than an hour at a time—if I can help it. I am enclosing two days' diary. I am not enclosing more because of the weight. I will try and send you them twice a week. Please keep the diaries, because I want to copy them into a proper book, when I get home. I am buying P.C.s of Brussels to put in it, like my summer holidays' diaries. You will see all the sins, etc., I have committed, in the diaries. I have put them all in, and I don't apologise one bit for any of them, because I have a clear conscience, and know they are not really sins! (x). I am writing this in a hurry before the literature lesson, so please excuse faults.

In music I am doing scales and *arpeggios*, and I must confess it fascinates me horribly doing them with a metronome! I can sit for any length of time playing scales like that, getting a bit quicker each time. It's simply lovely. Also I am doing an awful Loeschorn Study, Beethoven's Funeral March, and the next movement of the same Sonata; a Bach invention, and a Chopin Impromptu, which is the difficultest thing I have ever done, though glorious. I am enjoying my music most awfully, and I feel sure I am improving.

Last night I learnt how to make *Crème au Chocolat*, it is lovely, and so easy. You will have lovely food when I come home.

I adore fencing. I must stop now darling,—Your loving *fillette*.

Bunch, x x x

A. W. T. S.

A Letter to her dog

Chez Mlle Tobie,
18 Rue Dautzenberg,
Brussels, 6th November 1913.

My darling Kelpie,—Thank you so much for your letter, which

arrived this morning. You are a nice tyke to write to me. I'm so sorry I have not written to you before. I am so glad you are being such a good black dog while I am away. I am being very good too, though lately I've been having distemper, which was beastly. However, I am all right again now.

I think it was very sensible of you to run away a second time, when the missus said you were naughty. I should have done just the same myself. I give you free leave to bite her calves very hard. . . .

I am very glad you like the noises of Willy Wagner. I admire your taste. I hope you like Charlie Chopin too.

In the holidays we will have to try and make the acquaintance of the Skye terrier. I think he would be a useful friend, don't you? . . . In the holidays we'll have grand times, and you shall share my food. We'll have a fine time in the loft and stables too. Have you heard of Grey Gables? . . . There'll be no lofts and spinneys, and birk-crags and stables there, growler darling. It will be sad, won't it? But, of course, we two could run away and live in our house at Birk Crag on Harlow Car. I think we will. That would be lovely. I send you a hug and a kiss, my tykesome hound.—Your loving mistress,   Betty. Wags from me.

From the Brussels Diary

This afternoon, there were crowds of school children playing on the grass; the boys at one end and the girls at the other, with a strict space between the two. As far as I could see, the girls seemed to be playing marriages and hide-and-seek, and the boys, fights, burials, and general massacres. One little girl was gazing very longingly at rows of dead little boys being decapitated, etc., but she had not the courage to go too near. All the children, taken as a whole, were most picturesque and gay, and it was only when one looked very closely that one noticed the shabbiness. English school children would never look so gay and almost smart, as some of these little French poor children looked. It was not that the garments themselves were good, very much the contrary, but they knew exactly how to put them on. Each bit of shabby finery was arranged in a way which only French people, I think, know how. I have noticed it, on a much higher scale of course, in Brussels itself, the tilt of a hat or the turn of a ribbon, nothing more, and above all the movement of the body. I have not seen one really awkward or gawky woman or girl in Brussels. I noticed the movement with the poor children in the Bois. While playing unconsciously or copying some grown-up, every movement was graceful.

...Today was one of the days, when, if you are not very careful, you begin to feel homesick and other little unpleasant feelings like that. There was no reason for it, except that I think there was a mild *sirocco* blowing round the house, because certainly there is nothing else here except that to give one—

The hump, the hump, the camellious hump,
The hump that is black and blue.

...We met the little Princess Marie-Jose driving back from the Bois with her governess. She is such a dear little thing. She is only about eight years old, and she is very pretty. She has such heaps of short fair curly hair. It simply stands out round her head like a halo. She is extremely popular, and very amusing and mischievous.

...We had dinner at 6.30 as we were going to the opera to see *Carmen*. At 7.45 the cab came, and we all rolled off. It was thrilling. It was the first time I have ever been in a foreign theatre, and it was absolutely different from an English one. We could see everything quite well. There were a great many soldiers there. *Carmen* was just lovely. I have never seen anything like it before. In the first scene and in all of them the colours were really superb. The voices were gorgeous too. The chorus surprised me a great deal, having only heard theatre choruses. I was not prepared for such a burst of glorious sound....

...After lunch we went to see the "*Exposition de la Societé Royale Beige des Aquarellistes*." It was very interesting. It was the first day, and the ordinary public was not admitted, but we happened to have invitations, which was lucky. There were all the artists themselves there, admiring their own pictures, in long flowing hair and ties. Some of them were most awfully excited about their own pictures, and behaved just like a pack of children. Some of the paintings were lovely, especially the landscapes, and a great many little Dutch interiors, of houses, of course! On the other hand, there were some simply dreadful things, and of course crowds of dreadful futurist and cubist things. We stayed there quite a long time, and then we went into the town, and I bought some Christmas presents. On the way back I was nearly run over by about six trams and half-a-dozen drays! It was most exciting, but everyone was quite disappointed that I didn't swoon and faint, and that sort of thing....

... Mdlle and Helen and I went off to the Cirque Charles to see the animals. They were lovely. It is supposed to be one of the biggest circuses in the world, and it really was immense. There were over three hundred animals, and over ninety different waggons. ...

Next to the lions were the camels and dromedaries. There were heaps and heaps of them. They didn't have cages at all. There was just a fence in front of them on our side, and on the other the whole side of the tent was open so they could see out and get the air. They were all lying down on great beds of straw, and of course they were all hobbled. They were so sweet, and they just loved having their noses scratched. My hand quite ached at the end, because they all wanted to be scratched, and there were quite twenty!

In a partition to itself was a sweet Mrs Camel with a two-year-old son called Joseph. They were darlings and they loved being scratched. We didn't see them being fed. At the end of the line, also in a partition to itself, was a poor sick white camel. It did look so sorry for itself. It had a coat on tied with string, and it was lying down with its head on a filthy pillow, but still it was sweet! Opposite the camels was a cage full of water for seals. They were lovely, and had such lovely eyes. I simply couldn't imagine wearing one round my neck, they looked so dreadfully cold and damp.

Next to the seals were seven elephants. They were dears, especially one little one which had a great sense of humour. It kept on filling its trunk with sawdust, which must have been horribly uncomfortable, and then it went up to a big elephant, and rubbed up against it, and pretended to be ever so affectionate, and then all of a sudden it would blow all the sawdust down the elephant's ear, and then rush back to its picket with a squeal. It really was killing. The big elephant got furious, and made the most unearthly bellowings and trumpetings, and presently a man came along and tickled the big elephant's trunk, and brandished a stick in front of the little elephant, and after that peace was restored. ...

It was awfully funny to watch the different ways the animals behaved when they saw the food coming. The lions, of course, roared and walked up and down their cages and bit the bars, and so did the tigers. The bears had a funny sort of swinging movement from side to side, and when they got very excited and hungry, they polished the floor with their fore-paws. It was very curious to watch them. They all did it, rubbing and rubbing as hard as they could. The elephants positively danced up and down, with a funny sort of swinging; the camels groaned and sighed and twitched their lips; the seals made sounds as if they were suffering from *mal de mer;* the horses whinnied; the llamas spat, and the yaks, etc., mooed and flicked their ears. It was so funny to watch them all.

   ...The rest of us went to the Bois.... It was heavenly. There were very few people about, and as a result it was all very still and quiet. The trees were nearly all bare, and there were such lovely views through the branches, and in and out of the trunks. There was a lovely feel of Christmas in the air, and I'm sure the trees were feeling the same thing. They looked so sleepy and warm though the poor dears had no leaves. We saw a sweet little squirrel in one of the trees, who I suppose, was getting ready his winter store-house. Everything looked as though it was waiting for something to happen, and something that it knew would happen. Even the ducks on the lake gave one the same idea.

Chapter 2

Belgian Refugees

It was not long before the war touched Betty's life. Harrogate, like so many other towns, organised a Belgian Refugees' Committee to help to deal with the mass of refugees who began to pour into England in September 1914. On the 25th of that month she went up to town with her father and mother to help in selecting and bringing back some of the pitiful families who were temporarily camped out in the Alexandra Palace. On the 28th she came back to Harrogate in charge of a party of refugees, returning next day for another party, whom she brought back on the 30th. In this work she first made friends with Mr Henry J. Brice, who writes this appreciation of her:—

> ... I shan't forget the first meeting, how she looked me through and through with head erect and half-closed eyes, got my measure, and finally put her hand in mine as a fast friend. I was working for the Belgian Refugee Fund, organising the transport from Alexandra Palace. ... I had my car and chauffeur waiting outside, and Betty knew I was momentarily mad because a motor bus hadn't turned up to take three parties to various railway stations. Mrs Stevenson was there, and came to me and asked where Betty was, and I couldn't for the life of me tell her where, so I started a hunt. I found my car gone, and then one of the parties missing. It turned out that Betty had given the chauffeur instructions in my name, and dashed off with the refugees to Euston to catch their train. And the only apology she offered was: 'Well, you knew you could trust me, didn't you?'. . . . If I had ever had an impossible task to do, I would have put Betty to do it. And what's more, by her personality she would have got people to help her, and if she failed a hundred

times, you would have found her, head erect and smiling. . . .
Her judgment was always sound, and her happy confidence in
herself irresistible. . . . She just put her heart and soul into the
job in hand, no matter what it was.

I got her the post of driver with the Y.M.C.A., but though it
led to her untimely-end, I know she wouldn't have me regret
it, for she died, as she lived, the noblest and purest of souls. She
has joined the ranks of those to whom humanity owes an immense debt.

All they had hoped for, all they had they gave
To save Mankind; themselves they scorned to save.

Besides the refugees there was a group of wounded Belgians who had volunteered in the first days of the war, and who had been brought over to hospitals in Harrogate. There were international tea-parties in the big hall at Grey Gables, where they sang the "*Brabançonne*" and "Tipperary."

She kept up her music, practised much on her beloved Steinway, and began to teach herself Norwegian and Italian, with great success. Then after an attack of measles she went to Uxbridge to recuperate:—

. . . .I am writing this on the lawn under a great big chestnut tree. It is simply heavenly. On Tuesday Molly and I went to Hampton Court. . . .

The fields are full of ever such long grass, and heaps of buttercups and daisies and sorrel. They do look so nice. I long to go and rub my face in among them. At Twickenham we took another bus, which took us finally to Hampton Court.

By this time we were pretty fam., although it was so early. So we went along to a shop. When we'd got thoroughly in and seated, we found that they didn't cater for lunches, only teas. However we couldn't be bothered to get up again, so we just ate what they'd got. First of all we discovered that there would be some meat pies in soon, so we said we'd wait. We waited ages; I suppose they couldn't catch the cat! So we set-to on something else. We had a large awfully good buttered currant scone. When we'd done that, the pies arrived mewing plaintively. We had one between us. Jolly good. They loved having their noses scratched, the *bijoux*.

We then staggered forth to Hampton Court, Isn't it glorious?

King Edward's horses are quartered in the barracks there. We saw quite a lot. First we went right through the Courts and out into the gardens. They were just lovely. I have never seen such gardens. All the beds had several things growing in them. The bed would be covered with some bright low-growing little flower, so that no earth could be seen, and then lovely tall pink and white tulips grew out of them. There was every conceivable colour and they all harmonised beautifully. It made me long to be able to play it. I know exactly what it was, if only my fingers would do what my mind wants.

I bought a guide and then we went up the great staircase. It seemed putrid to be going up it in 1915. I did so want it to be the seventeenth century. I almost *saw* Charles and William and Mary walking about. The floor was stone. I wonder what they had it covered with. I'm sure they all got chilblains. The ceilings and walls were most gaudily painted with nymphs and satyrs, etc., and fat and overfed females, reclining on round clouds in an ultramarine sky. Then there were other females with yellow hair and pink extremities, playing harps and lutes. This staircase led into the King's Guard Chamber. It was all decorated with arms (fire!) in the most wonderful patterns. The guide-book says there are nearly 3000 arms used.

The next room was William III's Presence Chamber. There was a great big red canopy under which Willie used to sit. I wish I could have seen him. There were lovely pictures in all the rooms. In this room are the 'Hampton Court Beauties'; they are a bosomy crew! Some, however, were quite nice. Miss Pitt was sweet. There were heaps of rooms, all opening out of each other, which I won't describe. (You must be sick of this letter by this time.) King Willie's bedroom was thrilling. There was a huge moth-eaten four-poster covered with silk. I've forgotten the colour. The ceiling was painted with slumber scenes. There were sweet Pans whistling to drowsy goats, who were going to sleep on clouds with their heads on buttercups. There were fat females curled up in shells and sleeping on Dryads' bosoms! It would give me a nightmare on the spot to lie in bed and look at all that.

The queen's bathroom was weird. There was just a big marble basin let into the wall, with one tap. Naughty, dirty ladies! Not like Betty. Cardinal Wolsey's closet was ever so small, and all oak-panelled. In one corner was a little door which let into a tiny little room with no window, like a big box. It was all wired off and we couldn't go in. It simply reeked of heads and secret stairways. Last of all we went into the Great Banqueting Hall of Harry's in a different building. It is huge, with great stained-glass windows, with the arms of Harry and his six spouses on them. I didn't know before that all his wives could trace their descent from Edward I, but it is so. Teddy I. had two wives, French and English. We heard all about the ghosts. One is Harry's last wife: she walks down the hall; looks out of the window; takes her head off and chucks it out of the window. She was the only[1] wife who wasn't executed, so she probably does it out of pique, because she wasn't cut up too.

During this Uxbridge visit she amused herself with writing a little skit on a Charles Garvice novel, which had what she would call a *succès fou* among her friends in the trenches in 1917.

---

1. She forgot Catharine of Aragon.

CHAPTER 3

Kessingland

Then she went to Kessingland for a week with her mother and cousin, and went back again in August with her family for the summer holidays.

The mystery of all the naval operations brought the war a good deal nearer to her, as her diary shows.

13th July 1915.

We are at Kessingland-on-Sea for a week. The place is rather nice, four miles from Lowestoft. I am writing in a little wooden shelter right on the edge of the cliff. It is open at the front, making a lovely big "viewfinder." Quite a lot is going on at sea just now. Exactly in front of me a funnel and two masts are sticking up out of the water, about half a mile out. These are the remains of a cargo steamer, which was torpedoed by a German submarine a few days ago. She was carrying a cargo of wheat, and is now slowly sinking on the sand banks. The submarine gave the crew time to get away, and some of the wheat was saved. The people at Kessingland saw it all happen, and saw the crew climbing into the boats. We are indeed living in stirring times when ships are torpedoed within a mile of land.

Six little mine-sweepers are patrolling up and down, cabled together and energetically steaming along. They remind me of a child's train puffing along with the little carriages chained on. Yet they are the bravest little ships on the sea, these mine-sweepers, and are doing a great work. The other day they got a submarine entangled in their nets, and the bodies are still being washed up on shore.

On the far horizon are two cruisers which every now and then come into sight and then disappear again. In the morning there are a lot of fishing smacks out, but they dare not go out very far.

There are two villages at Kessingland, one a bit inland, and the other a coast fishing village. Both are full of old men and boys with sunburnt faces and blue jerseys. There are no young men.
...

I've just had a very good dinner, and we are all sitting in the hut again. The minesweepers have just gone by again, and each carries a mast headlight. They look so pretty, and yet they seem so much more important when it is beginning to get dark; they make one think of war, not of toy engines.

A big steamer is passing now, and she is just skirting round the sunk ship. She has two mast headlights, and she has left a long trail of ugly black smoke in the sky. It is beginning to get quite dark now, and the horizon is a black line. A soldier is walking along the beach playing a penny whistle, and throwing stones into the sea. I'm sure he is waiting for his best girl. She has kept him waiting nearly half an hour. I wish she would be quick.

There is a lovely smell of the sea here, and a seagull somewhere near is making such a sleepy chirping noise. It is getting cold, so I am going in....

14th July 1915.

We have just had a large breakfast, and are now sitting on the sands writing and digesting. We have just heard that a German submarine has been taken off Aldeburgh. We are all very excited about it.

Last night Mollie and I went for a walk along the cliffs as far as the coast-guard station. It was quite dark, and all the ships' lights out at sea looked so pretty. There was one big light which we were certain was signalling to another ship near by. It was a very big light. This morning Mr Banfield told us he had also seen it, and that at about 10.30 it had suddenly gone out. He was certain that something was up, and it was there that the submarine was caught.

There is such a pretty bush that grows on the cliffs here. It is like a privet with a purple star-shaped flower.

The family are bathing now and making a most unholy noise, especially my parent who persists in singing, "row, brothers, row."

The sea is lovely now. I think there is a storm brewing.

The sea is a dark purply-blue with bright green streaks. I think the green is over the sand banks which are guarded by two black and white buoys. The water looks hard though the horizon is blurred, and the buoys stand out very sharply from the water. It is just like an April day; bright sun and then lowering clouds.

Sitting here writing peacefully it is difficult to imagine the dreadful fighting that is going on just the other side of the water. We in England can talk about and discuss the war as much as we like, but we can't realise it. We look round and see the fields and villages and hamlets lying peacefully there, and we find it impossible to imagine what it must be like in Belgium—what we should feel like if our homes were ruined. The people of Scarborough and Hartlepool no doubt realise a little more what war is, and in big towns it is brought forcibly to our notice. But it is not the same thing, merely because we happen to be an island cut off from all the countries which are now in the thick of the fighting.

A Belgian wounded soldier recovering in England said it was extraordinary, the difference in the atmosphere of Belgium and England. That to see peaceful, quiet England made the horrors of Belgium seem like a terrible nightmare. Honour must indeed be a very sacred thing, if so much is being lost and risked for the sake of it, and it is not so difficult to sympathise with those who think that honour is a very secondary consideration, when human lives are at stake. And yet we are fighting splendidly, because we are fighting for our country's honour. We haven't a great army, or rather we hadn't, and yet we are doing great things. Germany has a great and efficient army, but she has no ideal to fight for, and the result is painfully and terribly obvious. . . .

We had heard that morning that four more Lowestoft trawlers had been torpedoed. It seems to me a coward's way of fighting. . . .

9th August 1915.

Last night there was great excitement because we had a Zeppelin over us. . . . At last I got out into the garden, and there I saw the Zeppelin sailing straight for us. It flew right over our heads, and then over the house, where it seemed to rest a few seconds, and then it changed its course and headed straight for Lowestoft. It flew very quickly and seemed to me to be just the size of a cigar held at arm's length. It was very long and narrow. By this time it was discovered by various females and fussy-buttons that I had bare feet, and had a white wrap on, which, there was no doubt, was illuminating the whole countryside, and was pointing out to the Germans the direction of Lowestoft!—so I was herded back to my room. Once there, I did not get back to bed again, as was insisted on by someone, but put shoes and stockings and one or two garments on, and also one of Daddy's big coats. This done, I repaired once more to the scene of action.

On the stairs I heard a big explosion which shook the house, and when I got out into the garden again I heard some more. These were bombs being thrown on Lowestoft. There were a great many flashes of light and big flares, and by this time the searchlights of Lowestoft were going—two from the pier, and one or two from two gunboats which are at Lowestoft. We saw some of the bombs being dropped. There was a flash from the Zeppelin when it was thrown, and then a big explosion and flare of light when the thing touched the earth. All this went on for some time, and then the noise of the Zeppelin gradually died away, and very soon afterwards the searchlights were stopped, and everything was once more quite quiet and dark again.

When she came back to Harrogate, she took over with her friend, Mrs Wedgwood, the charge of nine of the Belgian families, and she did her best to be guide, counsellor, and friend to them.

She also took lessons in motor-driving, in the hope that it would help her to do some war work later on.

Chapter 4

The Two Ships

This little rhymeless poem was written at Kessingland. It is inserted here because Betty's Vision of Life is in it, and has brought great consolation to those who loved her.

The moon was pale, the night was dark,
Scarce a sound disturbed the air.
Save the fitful cry of a sad sea-bird,
And the ceaseless break of the waves.

I sat alone by the sea that night,
And my heart was troubled and sore.
For my loved one had gone to the wars to fight,
And when shall I see him again?

Shall I ever see him again, I ask
Of the waves and the sad sea-bird.
And the waves they broke on the shingly beach,
"No more, no more!" they sighed.

The wind blew round me in hungry gusts,
And the rain began to fall.
I gazed on the sea and the cold black sky,
And a weird sight met my eyes.

A ship as black as a raven's wing
Came sailing by in the night.
At the helm stood a figure in shrouded garb,
A mysterious, ghostly sight.

My heart grew weak, and I strove to speak.
But no sound I made, nor sigh.
The ship sailed on, and nearer it came,
And the wind moaned dismally still.

I raised my eyes, and looked at that ship,
And trembled at what I saw.
The figure in black looked over the sea.
And met my terrified eyes.

Its face was covered, and yet its eyes
Seemed to pierce through mine to my brain,
"Look well, look well, O human soul.
And see what I have done."
So speaking it moved its shrouded head.
And pointed into the ship.
I looked and saw, oh, woe is me.
The figure of him I loved.

I sank me down upon my knees,
"Ah no, ah no! "I cried, "Good God!"
I prayed in agony,
"Eternal Father, save."

The figure laughed full loud and long,
"'Tis well, 'tis well!" it cried,
"Come, look on him you loved so well,
And see what I have done.

"I am the lord of all that is,
'Tis useless thus to pray.
Acknowledge me as lord of all,
I am the God of Death."

"I'll never bow to thee," I cried.
"For life, not death, I pray."
I raised my head and looked again.
And lo, the ship had gone.

The sea-bird flew around my head,
The waves broke mournfully.
And the wind moaned still its doleful dirge,
As I walked along the shore.

The morning came, and the sun rose high.
And the birds began to sing
But I laid me down with a heavy heart,
And closed my weary eyes.

I thought of that ghostly God of Death,
And the ship, and the face I loved.

When I heard a voice which seemed to say,
"Courage, there is no death."

"There is no God of Death," it said,
And it whispered soft in my ear,
"The world is full of life and love,
There is no room for death."

I got me up from off my couch,
For I knew that the voice spoke true,
And my heart felt light, and my heart felt gay,
For I knew that there was no death.

I lived that day with a cheerful mind,
And sang with the birds in the sun.
And saw in every blossom and bud
A thought of the God of Life.

The sun went down, and the moon crept up,
And once more I sat by the sea.
A nightingale sang in the woods beyond.
And the waves softly lapped round my feet.

I gazed around on the moonlit sea,
And up to the starry sky.
And everywhere I looked, I saw
The face of the God of Life.

And out at sea I saw a ship,
A ship of purest gold.
At the helm stood a figure in flowing robes.
With a sword of gold in his hand.

The ship drew near, and nearer still.
And I gazed on the wonderful sight.
And I knew as I watched this golden ship
That this was no God of Death.

The figure raised the sword in his hand,
And pointed into the ship.
"I am the God of Life" he said,
"Fear not, but follow me."

I stood me up by the lapping waves,
And I held out my arms to the ship;
And the figure in white with the flaming sword
Came to me over the sea.

He took my hand, and led me out
Over the rippling sea,
And I saw in that ship of purest gold
The figure of him I loved.

He held my hand, and we both knelt down
And worshipped the God of Life,
And we both of us knew in the ship that night
That there was no God of Death.

Side by side on that golden ship
We gazed out over the sea.
And far away in the dimness of night
We saw another ship.

Her sails were torn, and her rigging bent.
As she sank down under the sea.
At the helm crouched a figure: a cry rent the air,
As the ship sank under the sea.

And I knew that the ship that had gone in the night
Was the ship of the God of Death.
And we sailed away in our ship of gold,
Our ship of the God of Life.

The birds were singing above my head,
And the sun was shining bright,
As I woke and turned on my mossy bank,
And I looked at the happy day.

And then I remembered my ships of the night,
And the God of Life, and of Death.
And I rubbed my eyes and looked at the sea,
Knowing my dream was right.

And the sea-birds gay flew over the waves.
And circled around my head.
And the birds, and the waves on the shingly beach.
Sang to the God of Life.

And I knew that death disappears before life.
As the ship had sunk in the night.
And my loved one was safe, and would come to me soon,
And the birds, and the waves on the shingly beach
Sang "Soon, oh God of Life!"

August 1915.   B. G. Stevenson.

CHAPTER 5

A Story of Christmas
Written by Betty at Christmas 1915.

It was Christmas Eve, and the streets of the great city were silent, save for the gentle, drowsy sound of the falling snow. In the big houses the rich people were laughing and happy, preparing for the great feast of tomorrow. Outside in the snow a woman was standing with a child in her arms. She stood looking up at the lights of the great house. Seeing an open window, she moved nearer, and looked in, holding the child up, so that it could feel the glow of the light and the warm fire on its half-frozen little body.

In front of the fire in the big room the woman saw a lot of children. They were sitting very still, and were evidently listening to someone who was telling them a story.

The woman moved nearer, in order to hear the story to which the children were listening.

"And it was Christmas time, and the snow was falling, and everything was very cold and white, just like it is now. And the poor woman and her little baby had no home to go to, and no fire to warm themselves by, like you have. And at last, after a long time, they came to an inn, but alas! there was no room for them there either."

The woman outside in the snow gave a little cry, and began to move slowly away. From the house she heard children's voices and laughter, and presently the big door opened, and a blaze of light shot out, illuminating the snow and the poor woman standing there with her baby. The children came out and got into the motors and carriages that were waiting for them, and were driven away to their homes, where there were fires and good things to eat, and warm things to wear. The door of the big house closed, and the woman was alone again. She moved away, pulling her poor cloak more closely round the child, and was soon out of sight, away into the snow.

Outside the great city everything was even more quiet, and the moors and the woods, with their still, white covering of snow, lay there, waiting for the great day of rejoicing and happiness.

Away across the moors a little light twinkled and shone out across the snow. This was the hut of old Shuan. Shuan was a poor man who made his living by fishing. But now the rivers and pools were all frozen, and there were no fish to be had. It was night time, and the moon and the stars shone down on the snow, and on the path from the woods, causing the snow to glitter and glisten like a world of fairy diamonds.

Presently the stillness was broken by the sound of someone walking through the snow. A man was coming down the path from the woods. He was clad in a loose shepherd's cloak, which he was trying to hold together to keep some of the cold away. He was walking very slowly, and he looked sad and weary.

He walked on through the snow, and across the moors till he came to the hut of old Shuan, the fisherman. Outside the window he paused, and looked in. A miserable fire of peat and damp sticks was smouldering in the grate, and in front of it were sitting old Shuan and his dog Shemus, and he was reading out of a book. The man outside in the snow stepped nearer and listened.

"And the angel said unto them, '*Fear not; for behold I bring you good tidings of great joy, which shall be to all people.*

"'*For unto you is born this day in the city of David a Saviour, which is Christ the Lord.*

"'*And this shall be a sign unto you: Ye shall find the babe wrapped in swaddling clothes, lying in a manger.*'

"And suddenly there was with the angel a multitude of the heavenly host praising God, and saying, '*Glory to God in the highest, and on earth peace, goodwill toward men.*'"

The old man got up and moved slowly to the window. He held out his hand to Shemus, and patted his head, and together they looked out over the snow into the moonlight.

Then Shuan spoke: "Shemus, it is Christmas. A time of joy and thanksgiving. I feel sad and old, and this is my last Christmas. It is not for you and me to feast with good things. Times are bad, Shemus, and we are poor and old. We have read, and on this our last Christmas let us read again, of that first joyous Christmastide, when the child Jesus came to earth."

The man outside in the snow held out his arms to Shuan, and smiled. He moved towards the door, and opened it and went in. He walked up to Shuan, and laid his hand on the old man's shoulder. Shuan looked up and smiled at the man.

"Who are you?" he said.

The man from the woods answered: "My trade is the same as your own, Shuan. I am a fisherman."

"Ah, times are bad, and it is many weeks since the snow came, and froze up the rivers, so that I cannot fish."

"The snow and the frost," replied the strange man, "do not affect my fishing, Shuan."

"Stranger," trembled Shuan, "I am afraid. I understand not your speech. It is Christmas time, when everything is full of joy. I am old and feeble, and Christmas has no good things in store for me." The old man bowed his head.

The stranger got up and took Shuan by the hand. "Come with me," he said, "and I will show you the true Christmas. You are a fisher of fish, Shuan, but I am a fisher of men."

Old Shuan, trembling, got up, and was led to the door by the stranger. He opened the door, and, as a blast of icy cold air rushed in, old Shuan hung back, afraid. But the stranger reassured him, and together they walked out into the starlit night.

Suddenly Shuan felt no longer afraid. He looked up at the strange man and laughed. His limbs felt strong and healthy, and he knew he was young again. He looked again at the man by his side, and saw that his face was no longer sad and weary, but was smiling and full of joy. Shuan held his hand, and felt the warmth from the stranger entering into his own body and filling his whole being with a new and wonderful sense of happiness. Presently the stranger stopped and listened, and Shuan heard a sound like a child's voice.

He looked back, and saw a beautiful woman coming towards him with a child in her arms. She was smiling at the strange man, and as she came nearer he stretched out his hands to her. The child sat up in the woman's arms, and laughed at Shuan, and held out its hands to him. Shuan laughed too, and kissed the child. Suddenly the air all around was filled with music and the ringing of bells. It was Christmas morning, Shuan knew. He turned toward the woman and the man, and together they moved away into the great white woods, and gradually the music grew softer, as Shuan, a look of joy on his face, walked away with the woman and the Fisher of Men.

Christmas morning came with the ringing of bells and the sound of music. The snow sparkled on the trees in the woods and on the moors, and the sun shone on the hut of old Shuan the fisherman.

A robin, hungry for the crumbs that were always outside the hut on Christmas morning, hopped on to the window sill, with a sprig of holly in its beak. It flew in to where old Shuan, with Shemus the dog, were sitting. Shuan was asleep in his chair, an open book on his knees, and a smile of perfect happiness on his face. The little bird dropped the sprig of holly into Shuan's lap, and then flew away to tell everyone how happy old Shuan looked, although he was asleep, on Christmas morning.

B. G. Stevenson.

Christmas, 1915.

Chapter 6

St Denis

Early in January 1916 one of her aunts went to France to manage a Y.M.C.A. Canteen, and Betty was very anxious to join her. At first it seemed as if she would not be able to go, as she was only nineteen, which was considered too young. At last, however, she got her permit, and after a false alarm in the shape of a hurried departure to London with instructions to be ready to go to France, and a sad return home, Betty at last got her papers in order and started off to France, escorted by her father, on Friday, the 11th February.

Her letters and diary speak for themselves about her work, and her love of it, and the great pleasure and joy she found in being able to brighten the lot of the men for whom she worked so hard.

The passage was very rough, and Betty was never a good sailor. But nothing could diminish her joy in her great adventure, and her diary and letters are full of it. Who but Betty would have idealised "the friendly, insatiable little basin," or the life-saving waistcoat she had to wear, "in case Kaiser Billy's little sailormen might have something to say to us"? Her first letter to her mother the next day begins: "Everything is too heavenly for words."

Here are her impressions of Havre in wartime:—

> Havre looked just the same. I somehow imagined it would look different. Only there wasn't the usual civilian crowd watching the arrival of the steamer. There were several English Tommies and officers on the quay, several blousy porters, and lots of French soldiers. In the background was a tall, black-moustached French official, with his arms folded, watching everything.
> In the street behind the *douane* a little boy went by whistling 'Tipperary,' and several Tommies were trying to talk to a girl in

front of a shop window. . . . When everything was still, we got off, and went to the *douane*.

It was a fair-sized room with a long table running down the middle of it. Behind the table sat six officials—three bearded French ones, and three clean-shaven English ones. The passport passed down the table and so did I, and out at a door the other side. I felt I was going through a sausage machine, and as I came out of the door, a full-fledged sausage, I gazed back on the long rows of pigs and felt sorry for them.

We got a fiery-moustached little man who began washing his hands among my clothes. I produced my Y.M.C.A. brassard and he smiled and closed my trunk and said: '*Oh, c'est bien, mademoiselle, c'est bien, si j'avais su, mademoiselle, vous savez . . .*' and he waved his arms about and was no end of a wid.

Next day, the 12th February, she joined her aunt in the little hotel in the Boulevard Magenta, which was to be her home, and on the 14th she started her work at the St Denis Canteen.

Hotel Magenta,
Boulevard Magenta, Paris,
Wednesday, 16th February 1916.

Darling,—My letters all begin the same, namely, that everything here is too divine for words. Apparently I must say hardly anything about the camp, or the work, so I hope you won't mind. It will all go into a diary anyhow. However here is a time-table of what we do. We go up there every morning and afternoon alternately.

******

9.15 to 9.45.—Made my supper, ate it, read and smiled.
10.30 to 11.—Bed, and sleep like a pig.

******

4 p.m.—Made my tea and bought *éclairs* and other glorious things just round the corner.
6 p.m.—Am writing this!
7.15.—Shall go down the Boulevard to Duval's for dinner.
9.—When we like, sit and talk flowery French in the drawing-room with *Madame* and the other lodgers.

It really is a lovely existence. . . .

. . . Now I want to say something *really* important. Alice leaves in five weeks. Now I simply refuse to leave before my three *mois* are up, and I can stay longer if I ask Mr Coleman. I want you to ask anyone you think would come out to fill up Alice's place immediately she goes, and who would take on her room here. Well, look round for someone, there's a wid. ... It is a fair work and the tram service is awful, and you do want someone who cart be cheerful and understanding up there.

I do think Paris is too lovely for words—better even than Brussels, but I expect that's because I've got something real to do. I've just the comfortable time to lounge and shop and be lazy in, and just the right time to work in. There isn't too much of either. At the same time, the work is so interesting that I'd give up the lazing if I had to, though I think then I *should* be tired. At present I'm just right, and feeling as fit as a fiddle. It is lovely.

There are two very nice menials here, Lucie and Louis. Louis does all the bedrooms, answers your bell, makes the bed, and sometimes brings up your brekker. He puts in a corner things he thinks ought to go to the wash, and he has his own ideas as to how my frocks and coats should hang, and if I alter them, he always puts them back. He is such a wid. I hope this epistle isn't censored. *Please tell me if it is.*

"Up there" they *are* all so nice and grateful. Last night someone played the violin and I played the accompaniment.

The Gare du Nord is so interesting, though very sad. All the time there are soldiers either going back to the front, or going home on leave.

It is nice to feel you're wanted. Both Alice and *Madame* are too sweet for words.

I must stop now, we're going down to Duval's.—Love from your little   Betty.

It was not long before the work got more strenuous.

> Hotel Magenta,
> Boulevard Magenta,
> Paris, 24th February 1916.

Darling little Wids,—I'm so sorry I've been such a long time writing, but I really haven't had time. I'm living what Jars would call "Some Life," and I've never enjoyed myself so much before. Auntie says I'm enjoying it so because I'm working so hard. I know I am, but the fact is, the work's the nicest part. I've made heaps of friends up there! *Toutes sortes* and all castes. I'm longing to write reams about it all, but Alice says it's awfully risky, as letters very often go back, and so I'm not taking any risks.

Well, I don't really know where to begin with other news, there's been so much happening. Last Sunday (or Saturday—I've lost all count of time) there was a Zeppelin alarm. I told you in one letter how the *pompiers* and the *clairons* go round. Some of us were sitting in the *salon*, it was about 9.20 p.m., and Alice and I had just come in from our afternoon shift, when Louis, the nice valet, dashed in and said that a *gendarme* had been to tell us to put down our shutters, as it had come through that two Zepps. had succeeded in passing over the French lines, in the direction of Paris. There was great excitement, and all our shutters were put down, and when we looked out of the window all the street lights had been turned out.

All this was called an *alerte*. The *pompiers* and Co. only go when the little birds are within a certain distance of Paris. Several of the people here went upstairs and dashed their valuables into a bag, and then stood dithering in the hall. There is one old lady here of eighty-four, and her son. They are French refugees from somewhere, and their house is full of Germans. They had to escape at the last moment. The poor old lady always has her valise packed ready, and when she heard the *alerte* she sent her son for it.

Madame Christophe and I went on to the roof to see the *projections*, but there weren't any. We saw an aeroplane dashing off somewhere. It was a lovely clear night, and it was snowing. We looked right out over Paris and the avenues of roofs, all getting gradually whiter and whiter in the snow. It was simply wonderful, everything seemed to be waiting—as indeed it was. I shall never forget standing away up there, waiting for the Zeppelins, and looking right over Paris in the snow.

We came down and found Louis had got fresh news, that the Zepps. were coming to Paris, two of them. We then adjourned to the cellar. I say cellar, but catacombs is a better word—vaulted passages, which we all threaded our way through with the help of a lantern, and finally emerged into a fair-sized room which was fitted with electric light. As a result of previous raids, it was furnished with a table with a red cloth, a sofa, a chair, and a high plank balanced on two barrels. Round two sides were shelves filled with wine. In one corner was a heap of apples, and behind me a great heap of potatoes. Washing lines were hung from wall to wall, from which dangled linen, tablecloths, curtains, stockings and everything you can imagine.

The old lady was presented with the chair and a little footstool, and rugs over her, and her son stood beside her with a valise in one hand and a blue and red carpet bag in the other. He joked and was cheerful the whole time, and kept on encouraging his mother. On the sofa was an English girl in her nightclothes and a coat over them, and next to her another woman and a boy about fourteen, also French refugees from the same place as the other two. Then came me, perched up on the planks, with my head among the washing and my feet resting on a pile of potatoes. I was dressed all right, as I'd just come in from the camp. Then came Alice.

Louis kept on coming in with news. It was too funny for words really, in spite of its being rather frightening. We stayed there over an hour, and then as no *pompiers* had gone, we concluded the lil' birds must have been stopped. Alice and I led, and gradually one by one we dispersed through the stone corridors of that unwholesome cellar. When we finally arrived in the hall, Alice and I went in to Mme Christophe's office and had a large meal, composed of wine, biscuits and mandarines. Then we came to bed at 12.45. The lights were still out all over Paris, so I slept in a good many of my garments. Next morning you can imagine what we felt like when we heard the news. I suppose your papers were full of it? Two Zeppelins and four Aviatiks *en route* for Paris were stopped by the French aeroplanes. One Zepp. fell to the ground, the other damaged, and one Aviatik brought down and the others forced to turn. I've never been so excited over war news before.

All Paris was literally exulting. I must say I feel safer here than in England, though it will probably egg them on to revenge. (I've just remembered all this happened last Saturday night, 19th February.) On Sunday morning we went off to the Palais Royale, which is now a hospital, to see Mme Trouette who is nursing there. It used to be a great Course Hippique, and you go through avenues of stables to get upstairs to the wards. The huge circus is now a sort of main street. Mme Trouette wasn't there, but we walked round the ward and spoke to some of the soldiers and *infermières*.

Then we went to see the Musée d'Armee, where they had heaps of German guns and aeroplanes, and then on to Napoleon's tomb. It was simply wonderful; I can't describe it. It's like standing in the circle of the theatre and looking right away down into the pit, and there you see the huge brown wooden coffer. I wonder what Napoleon would have said to see all those people silently gazing down into his tomb? I think he would like it.

Paris is suiting me better than any place I've ever been in. It's extraordinary. I sleep like a top all night, and feel like a lion all day, no matter how hard the work up there. I'm doing everything I ought, and I've actually got red cheeks! We go up there by a tram which starts from just across the road, and we come back the same way. We often have to wait hours for a tram, and then hang on to a step by the skin of our teeth, while the conductress punches you and tries to knock you off. They really are awful Amazons.

I'm getting to know Paris ever so well now, and the more I know the more I love it. I went to Cook's on Monday for my chink, but it hadn't come, but I got it yesterday.

Alice and I live quite independently, and we join forces when we want to. Of course I don't mean to say I go trapezing about with strange youths, but I go about by myself, and I always wear my brassard, which means that I can go anywhere.

Now I'm going to jump into bed. I've had only two little letters from you since I left home! Write soon.—Your loving Widlet,

Bunçie.

P.S.—Auntie's been out all the afternoon and evening, and I've been writing so hard, I forgot all about dinner till 8.30. Places close at 8. I'm having chocolate, bread and camembert, biscuits and mandarines up here in my room, 10.45. Some life, as I said, and I'm as fit as a fiddle. I shall get up at 11.30 tomorrow, lunch at 12, then real lovely hard work and the knowledge that everyone is saying and thinking nice things about you, and is grateful for what you are doing. They tell about their families, and come for advice when they have tummy-aches. I do love them all, especially some!!

Next morning,—At 12 last night there was another *alerte* plus the *pompiers*. I vaguely heard it, but was half asleep and didn't bother. There's nowt int' papers, so I think it was a false alarm.

Hotel Magenta,
Boulevard Magenta,
Paris, 28th February 1916.

Darling Mother,—Thanks ever so for your lovely long letter, and the photo of Jark, and the Belgian Report which I got yesterday morning.

Now about the subject of food. . . . I'm never hungry and I always have enough to eat. ... I often go without tea, but that ought to please you and Paw, especially the latter! And then I have all the better appetite for dinner. Here's today's programme. (I'm writing this just before going to bed.)

9.20.—Breakfast in bed, *i.e.* cup of chocolate, chunk of bread, two *brioches* and butter and apricot jam. . . . 2 p.m.—Bowl of soup, three cakes, mandarines and chocolate, eaten off an overturned crate for a table, behind the counter of the canteen! (lovely).

... Sometimes when we are working up there in the afternoon there is such a rush that we haven't time for an evening meal, therefore when we get back I always have something in my room. I buy two slices of ham and some mandarines—get a chunk of bread and some chocolate granules from *Madame*—spread out my nightgown for a tablecloth—make the chocolate and have a fine meal. What more could you want? I don't want sardines and things. I like the slices of ham I buy, wrapped up in newspaper, two slices for 50 c. . . .

One of the soldiers up there is French and no end of a wid. He's lent me heaps of French books. I go home from the camp with my arms full of books and albums! So far they have all been quite *convenable*. If I find one that isn't—I shall just take it back and say that I haven't had time to read it. I'm reading one now called *La Jolie Infirmière*. It's extremely knutty and very exciting, all about this war. I've also got *Le Portrait d'Aimée*, and *Mignon*, the opera.

Betty's aunt had to come back to England, and the question of a successor was solved by her mother deciding to come out.

Hotel Magenta,
Boulevard Magenta, Paris,
7th March (Shrove Tuesday).

Darling Mother,—What perfectly lovely news. You simply can't think how excited I am about your coming out here. Of course you'll do the work splendidly....

Don't imagine you won't want pretty clo'; you will, so bring all you've got.... Life isn't all composed of blue overalls and brown boots. Bring lots of overalls for the work, but not ugly ones. You've no idea how "they" *love* to see something pretty. They're dead sick of uniforms, I can tell you.... You don't see any shabby people about here. They know that everything is so sad, but that it doesn't help anyone to look miserable and shabby. There's no silly extravagance, but every woman tries to be as cheerful and make herself look as pretty as she can, and there's more war work being done. Everyone's *infirmière*. Write soon.—Your loving

Wug.

You will love the work, and the appreciation of it.

Grand Hotel Magenta,
129 Boulevard Magenta, Paris.

Darling Mother,—What a long time since I've written to you, but as you will have got Alice's letter by now you will know that I've been *grippée*, I'm all right now, and would have gone out today if it hadn't been raining. Everybody at the camp has it or has had it, so now that I've got mine over, I can march ahead. The weather is very difficult to know—one day it is so hot, like summer, and the next day snow. But I'm learning.

Oh, I am looking forward to your coming, and I know you'll love it....

    Love. Bunçie.

A. W. T. S.

Hotel Magenta,
Boulevard Magenta, Paris.

Darling,—What a long time since I've heard from you, but you must be frightfully busy.... Oh! I am looking forward to seeing my wid again. You're to swear to bring J-A-R-S, and we'll get him in here... Donal's coming. Shan't we all smile? .. Be sure and wear your brassard at Havre because the customs won't bother you then...

A. thinks I've had a breakdown as well I've simply had *la grippe*—species of flu which every soul is suffering from. I've had it quite thoroughly, as I always do get things and now I'm

all right.
>   Write soon.—Your little

>   Love and a hug to the Wid.
A. W. T. S.

Bunçie

Chapter 7

Her Mother Joins Her

I went out to join Betty on 30th March. Fortunately my plans for going out on the torpedoed *Sussex* had to be altered, and I went a week later. It is almost like a dream now to remember what crossing the Channel meant in those days.

I shall not forget my arrival at the little hotel, about 10 p.m., walking into the room where Betty sat eating her supper. My journal says:

> Dear thing, she did look so sweet, tho' very pale. She fell into my arms and hugged me and said, 'You look about thirteen, and I love your hat,' which pleased me very much.

We had at first two tiny rooms looking into a narrow cobbled street. The noise of passing traffic was terrific, especially at night, when huge convoys of every description passed. Betty's room was a mass of "things." We moved very soon into one big two-bedded room, which had a tiny sitting-room opening out of it, about eight feet by six feet, and it was lovely to be able to keep Betty a little more comfortable, and look after her meals. She owned that she had got rather tired of eating a slice of *Jambon de Yorck* for her supper, "sitting on the edge of the bed and using my nightdress case as a plate." The hotel could provide no meals except *petit déjeuner*.

Naturally, after my arrival, Betty's letters home were much less frequent. She was tired, and I wrote most of the letters home.

On Saturday, 1st April, I got my permit, and started working in the canteen with Betty, and I'm sure no two people were ever so happy as she and I were that day.

The Y.M.C.A. Hut where we worked was a few miles due north of Paris, in a very poor and not too reputable suburb. It was set in the middle of a cinder-laid compound, and was surrounded by M.T. workshops, in which were motor-lorries and motor-waggons of every description, and wounded cars sent down from the Front for repair.

In our early days we used occasionally to get a lift back to our hotel in a car that happened to be going that way, but very shortly after I joined Betty, conditions in the camp became very different, and this was no longer done. One other lady shared the work of the hut with us. We used to work in alternating morning and evening shifts, *i.e.* one day Betty and I worked from after breakfast until 2.30 or 3.30, and the next day we worked from 5 to about 10.

Here let me try with a feeble pen to give some glimpse of the happiness we had inside that hut. It was absolutely the one bit of brightness in the men's lives there. It stood for home, and the decencies and amenities of home, and we knew it, and it helped us to keep going. I know it can be said of countless Y.M.C.A. Huts all through these past four and a half years, that they were little lifeboats on a vast sea of warfare, but I can never think that in any spot in the whole of the war area was a hut so needed as ours was.

When Betty and her aunt first went out, the hut was very ill-equipped. The only stove was at the opposite end to the counter, the water seldom boiled, and every drop of it had to be carried from one end of the hut to the other. After some weeks a real pukka stove was got, and "several miles" of piping were fetched triumphantly from a big stores in Paris by Betty and her aunt, driven out in triumph to the camp, and fixed up by the men.

We were helped by a wonderful little French woman, one of those capable, smart, attractive little heart-of-gold French women one meets all over France, beyond my pen to describe. Her husband had been killed in 1915, and she had one little girl. She could do everything, apparently, and do it well. The men loved to teach her English slang, and were enchanted when she called them "saucy puss."

Getting to and from our camp was simply a nightmare. We waited any time from half an hour to an hour and a half in all weathers at a corner close to our hotel for the tram, which was nearly always crowded, and we generally had to "sit on someone's figure" as Betty described it. After the night shift they had stopped running, and we had to walk about two miles to the nearest *Ceinture* Station, and get a train which crawled round Paris, and finally deposited us at the Gare du Nord. Walking through the station we had to be careful not to step on sleeping *Poilus en permission*, lying anywhere they could, dead asleep, coated with mud and laden with kit, straight from the trenches, country men perhaps, sleeping before they caught a train out of Paris. There were no benches for them. It was very late when we got home, and there were rough crowds about, but no one ever spoke rudely to us. We wore no uniform then, only our Y.M.C.A. brassards. It is true a wag once shouted to Betty, "*ee grec.—M.—C.—A.! Association de jeunes hommes Chrétiens!* Oh, shocking!" We used to climb the long flights of stairs to our room and flop on to our beds and sleep the sleep of the weary until it was time for tea or *petit déjeuner*, according to the time of shift.

There were French windows opening out on to the noisiest Boulevard in Paris, but there was a chestnut tree just outside, in whose branches a pair of pigeons built, on a level with our windows. Electric trams ran by, and as we were at the junction of four main roads converging on the Gare du Nord, the noise can be better imagined than described. But we always slept through it all. We both carry in our minds many pictures framed in that window. Joffre and Poincaré driving by together, convoys, endless funerals, crowds carrying bunches and wreaths of box on the *jour des morts*, more crowds, moved as only French can be, on the day of Galliéni's funeral. In the night, the clatter of horses' hoofs, and the passing of a company of *cuirassiers*, the lights shining on their brass-helmets with their horse-tails. They always made us think of the little French *duc* in *Trilby*, the friend of little Billee. And on Sundays, lots of our own men walking about and making the most of Paris leave.

It soon became clear that, with the best will in the world, we should not be able to hold out unless there were a better way of getting in and out to the camp, and especially as the weather grew hot and our feet became more and more like hot bricks. We therefore set about raising £150 to buy a second-hand Ford car. Kind friends at home gave £100 of this, and the Y.M.C.A. contributed the remaining £50. Betty soon picked up its ways, and drove it, and we took a new lease of life. Instead of arriving weary and breathless at our work and crawling back at night, we had the rush through the air to revive us. During the rest of the day the car was used at the Y.M.C.A. Headquarters. The old sentries at the Barrier were much amused the first time we passed there in the Ford, and Betty loved calling out "*Armée Anglaise!*" as we went through, and hearing one sentry reply: "*Tiens—tiens—tiens!*"

Betty's young brother came out to spend the Easter holidays helping at the canteen. At the end of April the camp had a great outburst of measles. Men would come in cheerfully, put a hand across the counter, give us a shake and say: "Well, goodbye Miss, I've got it, and I'm off to hospital in Rouen." It was perhaps not surprising that Betty and Arthur both got the "fashionable complaint." The canteen was closed, as the hut was "out of bounds," and the next fortnight was spent away from work while I nursed the two patients who were looked after by the kindest of M.O.s from the camp, who lent us an ambulance later on, so that we were able to take the air without infecting other people. There was a good deal of flute-playing at this time, and a good many jokes, and we were all three very happy in spite of measles.

On 15th May the hut was reopened, and Betty and I went up in the car and started work again.

To her Father

Hotel Magenta,
Boulevard Magenta, Paris,
20th May 1916.

Darling little Dumpos,—We're working again now, and it is so nice to be back. The men are such wids, and the day we opened the place was crammed, and we sold out everything. They all said such pretty things, and one old boy said: "If anyone ever says anything against the Y.M.C.A. again, I'll hit him." The car's going finely, and I do it all on my own now, including oiling. I'm going to clean it when I've time. Fords are going steadily up in price. While out in her, three people have asked if she was for sale, as they were looking everywhere for second-hand Fords. The people at the camp agree that they are the thing for army work. Light on tyres and petrol. She's got a perfect engine, really a find. It has been such a boon to us.

The weather is stifling and we'd never have borne the trams. In the afternoons I often do commissions for the Y.M.C.A. in Paris. I'm really nobby at traffic now! While we were in quarantine we went out in Capt. Rankin's ambulance. We used to go to the Bois and feed the ducks and swans. For 10c. you got a large chunk of bread from an old woman with a moustache any major might have envied. Did you know ducks could beg? Well, I made them. If you threw a piece of bread up in the air, the ducks all stood on their tails and pawed the surface with their feet. They were sweet. The other night Captain Rankin took

Jars and me out. I expect Jars told you ... we had a box at the Alhambra. It was a ripping show. Ventriloquists, singers, dancers, trick bicyclists, impersonators, and a man with a performing alligator. It was such a darling, and he was horribly harsh to it; kept on beating its nose. Still, I suppose you can't be too gentle and tender with a crocodile, or it might find you tender....
Ever so many loves and hugs.—Your wayward

Bunçie.

T.L.I.W.Y.
All these days we had to do double shifts, as the new workers had not yet come. It was fearfully hot.

Y.M.C.A.
c/o Army Post Office, S.5,
British Expeditionary Force,
26th May 1916.

Darling Dumpos,—We've been having it so hot we could hardly breathe, but it is much cooler now....

This morning I oiled and greased the car up at the garage, which necessitated taking up the floor boards, and sitting perched upon the seat with all the machinery underneath me, instead of the floor. It's very exciting and you get gloriously messy and covered with oil, and altogether it's fine. ... I must stop now, wid dear, as we're going out.
Goodbye, darling.

Bunch.

Chapter 8

Her Mother's Journal

Thursday, 16th June.

I had today a letter from Lady Bessborough thanking me for what Betty and I had done at St Denis—with a special message from Princess Helena Victoria. I was so bucked, and it was nice to get it at a time like this, when life was not too easy, and we had to get to and from our work once more as best we could, while the car was being mended....

Y.M.C.A.
Recreation Huts at the Base Camps in France
Hon. Secretary—Countess of Bessborough
23 Bruton Street,
London, W., 12th June 1916.

Dear Mrs Stevenson,—I am delighted with your interesting letter of the 4th. It is such a pleasure to have such an enthusiastic account as you give of your work in France for the last six months.

H.H. Princess Helena Victoria is greatly interested, and she and our Committee are most grateful to you and your daughter for the magnificent work you have done in the Y.M.C.A. Hut at St Denis.

Yours sincerely,   B. Bessborough.

Sunday, 18th June.

Today we were both going out to the Scottish Women's Hospital[1] at the Abbaye de Royaumont. But poor old Bet felt so tired I couldn't

---

1. *Scottish Nurses in the First World War* by Yvonne Fitzroy & Eva Shaw McLaren - *With the Scottish Nurses in Roumania* by Yvonne Fitzroy & *A History of the Scottish Women's Hospitals (Extract concerning service in the Balkans)* by Eva Shaw McLaren is also published by Leonaur.

get her to say she'd go, though I felt certain a day in the fresh air would do her a heap of good. So I had sadly to leave her behind and in bed.

It was a divine day. We got to the entrance of the glorious abbey and walked into the cloisters, at one end of which the staff were having lunch. I shall never forget the impression I got, of a glorious quadrangle of grey cloisters, in the middle a formal garden with tiny beds, box-bordered, a fountain playing in the centre, and blue sky overhead. At the end of one cloister was the staff; doctors, sisters, nurses, orderlies, all in blue at lunch.... The sisters with large starched handkerchiefs on their heads, the orderlies all in blue gingham with blue mob-caps; awfully becoming. A splash of red poppies and white daisies in the jugs on the tables. It was a lovely scheme of grey, blue and red. Mrs Hacon introduced me to the head, Dr Frances Ivens. She is splendid, and I became a humble admirer on the spot....

Wednesday, 21st June.

The car came back from hospital today! We were so delighted. When we got back from the morning shift, there she was, sitting outside the hotel. Of course Betty took her for a little run, up and down and round about.

At 6 p.m. Mrs Hacon and Daisy Davidson arrived on their visit. They looked so nice in their grey uniform. They brought us armfuls of glorious wild flowers: pink valerians, dog-daisies, meadow sweet, poppies. Our *salon* looks lovely with them, and we set aside the poppies and daisies to take to the canteen tomorrow. Then we all packed into the car, and Betty drove us.... We did feel happy! ... It is a great change for the S.W.H. to come into a city and see people and go to *cafés*....

Thursday, 22nd June.

...At 6 p.m. Betty set off to motor them both back to Royaumont. I felt it was rather an adventure for her, going so far and coming back alone, but I felt sure she would like to do it alone, so I stayed behind. I went across to the *charcuterie* and bought a very excellent cold pork chop, and had supper off it, with bread, wine and some of Mrs Hacon's fruit. It was rather nervous work as the evening went on, waiting for Betty, and I hoped she was all right. At ten minutes to ten I heard the horn and flew to the window, and there she was below in the Ford; I was glad to see her! She called up that she'd just stopped for a minute on her way to the garage because she knew I'd be getting anxious. So I flew round after the car to the garage and we walked back together.

She could hardly speak for excitement!

Royaumont had impressed her too, just as it did me, but the drive back had been the most wonderful of all, along the edge of the great forest, and there were gypsies encamped there. The guns were making a great noise, and Betty said she should never forget that drive. No wonder the guns impressed her. This was the preparation for the Battle of the Somme, which began eight days later.

2nd July.

This is a red letter day. It was gloriously fine, and Mr C. said we could take the car out to Royaumont with an easy conscience, as there is a lot of petrol due to us—thanks to the car having been laid up for so long. We started about 12, Betty in a clean muslin jumper, with a blue velvet ribbon; she looked so sweet, but dreadfully pale. We took for lunch some ham, bread, strawberries, two *gâteaux* and a bottle of red wine and Vichy mixed. We did feel so pleased with life. About three quarters of a mile from Rue Prudhomme we saw one of our big lorries crammed with the band which had been to play at a French hospital. We saw one vast grin, with familiar features behind. They'd run out of petrol. The sergeant in charge stepped out in front of us and we pulled up to hear what was the matter. Of course we offered to go back to the camp to get petrol for them! It was a proud moment for us, as they all make fun of the Ford. We tore back to camp and waited outside the gates, sending a Tommy in for petrol. After about twenty minutes the petrol tins were brought out, and we drove back to the band.

It is almost a straight road, but so lovely, and such views! Miles and miles you can see, with great sweeps of the Forest of Montmorençy. Bits of the road are awful, and we had to drive very slowly.... At last we came through Viarmes and pulled up at the back of the abbey wall. We walked round to the main entrance ... and found ambulances there, and wounded being lifted out on stretchers. So the long-expected big convoy was arriving today! At first we thought we ought to go straight back to Paris; then we tried to efface ourselves in a corner of the hall, while someone went off to try and find Mrs Hacon for us....

They knew nothing about this big arrival until 9 o'clock today! Then they got telephone messages for the ambulances to go at once to Creil (12 kilometres) to fetch wounded and to go on fetching them till every bed was full. They were putting beds all round the cloisters, and they would be slept in next night. We saw the wounded being brought, some on stretchers, lying so still—it was hard work not to burst into tears. One Moroccan, like a bronze statue, had a stick pushed into one empty boot and trouser leg. A few could walk one or two staggering steps, the orderlies helping them.

Every now and then Dr Frances Ivens appeared, in her white clothes, a figure of strength and gentleness. I saw her lay a gentle hand on a bandaged head and arm, and she asked a question or two, and then said what ward they should go into, and the orderlies took them away. One man wouldn't go to bed until he had told how he and his company had got into the 6th line of German trenches, just twelve hours before! ... A *chauffeuse* of one of the ambulances came and got a hurried tea; she hadn't eaten since 8 a.m. Soon after tea we went, as we were on duty at our hut tonight. Mrs Hacon came with us in the Ford as far as Viarmes, to order more meat and bread for the 400 *blessés*. . . . . It was such a divine evening. Our minds were very full of what we had seen. . . .

I forgot to say, even on this busy day. Miss Ivens found time to tell Betty how pleased she was about our bed in the S.W.H. . . . She said it had come just at the right time, and it should be used that night. I'm glad to think there is a *poilu* in it. It is in the Millicent Fawcett Ward. . . .

★★★★★★

In July we were sent away to take long leave. We went to a lovely little *plage* on the coast of Brittany, in Finisterre.

Betty's father and brother joined us here, and we had the most lovely holiday all together. We made hosts of friends among the nice French families there: most of all with three charming young French ladies, who each had a dear little girl—Lydie, Mercédès, and Lynette. They were so pretty, so charmingly clad in jerseys and tiny linen knickers which their pretty mammas made for them as they sat on the sands. Their fathers came *en permission* at different times, while we were there.

> Today we went down to the *plage* at 3. Betty bathed at about 4.30; she looked so pretty in her blue things. The Russian lady's husband is here *en permission*. . . . He talked a little to Betty as she came up from the sea, looking so sweet and with such a smile, her white teeth showing, and her face wet from the sea.
>
> While we were on leave in August, our Y.M.C.A. chief wrote and

offered us a "boss job" in what Betty called a "really thrilling place," much nearer the front line, because, as he said, "we had done our duty in hard circumstances," and I must confess that, left to myself, I would have accepted the new offer. But Betty sat and meditated about it, on the sunny *plage*, and she said: "Well, I know it would be thrilling to go to Abbeville, but I vote we go back to St Denis. We know how grateful the men are, and they know us now so well, and I somehow feel it would be mean to leave them for a new place."

So we decided to go back to our old hut. We were all very sad to leave this lovely place, where we had been so happy. We did not think then, that this was our last summer holiday all together. On Saturday 26th August, we said goodbye to all our kind French friends. We left many possessions in the care of the hotel proprietor, so certain were we that in 1917 the war would be over, and we would all come back again to this paradise. So there they still are: the tent, the chairs, the shrimping nets and fishing rods, and the enormous heavy and unnavigable raft, built by the Breton village carpenter, which would only hold one, and was generally attacked by four swimmers, and promptly submerged, to everyone's great joy.

In Paris we separated, Betty and I going back to our old rooms, and her father and brother crossing to England the following day. So we took up our work again at the canteen, and the journal says:—

> We were doggo when we got back. It is hard work, and no mistake, after such a long holiday!
>
> I had a lovely hour sitting on a chair in the Luxembourg Gardens today where I could see the flowers and watch the children playing, and there was no noise of traffic at all. I did like it, and the birds came quite close to my feet to pick up crumbs; they were wids, and one was just like Betty. I came away at 6, feeling refreshed by an hour of quiet and peace from Boulevard Magenta.

We went on with our old work until November, when our time was up. I feel I can only say, with the Victorian novelists, "*Over this parting I must draw a veil.*"

The cold in late October and November was the worst I have ever known. We had, for a long time, no coal or wood in the hotel, and fires were out of the question, until at last we managed to get some logs and light a fire in our tiny *salon*. We used to wrap our legs and feet up in spare coats when we were in our rooms, and occasionally go out and take a ride in a heated tram or on the Metro where there was always "a good fug on." The nights were frightfully cold, and everything in the room froze, that could freeze.

Before we left the men gave a farewell concert for us, and we said goodbye and came away.

We crossed from Havre to Southampton in a gale, and spent thirty-two hours in the Channel, of which perhaps the worst were twelve hours anchored outside Havre harbour in the storm.

CHAPTER 9

Étaples

From November 1916 to April 1917 Betty was at home, and the difference between life out in France and work at the camp, and life at home, is beyond my pen to describe. Everywhere we seemed to see all the old luxury and comfort, and "being waited on," which we had quite got out of the way of in France. It was odd to hear people complaining in shops because they had to carry parcels home.

Clean jugs, stair carpets, fires, and separate plates for two courses, seemed wonderful things to Betty and me for quite a long time. I thought perhaps Betty might decide to stay in England and find some work here. But, after a lovely time at home, and the happiest Christmas, she began to want to go back to France again and work for her beloved Tommies, this time as a motor driver.

There were many delays, as she was considerably younger than was required by the rules of the Y.M.C.A. for their drivers. However, finally, she was told she was to go to France to drive: perhaps the rule was relaxed on account of her 1916 record, a record of which her parents were very proud.

She and I went to London on 16th April, and she crossed on the 21st, Saturday. I came back the same day; the house was very still without her, and I thought of her setting out on her Great Adventure, alone this time, and having to make her own decisions and decide for herself what to do and what not to do: no one but her own dear self to rely on. I was not afraid for her. I thought back a good deal to 1916, to many, many occasions when she had had to do this in very difficult circumstances, and I remembered she had never failed. Times when there was no one to help.

It can be imagined how anxiously her first letter was looked for.

22nd April 1917.

Darling Mother,—*J'y suis*. I hope you haven't been anxious, but I simply couldn't send a wag from Boulogne. I sent one from Folkestone. . . . We got on board at about 11.30, got two deck chairs, put on our lifebelts, and started at about 12. The boat was packed, and we had a heavenly crossing, and I didn't feel a bit ill. We were met at Boulogne by a nice Y.M.C.A. man and were taken to a hostel to have a meal. We went in a car that was packed with luggage, and Miss Mackenzie and I stood on the step, and went flying along the quay, much to everyone's amusement. After lunch I was motored out here, which is about nineteen miles away. We brought two relatives with us who had come to see wounded relatives, and dropped one at Violet Solly's hospital, and one at the hospital here. I don't like to mention names. Then I was motored on to headquarters and shown my billet.

I am billeted in a house with a nice view over the river on the main road. I think I am the only female there, but I'm not sure. There are some Y.M.C.A. men there, and an English officer downstairs. The house is kept by an old man and his wife—filthy dirty, but very amiable. My room is the dirtiest I have ever seen, but is a nice room all the same, and the dirt isn't the sort that matters. I left my valise and things in my room, and then I was conducted along to tea. We all mess together in a room, male and female combined. They are all ever so nice, and make you feel at ease. I've met Joyce Scott, and her digs are quite close to mine.

We have breakfast 8-9; lunch 1; tea 5-6; dinner 8-9; and we all float in when we want to. I came back to bed directly after dinner last night, and slept like a log in a very comfy bed. This morning I have reported to the A.P.M., and am now waiting for a driving permit. Joyce and I went to church this morning. At least it wasn't church; the Y.M.C.A. have a service in a little room, and it was rather nice. Afterwards I bought some chocolate, and a blue tie and a flash lamp. The streets are pitchy dark, and I have to go up a windy stair to my room. I am going to stop now as Joyce and I are going in to Paris-Plage by train. Ever so much love to everyone,

Betty.

I feel I don't tell you much, but dear Mr Unknown, in the

shape of the censor, might object.

Diary

Sunday, 22nd April 1917.

Joyce came and whistled below my window at 8.15 this morning, and I joined her in a few minutes, and we toddled along to breakfast. After breakfast we went round to the garage and I was introduced to the boss of the mechanics. Joyce has been put on to drive a big Garford lorry, and at 9 o'clock she went out to have another practice on it and I sat on a tyre behind. It's a great big lumbering old lorry, and on these awful roads one gets absolutely pitched about. We were out about an hour, and it was great sport.

There are lovely woods all round, with little roads and avenues running right into them. At all these roads is a notice board up, either "Lewis Gun School," "Y.M.C.A. Hostel," "Les Iris," "Officers only; Out of bounds to all Troops," "No Road." It's all most tremendously interesting. When we came back we went and wrote letters, and after lunch we got leave to go to Paris-Plage. It was a ripping sunny day though rather cold, and we titivated ourselves up and prepared to enjoy life.

At 2.15 we sallied forth to the square opposite the town hall and waited for the tram. There was a huge crowd of officers, men, and nurses waiting for it. Presently a tram, or rather a light railway, with train carriages came along simply packed with officers. It was about a twenty minutes run and cost us 45 cents, each. At Paris-Plage we got out and made our way to the sea. It is a most divine place with a long promenade, acres of sand, then sand dunes, and no rocks. Presently we saw an aeroplane coming along, and we rushed along the sand to have a look at it, and everyone else did the same.

It came down so near us that we all had to fly for safety. The aviator was a nice little Frenchman, and he divested himself of his overall, or whatever the garment was called, and appeared in a most smart suit and a pair of brown boots. We watched for a bit and then we got back on to the promenade. A little way along we met Miss Bennett Burleigh, the war correspondent's daughter. She is here lecturing at all the different huts. She has been "twice through the German lines"—that is the title of her lecture. She went out to Belgium three days after the outbreak of war.

I haven't got a car to drive yet, because I have to have all sorts of permits and things first.

25th April 1917.

Darling Mother and Everybody,—I was so glad to get your letter last night and the enclosure.

I've unpacked my things and put out all my photos, and my room looks ever so nice. I am glad D.'s sister sent you his photo. He is with the Gordon Highlanders and is in "a damp muddy place, some way behind the lines." His base is here by the way, so I may possibly see something of him. I wrote to Uncle Lionel [1] yesterday, I do hope you have good news of him.

There is so much I want to tell you that I'm nearly bursting with it, but the Censor would I'm sure not allow it to pass, so I'll have to wait till I get home. All I'll say is that it is simply teeming with interest, this place. I shall never be able to tell you all I've seen. I haven't been given my car yet, but I am expecting it any day. I expect I shall have a Ford.

The woods round Paris-Plage are lovely and are full of wild daffodils. I haven't picked any yet, but yesterday I went out and bought some here for my room. I asked someone the way to the flower shop, and they pointed to a filthy-looking pub, packed with Australians. I went in, and was conducted through several bars to a back room full of the most lovely plants and flowers. I blewed 50 cents, on daffies. The water here isn't good, so I've bought some Perrier and Vichy. I had to go to a weird sort of cellar in a big warehouse to get it, and then carry the bottles home under my arm.

It is Anzac Day today, consequently there is an enormous excitement up at the big Anzac camp, and there are going to be great doings all the day. Sports and football matches galore. I am going up to see them at 1.30.

It is awfully cold. Today there is no sun *du tout*. My saucepan and Tommy's cooker come in very useful, as I can get no hot water here at all. The water is frightfully hard and simply peels the skin off one's face. I've bought some water softener. I forgot to bring my shoe-cleaning outfit, but luckily Joyce Scott has lent me hers. They clean her shoes for her at her digs, but they

---

1. Brig. .General East, C.M. G., D.S.O., killed in action 6th Sept. 1918.

don't at mine.

I live next to a cinema, and Joyce is over a carpenter's shop. At the other end of the town is another Y.M.C.A. hostel, where baths and other necessities can be got. It's a good long walk, but is all right when you get there. It's quite a long walk to our mess too, which is probably very good for us. It's great fun at the mess. There are two long trestle tables, and we are a gay crew. One of the Y.M.C.A. youths is awfully funny, and we all call him Tich. He makes us die with laughter. Another is known as Charlie Chaplin. Breakfast ranges from 8-9. This morning I overslept myself and didn't get there till 9.15. I was greeted with shouts and spoon thumpings, and Tich called out that I'd got a car at last. I was so bucked and asked which one. He said "Stephenson's Rocket." Rounds of applause; I was sick! They are all so amusing and kind, and don't give themselves any airs. Another of Tich's mots: "*Honi soit qui mal de mer.*"

My room is on the main street and exciting things are happening all the time. Thousands of Australians have just marched past, and ambulances and lorries all the time.

This morning I dashed out of the door of my digs and nearly fell over six or seven Australians who were sunning themselves on my doorstep. I've had some adventures which I will tell you in about four months! Lots of love and hugs.

Betty.

A.W.T.S.

CHAPTER 10

Anzac Day

Diary

Wednesday, *25th April* 1917.

Today is Anzac Day, and, there is great excitement among the enormous Australian and New Zealand camps.

The country all round here has been named by the troops, and as we got out we saw the painted board with Canada Park scrawled on it. We walked through a little bit of scrabbly sandy pine wood at the road side, and then we suddenly came to what we thought was a precipice. We walked to the edge and discovered that the ground all round sloped gradually down and widened out into an enormous flat expanse at the bottom, covered with short stubbly grass. But the grass was hardly visible because of the enormous crowd of khaki. It was a splendid sight. The slopes all round, and Canada Park itself, were one solid mass of khaki, and in the middle what looked like a wee little clearing space—this was the football ground.

It was a lovely sunny day but horribly dusty. The sand got in my hair, eyes, nose, and everything.

30th April 1917.

Darling Mother,—I haven't yet got my car, because it is in dock, and the head mechanic is in Paris ill. However I have been going round with Joyce, who is driving a lorry, and learning my way about.

I am afraid all my letters will be very dull because I simply mayn't tell you anything! I am sorry, but I'll remember it for when I come home. Although I haven't begun driving yet I love the life, it is all so different. I shall have no table manners when I get back.

Directly after lunch Miss Burleigh and I went up to a place called Canada Park where the sports and football were going to be. We went up in a lorry. I shall never be able to describe it all, but I shall never forget it. Canada Park is a big sort of plain with pine woods round, and is in a hollow like an enormous quarry. The place was packed, and we threaded our way through the biggest crowd of Anzacs, Australians and New Zealanders that I have ever seen. At one end was a Y.M.C.A. tent which had been put up for the day, and drinks and food were given free. Next door to Canada Park, in fact touching it, is the cemetery—acres and acres of little brown wooden crosses. They are burying at the rate of forty a day and the systematic digging is awful.

Three times during the afternoon the Last Post was sounded over some grave, and I shall never forget the impression I got when each time all the games stopped, and all the thousands of men sitting on the slopes stood up in dead silence while the Last Post was sounded, and then sat down again and continued their ragging. It made the most enormous impression on me. During the afternoon a huge long Red Cross train passed. They come every day, hundreds of carriages, and crawling along at a snail's pace. The event of the afternoon was the footer match between the Australians and New Zealanders. I have never seen anything like it. They half-killed each other! There were heaps of casualties, but after lying on the grass and having their clothes taken off they seemed to recover.

After that I had tea at one of the huts and then I went to a concert at an Australian hut, given by the men. At the end, the colonel made a speech, and it really was moving. He thanked the troops, and then he talked about Anzac Day this year and Anzac Day two years ago. I can't put down all he said, but I nearly wept. You see they'd all been through it. He had a horrid cold, but he was a perfect dear, and so un-English. He treated the men absolutely as equals, and when a bugle sounded in the middle he turned round and said "Shut up!" The men nearly stampeded. They love him. He talked a lot about Anzac Day two years ago, and said if it hadn't been for the help of a certain British division they wouldn't be there now.

After saying lots about the ——th, he said he was proud to say that one of the ——th officers was in the room and he would ask him to come on to the platform. I thought the men would go mad when the silent-looking little ———th colonel went on to the platform.

The Australian colonel took his arm and they just stood there while the men yelled and yelled. The men were moved right out of themselves, and I felt I oughtn't to be there. I was introduced to the Australian colonel afterwards, and he was a dear, and asked me to come up whenever I liked. You can't think of the difference in that way here from St Denis. If my letters weren't censored I would let myself go and tell you heaps of things, interesting, thrilling and silly, from Ian Hay to Charles Garvice! I can't hold up my head another minute.

    Goodnight,—Your loving

Bunçie.

A.W.T.S.

CHAPTER 11

The Day's Work

13th May 1917.

My darling Mother,—I know this will arrive late, but ever so many happy returns. I wish I was at home to give you a hug. I have moved from my digs and am now living with Joyce and two others in a villa right in the middle of the pine woods. We have a woman to cook for us, and a bathroom, and it is perfectly heavenly. We have our meals there when we have time. I have been driving a relative about to and from hospital. Poor man, his son died just half an hour before I arrived to take him back to the hostel. This relative business is simply too pathetic for words. We have to drive them to the funerals. A whole string of men headed by the *padre*, and then a procession of coffins draped in a Union Jack, laid on a little carriage and wheeled by two men; then the service round the grave and then the Last Post. A photo is always taken of the grave and given to the relative. There was an air fight here yesterday, and a Taube brought down. A piece of our own Archie shell fell outside the Y.M.C.A. Hut, an enormous piece. Thanks awfully for the woollies, etc. you sent out. I'm sorry I didn't answer sooner, but I simply haven't a spare moment. Could you send me out a pair of thick rubber gloves, size 7, ladies. My hands are getting in the most fearful state with messing about with the car.

The lamp blew up yesterday, and I turned round and saw the whole window in flames; I just had time to chuck on water and put it out. The curtains are burnt to bits.

I must go and work now, lots of love,

Bunçie.

A. W. T. S.

21st May 1917.

Darling Mother,—I was so glad to get your ripping long letter. I'm not allowed to mention any names of places, but yesterday I was sent off to the place where I landed, [1] to take relatives to the boat. I'd just come from church, and was expecting a free day, and the prospect of an afternoon in Paris-Plage, when I was suddenly sent off. It was quite a nice run, and took me about two hours. I had lunch at the hostel with another driver, took the people to the boat, loaded up the car with tins of oil, and toddled back here. I then discovered I wasn't wanted till 5, so I went up to the Australian Hut and had tea. At 5 I went to a big camp about six miles away, where V. S—— is, to bring back some relatives. When I got back a fearful thunderstorm came on. The lightning was awful, and I got soaked to the skin. At 7 there were more relatives to take from the hospitals to the hostels, and we got in about 10.

We have our breakfast here at the villa always, unless we are given an early run. Lunch we get where we happen to be, likewise tea. By that I don't mean we don't get a proper lunch. We always do, only we never know where we shall have it. Sometimes at a hut or a hostel or a hotel. We very seldom go without a sit-down lunch, and then I take something in the car with me. I have an awful appetite and eat pounds. Supper we have here at home whenever we get in, sometimes 8, sometimes 11. We bring a car back last thing at night. It is generally mine, and I collect the others at headquarters.

I do wish I could write and tell you everything, but I can't, and even if I was allowed to, I should never be able to describe it all. I do wish you could see it all. My diary is very spasmodic, as my only time is at night, and I'm too tired. I am as fit as it is possible to be in every way, but I am tired; I always sleep like a log, though. It is being out in the open air all day, and the excitement all the time which is tiring, but I do simply love the work. I was out the other night up in one of the camps, and I could see the flashes of the guns the whole time, and hear them too. It was thrilling. It is 11 o'clock, and I've just had supper, and must go to bed. Goodnight, darling.

Betty, x x

T. L. I. W. Y.

---

1. Boulogne.

Diary

Wednesday, May 1917.

It is simply freezing this morning and I'm wearing all the clothes I can lay hands on.

We had the most awful business starting up the car. Joyce and I took it in turns, and cronked and cronked till we were nearly blue in the face. We got so tired, that in the end we gave it up, and I said I would go along to the end of the road and try and get hold of a soldier to come along and help. So I went along to the main road and waited. Presently I saw two dispatch riders coming along. I felt I simply couldn't stop a dispatch rider, but when they got closer I saw that one of them was a particular friend of mine. Some time ago I nearly ran over him at Camiers, and we have been firm friends ever since. Accordingly I gave him a smile and a wave as he passed at about sixty miles an hour. However, he pulled up suddenly just beyond me and looked at his engine, so I tore after him and told him that we had been winding away at the Ford for hours, and that we were simply worn out and, would he mind awfully coming to help. He is very good-looking, with a very brown rather thin face, and light curly hair, a lovely smile and two rows of very white teeth. He smiled and said "Surely," which reminded me of Geoffrey, and turned round his machine.

The other rider turned round when he saw all this excitement and we all came back together. Miss Brodie was looking out of the window wondering whatever I was doing, so I told her, and we then trooped into the garage. I sat in the car and "worked the effect" while they ground her. It took some time, but in the end they did it, and then with many smiles and thanks and jokes they went off. Of course we arrived late at headquarters, but luckily I wasn't put down for a 9.30 run. At 10 I took the husband of the old lady I took yesterday, to join his wife. They couldn't get their permits together, as there was some muddle or other, and she came on alone. Their boy is in the Baltic Hospital in Paris-Plage.

He is an amusing old boy. He's in a shipbuilder's yard, I think. He was very surprised when I told him where I came from. "Well," he said, "I thought yer moost 'ave coom from the south, yer don't talk broad at all."

On the road to Ignotus we passed thousands of New Zealanders resting by the roadside. He was very interested, and wanted to know all about them. They all cheered as we passed and they did look so hot and tired, poor dears. The men were wearing their tin helmets, and the officers the nice big cowboy hats with the red and khaki band round. When we got to Ignotus, he said he wanted my name and address, so I gave it him and he said I should hear later. I do hope he's not going to tip me! He's only a workman, but after all I'm only a chauffeur. I am longing to know what's going to happen.

Then I went to the corner shop and bought some chocolate. It is forbidden to sell chocolate on Tuesdays and Wednesdays, but the girl in the shop is rather a friend of mine, and always lets me have what I want, which is, as Jars would say, "s'nice but s'naughty." Then I went into the General Post Office and talked to them there. Mr Home was sitting at his desk censoring all our letters, and he beckoned me and said he'd got my part for me and he handed me the book. The play is called *A Case for Eviction*. It is for three people, and I am to be a saucy charming parlour-maid. (Loud cheers!) Then Lady Cooper arrived, and I took her and the two Miss G.s to the Walton.

My special M.P. was this side of the tunnel, and he saluted and grinned and I did the same. Lady Cooper was very much amused, and said he seemed a great friend of mine, so I said he was. I stopped my engine once at a cross-roads where he was guarding, and he assisted me, so we are sworn friends and salute each other in the most military fashion. Whenever he sees me now he makes all the other traffic stop and waves me past. It's screamingly funny. The other day he made two Rolls-Royce cars full of staff officers pull up, while I sailed past in my broken-down old Ford. One car full of staff officers looked furiously angry, and the other car load roared with laughter—so did I.

When I got back from the Walton I discovered there were no more runs written down for me, so I came along to my old room where I am writing all this.

CHAPTER 12

Mumps, and Stories of the Day's Work

Saturday, 26th May 1917.
My Darling Mother,—Isn't it rotten luck? But I'm not really ill, and am feeling better today. On Wednesday I felt so bad that I reported at headquarters, and I was told to go and report myself to Colonel Raw at one of the hospitals; he couldn't tell me then if it was mumps or not, but he said he would come round next day, and so I finished my day's work feeling an absolute wreck, and then went straight home to bed.

There is a parrot outside my window which shrieks out long French phrases all day long. The only words I can hear with any clearness at all are "*Cochon bon jour p'tite cocotte.*"

I blush as I write, but of course it is all much appreciated by Madame & Co. Anyhow it keeps me interested for the greater part of the day. *Madame* comes in to talk a lot. Her gossips and scandals are too thrilling for words.

You will notice the style of this letter; that is because the Y.M.C.A. are not censoring it.

I must describe my effects. On the mantelpiece is a large vase of lilac and a large *ditto* of cornflowers. On the washstand a large vase of lilies, on the table by my bed twelve oranges, a pink box of chocolate creams, a big bag of enormous chocolates, eight books, two French magazines, some letters and one *billet doooooo*. On the bed more letters and a box of cherries. On the item of furniture at the other side of my bed a bottle of *Eau de Cologne*, and a wooden box of apricots, also some cigarettes, all of which, dear mama, have been presented to your little cheeild.

I'm too hot to write any more.—Your loving, though swollen,
                                                    Bunçie.

A hug to the Dumpos.
A. W. T. S.

                                                  May 1917.

My Own Wuglet,—I am feeling a bit better today, so *voici une lettre*. The last three days I have been feeling an awful bit of chewed string. My neck and face still feel as though they might burst at any minute, but the dreadful aches have gone. The doctor hasn't missed a single day. He's given me a bottle of filthy medicine and taps my manly chest, and then he sits on the foot of my bed and cheers me up. Yesterday at 7 p.m. I'd given him up and at 7.30 I was waked up by a voice saying "Well, Betty, here I am at last." I was feeling beastly, so just groused at him. I'd got a temperature. . . . He didn't stay long, as a big convoy of wounded had just come in, and he only had time just to fly down and see me. He'd been doing operations all day, and he was worn out.

—— has sent me in a lovely lot of lilac, red and white peonies and snowballs. My room looks lovely. Everyone is awfully good to me. I think I may get some sick leave after this, wouldn't it be lovely? The weather is simply freezing again, and I've gone back to pyjamas, a hot-water bottle, and two rugs. I've never known such changeable weather. Before I took ill, I used to have to do things that would have given me a bad chill at once at home, but which had no effect on me here. It shows how healthy I was. For instance, I have had to drive in the rain in a linen coat and get soaked to the skin, and stay soaked, and I haven't had the slightest cold. If I did it in Harrogate I should probably be in bed for a week.

I had a smash before I got mumps, but it wasn't serious. I was going round a corner, and a general's car came flying past. There was just enough room, really, but the driver lost his head and put on his brake suddenly, and the car skidded, and smashed poor little me flat against the wall. My wheel and mud guard were bent, and all his glass smashed. He was very apologetic, and so was I, and I managed to stagger back to the garage and in four hours was on the road again.

I had a most amusing time the other day. I was taking a lecturer and three other youths out to a camp about five miles away. I was going gaily along the road quite near to the camp, when suddenly the car began to jib and splutter, and finally stopped dead. I hopped out and began to crawl about inside her and started winding her, but awful explosions took place, and then I began to swear. I tipped my car load out and made them work, but still nothing happened. Then out of nowhere appeared five young officers and offered to help, so we began again. By this time it was getting late, so the lecturer thought he would walk on. So off they all started lugging the magic lantern with them.

Then I and the five lads set to work. They laid their sticks and caps and gloves on the bank, and we wound that beastly Ford till we were blue. Then a Y.M.C.A. car passed, and the driver said she would stop at our garage and send out a mechanic. However, in about another ten minutes we got the thing started. We all lay on the bank from exhaustion and then I dressed myself again, and then amid cheers and wavings of sticks I honked off down the road. I picked up the disconsolate party of Y.M.C.A.S and tootled them to their camp, and managed to get back to the scene of the accident in time for the mechanic. Joyce had run him out in her car.

I am in a house where the New Zealand girls are, and they are dears. They aren't New Zealanders, but they work in the New Zealand Hut. There are four of them.

There are heaps of German prisoners here and they work on the line and on the road. The other day a gang of them were working under the windows of one of our messes, and a Y.M.C.A. flew up to the sitting-room and began playing the "Watch on the Rhine," and other ditties. The Germans got awfully excited, and in the end they all stopped working, and listened with sheepish smiles on their faces. Some of them are fine-looking specimens. They wear blue linen trousers, and white linen very loose jumpers, with P.G. and a number below. It ought to be P.I.G. I think. They wear such silly little caps perched on the top of their heads. I hope the Censor won't scrabble all this out. I don't see why he should.

I have been sent *Mr Britling*, but the doctor says I'm not to read it till I'm well, and it's too serious. The soldiers must love him.

SOMEWHERE IN FRANCE
BETTY AND 'ARCHIE'

He's a person you could trust to the last gasp.
It's quite time I got a letter from you. Do write.
I will try and give you an average day's programme, though of course I can't mention names. (I mean a work prog.)

7.30.—Marie brings hot water, and tries to wake us. 8.30.—Wake up. Discover the time and fly out of bed. We are supposed to be at headquarters at 9.30.

9.0.—Powder our noses frantically and collect our belongings for the whole day. Books, money, nose bags, safety pins, combs, etc. The big pockets of the overcoats are very useful.

9.-9.15.—Persuade the car to start. I always bring mine back at night, and bring Joyce with me.

9.30.—Arrive at headquarters. Fill up with petrol, and then go in and look at the motor programme which is chitted up in the hall.

9.30-10.—Take a relative from headquarters to a hospital in P.-P. Nine miles altogether. Take some canteen workers to a hut up in the camp. 10.30.—Quarter of an hour free. Look at the car, oil and grease. Fly to the corner shop for a pennorth (chocolate).

10.45.—Drive Lady Cooper, Lady Superintendent, to another hut.

11.15.—If there don't happen to be any more relatives, I report to Stores. Take up stores of all sorts to the various huts in the camps here and also a good way away, nine or ten miles. This is rather nice work. I get fed at all the huts, and am bribed for particular stores in the most shamefaced way. One day my total haul was:—

1 bag large sweets.
I tin peaches with tin opener.
1 box dates.
6 cakes.
1 khaki handkerchief.
1 pocket comb.
1 pocket glass.
3 packets biscuits.
Numerous invitations to tea!!

2.0.—Got back rather late and found an important run to

M—— waiting for me. No time for lunch, so on the way to M—— I stopped my car and ate the things that had been given me in the morning. I ate the peaches with my brooch, and wiped up the mess with the khaki hanky, and then powdered my neb with the aid of my pocket glass. I had a puncture on the way and had to change the wheel. In the middle of it I heard shooting just behind me. I fell over backwards and discovered a Lewis gun class going on behind some bushes—machine gun *ditto* on the other side—and bombing in the middle. I nearly died of fright. I wish I could tell you the name and all about the place I went to. You are not allowed inside. Everyone stared at me because they never see a girl driving. I bagged some food from the Y.M.C.A. Hut, and ate it in the car coming back.

5.30.—Back at headquarters. Drive a concert party out to St Omer. Wait during concert and drive them on to N——. This is rather fun. I eat heartily in the hut leader's room—and then get the benefit of the concert. There are no women in these huts. They are nine or ten miles from here. After the concert at St Omer I drove them on to N—— for another concert.

8.30.—Drive them back to Paris-Plage, where they are staying.

9.0.—Take some relatives from the various hospitals back to the hostels.

9.45.—Pick up Joyce at headquarters and drive home. Feed—bed—sleep. All my days are different, and I simply love it. I love the uncertainty. Last Sunday I did this.

9.15.—Arrive at headquarters. Nothing doing, and the prospect of a day off

10-11.—Service.

11.15.— Going to P.-P. with a Y.M.C.A. youth and Joyce for lunch and tea, and have a well-earned holiday. My boss was out, so I waited to report and see if all was correct.

11.25.—Enter boss in a great hurry and says there is an important run for Boulogne, and will I make preparations for a long run. I was awfully annoyed but rather excited. I filled up with oil and petrol—got some spare wheels and started off. I picked up two relatives at the Rest Hut and took them along to Boulogne. I got there about 1.30 and found the hostel after a good deal of bother and deposited the relatives. The boat didn't go till 2.30, so I went into the mess room where I found two Y.M.C.A. men and had lunch with them. Then I went round to the garage and filled up the back of my car with tins of oil, and then I took the two relatives down to the boat. It was awfully interesting; all sorts of people going on leave and all in such spirits. I waited a little and then I came back here.

3.45.—Back at headquarters—free till 5.30 to walk up to the Australian Hut and have tea there.

5.30.—Off to Camiers (where Violet is) to bring back some relatives and take them to P. -P. where there is a hostel.

8.0.—Relatives from a hospital to headquarters.

8.30.—Fetch a woman from a hospital whose husband had just died. This driving of relatives is awfully sad. She was an officer's relative. I arrived at the hospital and went in and found that she was with the *padre*. I simply couldn't say I was in a hurry, so I told the nice sister I would wait. I sat in the car till 9. In fact I went to sleep for a few minutes, and she came at 9 and I drove her away.

When I say "hospital" I expect you imagine a big building, but they are only huge tents, sometimes a wooden hut. They are just planted along the roadside, like a huge town of tents and huts, each side of the road, and at the back is the railway and the ambulance sidings. The name of the hospital is painted on a white board outside each set of marquees and huts. During the day the men all lie out on the roadside outside their tents, with Japanese umbrellas. There is the tent, and then a strip of grass or garden roped in, and then the road. They always wave their hands when I go past.

I must stop now. It's now 2 o'clock and I've been writing since 10.30 and am worn out.—Your loving

Bunçie.

T.L.I.W.Y.

Sunday.

Darling,—I've just got your letter about D——, and feel so miserable about it, I don't know what to do. I do hope he's all right. How awful his people must feel about it. I'm glad Fred is all right.

The nice colonel can't come today as he is going to another

place. He's such a darling, and comes in every evening and sits with me and cheers me up. Yesterday I upset a jug of milk, and he hopped round and spooned it up. He's a Liverpool man and ever so clever. He saved a Y.M.C.A. girl's life last year who'd got spotted fever; he sat up three nights with her. He'd just been doing a big operation on a boy who'd got shrapnel in his lungs and liver, before he came to me yesterday, and he said it was a nice change to come and scoop up milk.

The heat's fearful again today and I don't feel very grand. My neck's very sore, but by the time you get this I shall probably be all right. I shall be up in about a week, then three weeks' quarantine. I may get some leave, but am not sure. Wouldn't it be lovely?

I can't write any more. I do feel bad about D——. Love.

Bunçie.

A.W.T.S.

CHAPTER 13

More Reminiscences from Maison Mumps

3rd June 1917.

My Own Darling Mammy,—I've just got your letter, I was so glad of it. I am so sorry to hear about Alec M——. There'll be nobody left soon. I can't get the thought of D—— out of my mind. Thank the little Dump Wid ever so for his letter, and I'll write to him next.

E. C. G. really is "it," isn't he? I can't think how he does it. There's a large picture of him in the 23rd May *Tatler*, do get it, also a lot about him in Eve's letter in the same number. I suppose he'll now appear in the latest naval uniform. He's really rather great, isn't he? . . .

The doctor was very pleased with your letter, and is going to bring it to show me. He comes every other day now but he won't let me get up yet. I've had the disease a fortnight now. I had it three or four days before I reported, really, and I've been in the house about ten days. I'm feeling heaps better to-day, though I'm wobbly on my legs still, and my face isn't quite normal yet; it still has the effect of having slipped somehow in the making—and I don't think it did really, did it?

We had a great excitement here the other day, but I really daren't tell you what it was, because Patrick, the wild Irishman, who takes our letters for us would get into an awful row if my letter was censored. However I hopped out of bed and watched 'em, and they whistled past my window with the noise of a strong gas escape, mingled with a piece of linen being torn. I nearly died of thrills. The pickets were out making everyone go indoors.

I'm rather longing to get back to the villa. The drains in this place make one ill. I must describe our villa. Firstly it is called "*Le Réve d' Antoinette,*" it's on the way to P.-P. A little glade branches off from the road, and two little villas are sitting right at the end of it, right in the woods. The other is called "*La Flore des Bois*" I'm not sure if there's an "e" at the end of Flore or not, but anyhow what does it mean? There is a little white railing round ours and a gate, and a patch of grass, and you go up a little flight of wooden steps at the side to get in. It is just like a Swiss chalet. Inside are just bare boards, beautifully clean. There are two rooms on the ground floor, a dining-room and a sitting-room opening out of it, and a kitchen. Upstairs are three bedrooms, and a bathroom.

Joyce and I share a front room looking right into the woods—not civilised woods, but real wild woody woods with little fluffy green bushes and pine cones, and squirrels and piney smells. It's heavenly, and we spent our first night with our heads out of the window smelling all the nice night smells. We used to share a bed, which was rather awful, as only small single sheets were available. It was only the fact of our being so dog tired at night that enabled us to sleep at all. We never had any clothes on us when we woke up. Now we've got two little single beds, which is tons better, though we only have enormous straw mattresses which prick, and no under-blankets. There is a Belgian refugee called Marie who cooks and cleans for us. She is a dear old thing, though she has lost everything and everyone. She never tells us much. There are two rooms over the garage, and she sleeps in one. The other two people who share the villa are Miss Hall and Miss Brodie.

The other day I was having an afternoon bath when I suddenly heard voices under the window. I was sitting on the edge of the bath and I looked up and saw, as I thought, the whole Y.M.C.A. staff under the window waving their hands to me. I gave a wild whoop and lay down flat on my back on the floor. I collected a few garments round my upper beam end and then knelt on the floor and looked out of the window. There were heaps of them all going for a picnic. I did envy them. They stayed and talked hours and I thought they'd never go, and then one very nice boy asked what on earth I was doing in that weird position. I flourished a loofah at them and said that I was in the middle of a bath and would they please go? And they did with great hilarity and alacrity.

I'm longing to get back to my driving as I do have such an exciting time. In the huts a long way out there are no women workers, sometimes because there's no suitable living place, and sometimes because it's a zone where women aren't allowed. The other day I was driving a lecturer with a lantern and operator to one of these far distance huts, and I had orders to wait the lecture and drive 'em back. I came across a lot of W. Yorks men there.

I had an exciting time driving one concert party about. One night I had to go with my car to fetch them away from a concert they were giving at an officers' hut. It was fairly late, 10.15, and they had been told not to go to the officers' mess, because the drivers weren't to be kept waiting. The drivers have strict injunctions not to go to messes. At 10.45 I began to be rather sick of waiting, so Mr B—— who had come with the second car went off to hurry them up. He was gone ages and I sat shivering on the step of my car. I was furious, but it was rather interesting all the same. It was a pitch dark night and the searchlights were going in the distance and kept on lighting up some soldier or other on sentry go. It was weird and quiet.

The guns booming right away in the distance, a sentry challenging someone, and a sudden burst of applause from the hut on the other side of the camp, and funnily enough a nightingale going strong all the time. This particular place is a certain gun school for officers, and the little camp is dumped down in a sandy, hilly, eerie sort of place. On the ground at my feet was a pile of officers' kit—sacks, helmets, swords and odds and ends. I'd been using a tin helmet as a most convenient footstool. Presently I heard voices and saw two little lights coming towards me, and two orderlies came and collected up the things, and took them away by flashlight. They didn't see me, so I spoke to them before they quite walked over me. I talked to them a little and then they went away. There wasn't anything in it, but I shall never forget it.

I just caught sight of them once when a searchlight caught us, and we all had a good look at each other, and then it was all icy black again. When the searchlight came it lit up the camp and struck a sentry on a little hill on the horizon. The whole thing was like that picture in the tank film of the sentry at dawn. It was wonderful. When the orderlies had gone, two more men passed, and they stopped when they realised I was there, and talked. They were kilties and very nice, but it was only afterwards that it dawned on me that we had been whispering the whole time. One somehow whispered instinctively.

Mr B—— came back with the news that the concert party were in the mess and looked as though they meant to stay there. However in a few minutes we heard footsteps and presently a voice said "Er, where are the, er, drivers of the Y.M.C.A. cars?" So I said in a cold voice, "Well one of them's here and has had enough of it." I then discovered two officers. They came up to my car, in fact they nearly got in, and began cajoling and bribing me to go into the mess. At first I was amused, though quite definite in my refusal. Then I began to get annoyed. They wouldn't go. In the end I was rude and they went. Still the concert party didn't arrive. Presently the two officers came back, one carrying a bottle of liqueur, and the other some dessert plates of chocolates. They begged me to have a liqueur but I wouldn't. In the middle of all this the concert party condescended to appear, and amid their tender farewells I managed to get a move on.

It was now 11.30. I had to take them all the way back to their hotel in P.-P., and then go all the way back to Étaples and report. I left my car in the stores for the night, (this was before we went to the villa), and began to walk round to headquarters to report. On the steps of the mess, however (our mess), I saw two men. They came towards me, and at first I thought they were drunk *poilus*. However they turned out to be two nice English officers. They asked me if it would be possible for them to get beds at our mess. They thought it was a *café*. I directed them to an hotel where I thought they'd get beds for the night. It was now midnight. I went into the mess and got some coats I'd left there, and then I walked down to headquarters *via* the *Place*. It was all very quiet and empty and dark, but in the big market square I saw two solitary figures standing, and I was sure it was my two poor officers.

I walked on a bit and tried to make up my mind what to do. In the end I decided to risk it. So I walked back to them and flashed my torch right in their faces, and it was one of them, and a military policeman. They got an awful shock and I apologised and explained that I hadn't been quite sure if it was they or not. They hadn't found the hotel it seemed, and the other officer had gone off to have another hunt. They'd got all their kit slung over their shoulders and they were dead beat, so I said they'd better come along with me to headquarters and see what the Y.M.C.A. could do for them. So off we started. The poor dears had just come back from leave and were on their way up the line. I left them outside the headquarters and went in, and luckily found some men there, who came out and sent them off to an officers' rest hut somewhere, and then they saw me home to my digs at 12.30. Some night!

Will you promise to tell me always when my letters are censored and exactly what part of them was scrabbled out. Don't forget....

I simply can't write any more. I've used up about ten pencils, but there's heaps more to write about. I can't stop.

For continuation of this thrilling serial of such real life interest, see our next....

Maison Mumps,
8.45 pip emma,
7th June 1917.

My Own Littlest Widlet,—I was so glad to get your letter to-day. As you say I think I can't have been getting all yours. I hope you've been getting all mine?

It was so stifling yesterday that I simply didn't know how to exist. I lay on the outside of my bed the whole day and gasped. There was simply no air to breathe. I felt ill with the heat. It ended up with a terrific thunderstorm in the afternoon. I've never seen such rain. It cleared towards evening and the thunder growled away in the distance. It came on again during the night, and I've never seen such a storm in my life. It lasted hours, and the thunder simply crashed over the house. I thought we should all be smashed to bits. I've never imagined such a noise to be possible. It went on till about 1 ak emma. The lightning simply shot round the room. In pre-war days, I am sure, I should have been terrified—it was so stupendous, but last night my one feeling was one of safety—that nothing could drop on my head in the way of bombs or archies.

All day today there has been gun firing—practising I think. It's gone on continuously till my head buzzes. The dear doctor has been in today. He came in dead beat. They've been taking in wounded all day—every bed's full, and he's been doing operations all day—till he says he feels full of ether. He took his coat off and I fed him with chocs. He was absolutely dead beat. They've got some very bad cases in just now. Several officers who have gone mad from shell shock, and from the results of an awful new gas against which gas helmets are no good. Oh! how I loathe the *Kaiser*. I shouldn't think one single man has ever had, or ever will have, so much to account for as the *Kaiser*, when his time comes. The recording angel will have to take it all down in shorthand, and even then the heavenly editor will have his work cut out....

It's 10 pip emma and I'm sleepy. More *anon*.

8th June 1917. 10 ak emma.

Good Morning, Darling.

I hope you've slept well as I have, thank you. Thank heavens it's not going to be so hot today...

9th June.

I don't seem to be getting much forrader with this letter, but now for a final effort. It's boiling hot again and I can hardly exist.... Everyone is so kind to your little Bunçie.

I have been reading *Philip in Particular*, by W. Douglas Newton. It's a little cheap war book, and you must get it to add to our collection. It has made me laugh out loud, and I do love a book like that. You'll see that I have cut out the bathing dress that has struck my fancy. I know all my letters are full of demands, but I hope you still love me in spite of it.

I had a most amusing time the other day before I "took ill." A man asked me to have tea with him in P.-P. one Sunday, so I said I would and bring Joyce with me. We said we'd meet him outside Skindles at 4.30. Joyce and I had a free day for a wonder, so we walked back to the chalet for lunch. We decided to go to P.-P. by tram directly after lunch and have our heads washed and do some shopping before we met him. Accordingly we cleaned ourselves and sallied forth in clean khaki overalls, and our black shiny hats with elastics under our chins, and a stick each, and feeling very smart and tidy. By the time we got to the *arrêt* it was about 3.30, and as there wasn't a tram for hours we decided to walk, and we did, and arrived outside Skindles' tea shop, panting, at 4.45. . . . The trams run every half hour and there is usually one closed truck and two open ones—it's really more like a light railway. There's always such a rush that everyone runs after the tram and gets into it before it stops. It's the only way to get in at all. I am quite expert at it now. Accordingly, coming back, Joyce and I tore along in company with thousands of the B.E.F., jumped on to the footboard and clawed our way along to a seat.

I was rather late, but three officers sat on each other's knees, so I got a square inch on which to sit. Three more tempys sat on the chain across the doorway and several more on the floor, while lots more stood all the way along the foot board. When we had calmed ourselves down a bit, I looked round and took notice generally. I found what most of me was sitting on was not the seat, as I had imagined, but the knee of an officer, the rest of him was hidden by a kilt which belonged to someone else, and a pair of bare knees which I made out belonged to someone else. My feet were resting on the skirt of someone else's tunic, and I was firmly grasping, not my own stick, but a cane—the owner was somewhere under the seat. Joyce was nowhere to be seen, but I presently discovered her at the other end of the truck; I could only see a small portion of her, framed in trench boots and cowboy hat.

We sorted ourselves out a bit and I smiled apologetically at the face I thought belonged to my knee, and it (the face) promptly asked me to tea! In this be-officered town, you've only got to breathe and someone promptly asks you to tea. I said *napoo*, and I was sorry, and that I couldn't, and had had tea, etc., but the face persisted—and so did I. The face felt it couldn't be eloquent enough in such a position, so with a great upheaval the whole of him appeared—like what's his name from the waves—the waves in this case being trousers, and to my surprise I found that the knee I was sitting on still stayed where it was, so the face hadn't belonged to it after all, and my apologetic smile had been bestowed on the wrong face.

Awful consternation on the part of the modest and retiring young girl (me). The face, which had now resolved itself into an Irish tempy of doubtful extraction, continued the argument about the tea, till I got quite fed with him. He said then would I come out with him one day during the week, so I said nope: I was working far too hard during the week to tea out with anyone. When the ticket boy came round there was the most awful upheaval, as everyone was sitting on their own or someone else's pocket. When we were re-sorted, the doubtful one was a little further away, though he still kept it up. The tram passes the end of our glade in the woods, and Joyce and I hopped off and went and lay in a tepid bath all the evening. I've wandered miles from the point, as per; when I began, I meant to tell you something quite different. . . .

To her old governess

8th June 1917.

Darling Woodie,—I was so glad to get your lovely long letter this morning. At present I'm recovering from mumps! I'm having the most frightfully thrilling time here barring mumps—but I'm not driving an ambulance, I'm driving an ordinary Y.M.C.A. car. Taking concert parties about, taking relatives of wounded to the different hospitals—I go into Boulogne and collect them from the boat—taking round stores to all the camps, and in fact driving anything and everything all day and half the night. I pass Roger's hospital a hundred times a day. It looks a ripping place from the outside. It's a big brown wooden place—most stylish—most of the hospitals here are just tents and marquees. I'm hoping to get a bit of leave after this, but I'm not quite sure about it yet. . . .

I used to be billeted in this town in a filthy old house by myself (except for numerous officers), but now four of us live in a little villa in the woods just a little way out, and a woman cooks and does for us. It's simply ripping. I share a room with a very nice girl. We have our breakfast there, and we have to get our other meals when and where we can. It's most exciting. Sometimes I feed in my car, sometimes by the roadside, sometimes at the mess, and generally at the various huts in the camp. We get our supper whenever we get in at night—sometimes 8 p.m., sometimes 12 *ditto*. It's an exciting life, and you do see such thrilling things, which I can't tell you because of the censor, dash him. The other day my lunch consisted of a tin of peaches which had been presented to me at one of the huts. I'd nothing to eat them with, so I had to scoop them out with my brooch and catch them on the point! You hear the guns quite loudly here sometimes, and at nights up in the camps you can see the flashes in the sky. I'm so tired I can't write another *mot*. Goodbye, and thanks ever so much for the letters and photos, and write again soon.—Lots of love and a hug,

Betty G. Stevenson.

Chapter 14

At Work Again

10th July 1917.

My Darling Mother,—I am awfully interested to hear about the house-letting, but I do hope all my wids won't get bombed. If the house is let to Sept. I shall leave here on the 1st, all being well. I do hope that can be arranged because I do want awfully to be home for my (21st) birthday,[1] and if I leave here on the 2nd it's running it rather fine....

I have decided to come back here after my leave. I do hope this meets with your approval, if it doesn't of course I won't. I don't know that I really *want* to come back, but I shall all the same. The work is so full of interest and thrill that I don't feel I could bear to leave it for good. I am going to squeeze as big a leave out of them as I can. I am getting up at 5 a.m. these days.... I have an egg and a cup of coffee before I start, and then I generally come back for another breakfast at the villa or have one in Étaples. I wish you could see your lazy Bunçie getting up at 5 and going to bed at 10. I shall spend all my leave sleeping!

I happened to be at C—— the other day so I looked up Violet Solly; she was on night duty, and was sleeping, so a nurse took me along to her hut, and I sat on her bed and ate biscuits. She lives in a little hut like a hen house, with another girl. There are no windows, but the sides hinge up like nesting-boxes, and her bed is just beside this hinge at grass-top level from the ground. They are funny little things.... I went with Miss Brodie, by special invitation of the colonel, to a dance. He is an old dear. We danced in a ripping recreation room to a divine band, and then we all sat out in a piece of garden with the entire C.I.B.D.

1. September 3rd.

looking on. We all had our uniforms on, and the canteen nurses looked too lovely for words in that delicious blue uniform and brass buttons. We had a fine supper, but I couldn't stay very late because of my early morning start. I am going to some sports at the C.I.B.D. on Saturday, and, tell it not in Gath, I believe we're going to dance afterwards; won't it be divine?

I had the most agonising time the night before last. I was miles away in the car with Mr Smith, our business manager, when I got a puncture. To my horror, my spare wheel didn't fit, and I had no tyre-repairing outfit. I decided to run on the rim to one of our huts in a camp quite near. We arrived there at 9, and Mr Smith went off to the mess to telephone to C—— to tell them to stop the next Y.M.C.A. car there, and we would walk out to it. While he was doing this I went into the Orderly Room and played dominoes with the orderlies! Then at 9.30 we raked up a dinner of tea, bad meat-paste and bread, and then the hut leader came . . . and we all set off in the dark to walk to C——. We arrived there about 11 p.m. and to our joy discovered the lorry waiting for a concert party. We had to drop them at their various messes, and I didn't get in till 1. I left next morning at 5 a.m. with another tyre, mended it and came back to breakfast. I was tired. I'm just going out. Goodbye, my own wuggy,—Your

Bunçie.

T. L. I. W. Y.

P.S.—Mr Yapp has been here. When he discovered you were my mother, he said what a success the Buxton campaign had been, and that the Derby people were splendid fellows, and he wished you all success, and asked to be remembered to you when I wrote.

26th July 1917.

My Own Darling Dumpos,—The time here goes so quickly that I really can't keep pace with it. I do love being here. At the time of writing I am in a very jubilant frame of mind. I have just been on a long run to Abbeville where Uncle Lionel was. Started at 1.30 and got back at 6.30. Hard driving all the time. It was thrilling. I am driving a lovely Ford now, with a new electric lighting set on it, and I feel no end of a swank. We are having most fearful rain and thunderstorms just now. I've never seen such rain. It comes down in bucketfuls. My mackintosh lets the water in. Yesterday I was soaked to the skin before I'd done any runs, just with getting the car started up. I was literally soaked to the skin, and it's not good enough spending the day in sopping clothes. Could you ask mother to get me a macky? I want her to get me one called the Quorn, and I am trying to get hold of a picture of it for her. The rain here is extraordinary. In an hour the roads are nearly a foot deep in water and mud. There is a lot of sand in the camps, so you can imagine the state of things. We all wear gum boots, of course. We have now got two very nice girls living with us, called Miss Marriot and Miss Gray. They are such dears. I can't think why everyone is so nice. The whole base tries to look after us. You see we are the babies of the base, and they have told us that they are proud of us....

... I have been getting up at 5 a.m. and going out to the sidings, and selling things to the men going up the line. Train after train of them. It's the most interesting work I have ever done, but most horribly sad. I want to weep most of the time, but find myself making jokes and laughing with the men when I feel most dismal. I'm sure we cheer them up. I can't sell quickly enough. I get on the footboard of the train and they all fight for things. What with English, French, and Belgian money, it's most awfully difficult to keep one's head and remember the rate of money exchange. Last time I clung to the train till it was moving horribly quickly, and I flung myself off into the arms of an officer who was standing on the ground. There is a little shanty at the sidings which is open all night till 9 ak emma and the drinks are given free, and we sell the stuff in trays along the train. Magazines and papers are given free too. It gives you a rampant appetite for breakfast, I can tell you. The guns are going hard all the time now. There must be a big strafe going on. At night from the camp you can see the flashes of the guns.

There are some big Étaples Administrative District sports on next Sunday at the polo ground, which is near our villa, and Joyce and I have been asked to sell in the Y.M.C.A. Officers' and Sisters' tent, which will be rather fun. I sold flags at some Canadian sports the other day, and had a fine time. We had tea in the Canadian mess afterwards and enjoyed ourselves hugely. I've heaps more to tell you but I must get this off.

Au revoir à Sept. 1st and thank you awfy for the *cinque.*, darling. T.L.I.W.Y.   *Ta Bunçie.*

5th August 1917.

My Own Darling Mother,—Do write and tell me everything that's happening. I hope awfully to be able to get home on leave on Sept. 1st, but it's quite possible I shan't be able to. There is a fearful amount of work just now, and we are driving all day and all night, and I've been having a very strenuous and exciting time. We meet the boat in Boulogne every day. Lately the boats have been getting in about 8 or 9 pip emma. We park our cars with all the military cars, and then go to the quay and pick up all the relatives who happen to be on that boat, and drive them along the quay to the Y.M.C.A. hostel. There they are fed and sorted out. Some stay in Boulogne, others go to Étaples, others to Camiers, and others to Le Tréport—sixty miles away.

Three of our cars generally meet the boat, and, needless to say, Joyce and I go as often as we can. It's a twenty mile run and very interesting. We arrived at Étaples the night before last, each with our respective loads, which contained twelve for Le Tréport. Of course they are taken straight through. No time is lost. Joyce and I and Mr M——, such a nice boy, were told off to do the run. We three tore round to the mess and grabbed some food and then tore round again and fitted up our cars for an all-night run. We all borrowed coats and rugs and then we got our relatives in, and at 10.15, with the whole base cheering, we set off in a convoy.

As there were so many, a fourth car-load, driven by Miss Gray, who lives with us, was sent on before us. M—— led the way, then me, then Joyce. M—— is a brick. He had a commission and was badly wounded and got shell shock, and he has the most dreadful stammer and can hardly speak at all, though he sings beautifully. He is so brave and cheerful about it, that I have got not to notice it at all. When he gets absolutely stuck, he has to write what he wants. It's so pathetic. . . .

We had two breakdowns on the way, but we repaired them all right; then M—— got in the ditch, and we had to push him out. Then my light collapsed. It was awful. It was pitch, and I couldn't see a thing in front of me. Accordingly, once I took the wrong turning: I heard a frantic tooting behind me, realised my mistake, and turned round and charged up the right road by the cathedral at R. . . . Two inches in front of me I suddenly saw M—— swerving over a high kerbstone, in his frantic efforts to turn round, as he had discovered we weren't behind him. We settled ourselves eventually, and then his lights went wrong, and we only had Joyce's, which luckily were strong acetylene, to guide us. It really was the most appalling run I've ever had. My eyes were simply starting out of my head, and when we arrived at the hospitals at 3.30 a.m. my nerves were really on end. We left the relatives there, and then drove down to the hostel, which is a lovely house in a divine garden. We had some bread and cheese, and then Joyce and I tumbled into one spare bed, and Miss Gray slept on chairs, and poor M—— had to go all the way back to the hospitals' hostel and sleep on a form. When the relatives came back they slept in our cars. There wasn't room for them anywhere else.

Next morning it poured for an hour before breakfast. We drove relatives from the hostel to the hospitals, without stopping. We then had breakfast, and we were literally soaked to the skin. The water squelched out of our clo'. Miss Gray had to go back *via* Abbeville, so she started about 9.30. We three filled up with homeward bound relatives, and left at 10 a.m. We arrived at Étaples at 2, had lunch, and dashed them on to Boulogne, the boat leaving at 4. Met the boat from Blighty arriving 7.30. Back at Étaples at 9, and bed at 10.30. Worn out. We had a bit of rest the next day. I went to Le Tréport again the night before last. Left Étaples at 11 p.m. and arrived at Le Tréport at 4 a.m. Hard driving the whole time, in pouring rain, wind and mist. Three hours back to Étaples at 10, arriving 1.30, lunch, leave for Boulogne at 2. Missed the boat, so relatives had to stop night at Boulogne. Bed 11.30. Today I've been given a whole day off. I'm half asleep. They are all dears, though. Joyce and I are getting swollen heads. We are far more popular than is good for us. . . .

The weather is dreadful; deluging rain, and one day hot and the next frost. I'm having to get no end of things, and knapsacks and washing things, and spare things for these night runs. We have to be always prepared. We never have time to come back here to get our things.

I have just washed my hair, and am having such a lovely lazy time.—Goodbye, my own darling.   Bunçie.
T.L.LW.Y.

19th August 1917.

My Own Precious Lamb,—What a lovely long letter. I hug you for it. I'm nearly bursting at the thought of Sept. 3rd. I am arranging so that I shall be back for it and I think things will be all right. However, we are very short of drivers. One has gone on leave, and Mr M—— has had to go back because his father has just died. Now Joyce's father is ill and may have to have an operation, so of course she wants to go home. We are going to see if she can go off on Thursday, and then I can come on Sept. 1st when one of the other drivers will be back. Mr Scott is being a brick about it, and is going to do his best, and I am all hopeful. I couldn't bear to have my 21st birthday anywhere but at home, especially when you've asked such a houseful of wuggies to be there. . . .

Uncle Lionel is a perfect darling. He came to see me last Wednesday. He told me he would come if it was fine, so as it was pouring rain I didn't expect him. When I happened to go round to the garage during the morning and saw a gorgeous car draw up, and Uncle Lionel step out, I nearly died of joy. He was a gorgeous vision in khaki and red tabs and gold lace and ribbons. He was a thorough wug. He had come down from the line early that morning, had breakfasted at G.H.Q. (where R. L. W. is). Mr Scott was a brick and gave me the morning and afternoon off, till 6 o'clock. I then introduced them to Joyce, and we all got into their car, and I drove them out to their villa. I was stopped by the sentries, and they got very hectic, but in the end let us pass.

At the villa Uncle Lionel and I and "Light Railways" stopped, and Joyce drove the car back to H.Q. with the chauffeur, as she had a run. She got into hot water with the picket, who took her name and made all sorts of fuss, not being worried by the presence of the general. By this time it was pouring cats and dogs, but, nothing daunted, we three took the car and went to P.-P. We then took the car and went to the St John's Hospital in Étaples. We had a sort of inspection, and Uncle Lionel and the C.O. walked in front, and "Light Railways" and I formed a sort of rearguard behind. Then it was time for them to go. At H.Q. we met Joyce, so we all got into the car and went along the road a little way with them, and then we got out and walked back. It was a ripping day. We went straight away and told Mr Scott all about the trouble with the sentries, and he said he would protect us, and that it was all right....

Yesterday morning I got up at 5 and went and helped at the sidings again from 6-10 minus breakfast. In the evening right out in the forest near B—— I had engine and lighting trouble, and had to come back at 10 pip emma with the car load of a cinema and two boys, one of them standing on the bonnet and holding up a little lamp. My oil all leaked out and I had to fill up with revolver oil from one of the camps. I arrived at 11.30 and as a result I've got a day off today....

I am sorry to hear about A—— S——, I don't feel there will be anyone left soon. I've made such a lot of friends out here, but I'm almost afraid to, it's so awful when they have to go....

Bunçie.

T. L. I. W. Y.

From Brigadier-General East

19th August 1917.

... Here I am writing in Betty's sitting room. I came to this part of the world about some business, and have come on here.

I met her at the garage to which she drove her Ford, and she then insisted on driving my car, a Sunbeam, and stopped the engine five times before starting, and then stopped dead in front of a picket, and I expect I shall be court-martialled, but of course it would be worth it.

I am writing at her writing-desk: it is about 2 feet by if feet. At the right-hand top corner are two books, and envelopes, in the middle top a basket crammed with all sorts of things, soap, paper, string, etc....

Betty returned at that moment, so of course I had to stop. She wants mosquito nets badly. I do not know if I can get any near here, but they are frightfully worried at night, as their house is in a wood....

CHAPTER 15

Coming-of-Age Leave

Betty's twenty-first birthday was spent in Boulogne after all. She could not cross on Monday, 3rd Sept., the boat was crammed. Some of her kind friends tried to console her for her disappointment by giving her a birthday dinner in Boulogne.

General East wrote:—

4th Sept. 1917.

I do hope that your poor Betty is getting over today all right. She will have told you about her birthday before you get this, I tried to make up to Betty for her disappointment. She was very plucky about it.

On Tuesday the 4th she and her escort crossed, and arrived in London to find an air raid beginning, through which they had to walk from Victoria to Morley's Hotel, and there was not much sleep for Betty that night until the "All Clear" was sounded. Wednesday the 5th she arrived, along with the first batch of visitors for the twenty-first birthday party. She had slept in the train, but I don't think any of us in the least realised how very tired she was. She blew in at the door looking simply radiant, flung down her khaki bag, which had "Stevenson & Scott, Y.M.C.A. Étaples" painted on it, and which promptly burst open and disclosed every kind of contents, including paper money, and all she had had to "live in" for four days, and we all felt so happy to have her back, we could hardly bear it!

The birthday party lasted for three days, and was called "The Great Push" by one wag who helped at it. On Wednesday, twenty-four of us sat down to a festive dinner. Birthday speeches were made, and I do not think anyone present will forget Betty's happy smiling face, as she sat at the end of the long table, beside her father. Nor will some of us ever forget how she had to come down to her party, wearing what was *not* the *dernier cri*: the pretty frock which was a birthday present, and was laid out ready for her in her room, did not quite 'fit' alas! So she had to appear in an old skirt, and a blouse she had made herself in 1916, and which was, as she said, a trifle *passée*. But it never spoiled her evening, though she simply loved pretty frocks, and there were so many there that night.

On Thursday the 6th, a big party went to the swimming baths, which we took for our own party. In the afternoon there was tennis, and in the evening we went to the theatre.

After the three days, the party broke up, and Betty settled down to make the most of her leave, and to rest. How she slept! But I don't think we ever realised how hard she had been working, and how disturbed her nights had been. Her leave simply *flew*, and she crossed back to France on Saturday, October 6th.

CHAPTER 16

Winter, 1917

Étaples, Oct. 1917.
We have a fire in the evening of fir-cones and wood, and we all sit and toast our toes and are very pleased with ourselves. We are all very busy and most of us are driving several cars. I'm driving two. The cold is awful already, with the most beastly soaking rain. It's lovely if you're only walking. I find it very hard to keep warm, even with all the warm clothes I've got. Drenching, pouring hail, and rain which soaks through everything till you haven't a dry rag. The other night coming from Le Tréport at about 3 a.m. before dawn I nearly cried with cold. I felt as tho' I had nothing on at all, and yet this is what I had on:

Leather coat.
British Warm.
Mackintosh.
2 Scarves.

I've always heard it's fearfully cold just before dawn. It was a wonderful drive. I got off from here at about 10 pip emma and arrived back here at 6 ak emma, 120 miles.

The two following letters are inserted here because they refer to one of these memorable drives:—

Y.M.C.A.,
A.P.O., S. 11., B.E.F,
13th June 1918.

Dear Mrs Stevenson,—I don't know if you can bear to have letters from people who loved Betty, but I feel I must write one word. She just came right into my heart and stayed there and kept it warm through weeks and weeks of last winter when life seemed very black.

I don't think I've ever known anything to equal Betty's radiance and her delicious naughtiness.

All the time she drove she was a delight; turned up smiling for every run, and her way with the relatives was just a joy. One most memorable run I had with her when I was allowed to "*chaperon*" her to Tréport, and we came back without lights the same night. Her driving and her spirit were amazing, and I sang folk songs to keep us awake. "No one could sleep with that row going on," as Betty said, and then at 3 a.m. we tumbled into bed at the villa.

We shared the big room at the Dacquet for a month before she went on leave, and she was the sweetest companion. There are lovely pictures of her in my memory . . . and then lots of times when she got suddenly serious, and one felt "Tread softly, because you tread on my dreams."

It would be an absurdity to try and tell you what an emptiness there is there. Our hearts ache for you.

Please forgive me for writing such an inadequate letter. I did love her so.—Yours very sincerely, Lois Vidal.

On Active Service

B.E.F.,
A.P.O., S. 11, Saturday.

My Dear Mr Stevenson,—We are very fed up here at present with rather a lot of night runs, and always to the same place . . . which I'm sure you have heard Bet mention. How we used to love going there at first; we thought it so fine to be allowed to go for a really long run, often at night, too, and Bet was such a ripping person to go with, so cheery, even though we did squabble violently at times as to which was the right way! I remember once we came to some forked roads; I swore we ought to take the right-hand one, Betty said it was the left-hand one. We ended in each going our own way, but as it happened the two roads joined together again a little further on, and we only just missed rushing into each other as we came down our different roads. . . .

Goodbye.—Yours very sincerely,

Joyce S. Scott.

Y.M.C.A.
A.P.O., S. 11, B.E.F.,
France, 22nd Oct. 1917.

Darling Dumpos,—You must all have wondered why on earth I haven't been writing, but we have all been head over ears in work, and I have been to Le Tréport three times this week, which has taken up the whole week. I am writing this at the hostel in Boulogne, where I have just brought in a car-load of relatives, and I have just missed the boat, which is bad luck. The N.Z. girls have taken a studio bungalow just behind us, and we are having a lovely giddy time there in our spare moments. They've got a ripping little garden, and have adorable dances in the studio. Yesterday afternoon we had the gramophone in the garden, and danced there on the grass. A man there danced divinely, although it was rather skiddy work on dampish grass. I was dragged away in the middle to come here. It was quite dark when I arrived, and my lights went wrong, and also my horn broke, and I nearly wept with rage and despair. However, by dint of shoving a hairpin down the jet, I got the lights working, and arrived home at 9.30, after starting at 5.30, and it's only forty miles. . . .

We're having rather a nasty time at night now, with night birds, and in the day time as well, and it's rather nervy work driving about during a strafe or alarm with no lights, and I don't enjoy it. Our villa is quite close to the Anti-Aircraft Camp, and the other night we had an awful time, ——s flying past our windows, and flames, and explosions and goodness knows what. I suppose I shall get used to it. A thousand hugs to everyone.

Bunçie.

T. L. I. W. Y.

From General East

3rd Nov. 1917.

. . . Directly I got in, I started off from Étaples, and saw your Betty. She was looking sweet, in her brown suiting, with the famous boots. In the evening we were dining at P.-P. and she had just said how nice it was to sit down to a good dinner, when a girl came to say Betty had to drive relatives to Tréport, sixty miles away. The girl murmured something about the war, and I heard Bet say: "Hang the war!" but she was too sweet for words, poor child, though she had to go off with her relatives. I had meant to stay with her and Olive till about 2 a.m., but of course I had to clear out early.

60 Castle Street, Liverpool,
15th June 1918.

My Dear Sir,—. . . I happen to be the architect of the Liverpool Hospital at Étaples, and on more than one occasion your daughter gave me a lift into Boulogne. I remember coming back last November and telling my friends how one evening, it was Saturday, 3rd November (I have found it in my diary), your daughter had taken me in, and said she hoped she would have room in the car to take me back if I called at the H.Q., Y.M.C.A. about 7. I *did* call, and saw her, but she told me she was awfully sorry but she had parents to take to Le Tréport. It was an *awful* night, no light anywhere and tremendous rain; however, it never *struck her* that there was the least difficulty. I remember asking her where she was going to sleep—she only smiled and said, "I really don't know, but I will be all right, thank you. . . ."—I am, yours sincerely,

T. E. Eccles.

A.P.O., S. 11,
B.E.F., 9th Nov. 1917.

My Own Darling,—I have got a slight touch of influenza, and am having a few days' rest in bed, and it is gorgeous. I am in Mrs Stewart-Moore's room at one of the messes in Étaples. I've got a fire in my room, flowers on my table, and roast chicken in my inside, and I am thoroughly happy. Col. Raw comes down to see me every day. I think I shall be up on Monday.

Uncle Lionel is coming down today. He goes to Blighty tomorrow, and Chappie is going on leave, so they are going together. Chappie is my name for Mrs S.-M., originating, I believe, from chaperone. He is spending the night here, and was giving us both a spree, but of course I can't go, so he will have to spend half the evening, at least, here in my room. . . .

Chappie and I had a fine time at the villa. Last Sunday we were free all day, and we were mousing about in the kitchen cleaning up at about 3 pip emma, when a motor bicycle appeared, and presently one of Uncle Lionel's sweetest dispatch riders appeared with letters. We brought him in and found he'd eaten nothing since 8 ak.

He's such a nice D.R., and is perfectly at home anywhere. He sat down with his head among the washing, which was slung across the kitchen—the remains of Marie's rule—and tried hard not to notice my wincey knickers which were tickling his nose—while we fussed about getting a meal ready. We slung everything off the kitchen table, which is about an inch square, and produced a clean cloth. He and I ground coffee, and Chappie boiled the water. I ransacked the house and produced butter, bread, Libby's veal mould, cheese, and bully beef, and then with great *éclat* I produced three eggs and scrambled them for him....

Uncle Lionel came down the other day and we had great fun. We had tea at the villa, and he and I sat on the kitchen floor while Chappie made the tea. I had to work after tea, but at 6 I was free, and we three went in Lionel's car to the Continental at P. -P., and had a lush dinner. We'd hardly finished when one of our girls appeared and said I was to go to Le Tréport as soon as poss. I was disappointed, as we were going to amuse ourselves at the villa until the early hours. The girl. Miss Vidal—a perfect dear—and I went back in Uncle Lionel's car—picked up my things for the night, and went on to headquarters, and then I set off with four relatives. I didn't get there till 1 ak. Uncle Lionel has brought us some lovely shells, and a general's crossed swords for a brooch.

Mr Scott and Dr Macaulay, the head of our *padres*, and a great friend of Uncle Willie's, come in and give me "spiritual advice."

I must stop now. A thousand loves.

Bunçie.

P.S.—At a town on the way to Le Tréport about forty miles away, I came across one of our old St Denis[1] men—I can't remember his name. We were so pleased to see each other. He says the old camp is all changed, and hardly any of our boys are there. A good many of them are round here. He told me heaps of news; old Étaples is in Africa, and young Étaples up the line. Lodge is quite close to me. Capt. Grant has gone.... I was so thrilled, of course, I quite forgot to ask after Jim and Carr and Johnson.

---

1. Where Betty and C.G.R.S. worked in 1916.

A.P.O., S. 11,
B.E.F., 11th Nov. 1917.

Darling One,—I am up now, but am not to begin work again till next Saturday at least. Col. Raw said that I had been working too hard, and must go easy for a bit. People are dears, and bring cakes and come and give tea parties for me.

I am very thrilled because we are going to have a fixed half-day off per week. You don't know what a difference this will make. I shall do so much better work if I feel I can look forward to a definite free time. It's wearing to have to snatch minutes here and there. . . .

I've been reading a ripping book—*The Dust of the Road*, by Marjorie Patterson. Col. Raw sent it me. He knows the writer. The book is about acting. Do get it and tell me what you think of it. It's fairly old, 1913, I think. I think it's very clever, but I feel the writer has funked it at the end. One feels it's unsatisfactory somehow. Anyhow get it. I've also been reading *Mr Sheringham and Others*, Mrs A. Sidgwick. Of course it's lovely—short stories. . . .

There is a military policeman here who's such a dear (one among many). I keep in with them all, because it's a sound thing to do. In private life he's a stockbroker. . . . I smuggle him out buns and food, which he eats secretively, when no officers are looking.

You do get some shocks among the men. It's much more classy to be a private now. Take my word for it.

The other day I was out before breakfast to take two relatives to a funeral. Officer's relatives. I've had to take thousands to funerals but I've never felt so miserable as I did at this one. It was a mother and such a pretty daughter. I'd been driving them up to the hospital for quite a long time. They thought the boy was getting better, and then he suddenly died. I could hardly bear that funeral, and how they bore it, I can't imagine. The cemetery is in a big sandy hollow in some pine woods, just off the road, and on the other side is a big hutment consisting of the mausoleum, the *padre's* rooms, and the orderlies' rooms. I sat in the car shivering, on the coldest morning I've ever known, with very few clothes on, as I'd dressed in such a hurry, and watched it.

First came a piper (they always pipe the officers to the cemetery), and you know what a piper makes one feel like. Then two buglers. Then a young *padre* with his white robes all blowing about in the wind, showing trench boots and little glimpses of khaki. Then the coffin covered by a Union Jack on a two-wheeled cart, like a stretcher, with two men in front and behind, wheeling it, and then my two poor relatives and a Y.M.C.A. lady with them. They walk very slowly, and had to walk behind those pipes for at least ten minutes before they reached the grave. I couldn't see any more then. The cemetery is always full of soldiers, and they all stand at attention while the sad little procession passes, and all traffic is stopped until they have passed.

While the service was being read, one of the orderlies came up and spoke to me. He saw how cold and miserable I was, and he deliberately set to work to cheer me up. I love him—such a nice Scotch boy with a burr. The first thing he said was: "The push must go on, you know." I told him how hungry I was (I had no brekker), and we set to work imagining the most wonderful meal, till we began to laugh, and I pointed out that it only made me feel hungrier in the end. He advised me to read something of Keats about fruit and food, I don't know what. Then he began discussing the various *padres* who took the services—how some always hurried and hustled: "no religion about it," and how others made one feel that they meant each particular service that they read, sometimes forty a day. He cheered me up a lot, and then the Last Post went. Everyone stood to attention, the passers-by stopped, and the men who had been lying about jumped up. Then they all came back, and the *padre* bicycled away to breakfast with his robes rolled up under his arm.

I was numb with cold, and I didn't get my brekker till 11 a.m. On the way back we called at the hospital and got the boy's belongings—little notebooks and trumperies—a pathetic little bunch of things, which the mother couldn't hold tight enough. I shall never forget that Scotch boy; he was a true brick.

Bunçie.

T. L. I. W. Y.

Y.M.C.A.,
A.P.O., S. 11, B.E.F.,
France, 19 Nov. 1917.

Dumpos Darling,—I crave to call your attention to the fact that £— is due to me on 24th Nov. as per arrangement of £— per month, I having rejoined my unit on 6th Oct. and the first £— having been paid on 27th Oct. Also I should like to humbly point out to you that £— is due to me on 1st Dec, and will be thankfully received on that date. Having got that off my chest, I will write you a respectable letter.

The top part has rather a Jewy look, I admit.

I am not driving yet, but I hope to begin again soon.

I had such a lovely time yesterday. Uncle Lionel came over from Blighty, and I got a lift to Boulogne in one of our cars, and met him. It was quite dark when the boat got in, and I was so afraid I'd miss him. No lights are allowed on the quay, only a flare, and I conceived the brilliant idea of standing right underneath the flare, and Uncle Lionel saw me before they were even moored. Uncle Lionel was O.C. the boat, and he came off the very first. My foot slipped, and I knocked everyone down, and flung myself down the gangway into his arms. He said it was a very embarrassing exit for the O.C. of the ship. We all got into his car and went to a *café* for tea, and Uncle Lionel bought me some chocs. We did it to waste time while the luggage was being got off. After tea we secured the luggage, and then had a gorgeous drive back here to Étaples.

We went to H.Q. and picked up another girl, a crony of mine, and then we all squeezed into the car—Effie and I, one on each side of Uncle Lionel in the back, and B. in front. We went to a heavenly place called Cigale at P.-P., and had dinner in a private room with a balcony—especially the balcony! There is a new order here that everyone must be out of restaurants at 9 p.m., so unfortunately we had to be hoofed out after the meat. We had *hors d'oeuvres*, soup, fried sole and pheasant, and there we had to stop.... After dinner we got into the car and drove to the other end of P.-P., and there we got out and sent the car back to the Cigale, and said we would walk back there.

It really was most thrilling—pitch dark, with the lighthouse flashing behind us, and a long line of lighted-up little fishing boats right out at sea. We all held hands and stumbled along the dunes to the beach. We kept on falling down. We were walking along quite gaily, when suddenly Effie disappeared with a shriek. We all rushed after her and suddenly felt ourselves sliding down a steep stone slope.

We all arrived at the bottom . . . when suddenly a flashlight appeared above us. We sat up and took notice, and discovered that we had missed the steps down to the beach, and had come down a stone slanting sort of wall. The flashlight moved off after a bit.

What they thought I can't imagine—a general and a staff officer and two Y.M.C.A. workers minus hats lying in a confused muddle at the bottom of a stone shute, howling and sobbing with laughter, and making frantic though feeble efforts to get up. . . . Uncle Lionel rushed about like a two-year-old. He can run most awfully fast. Eventually we discovered ourselves in the sea, so we bore off to our right and made for the Cigale. . . . We seemed to walk for hours, and every now and then we came across great channels of water, and Uncle Lionel carried Effie and me across as though we were babes. After many vicissitudes we arrived at the Cigale, fell into the car, and went back to H.Q. . . .

We were all dropped at our various *maisons*, and this morning are feeling wan and weak, but strange to say are not all down with pneumonia. . . .

Truly there is a war.

23rd Nov. 1917.

I'm going to begin driving again on Monday. I've had a lovely rest.

This afternoon V. and I went into P. -P. and walked about on the beach. I do wish you'd been there. The aeroplanes came and hopped about over our heads, and the pilots waved to us, and we got so thrilled. . . .

My leave comes 6th February. I shall be homesick at Christmas. If you're thinking of sending anything out to a young girl in France, I know one who wants a wee leather valise, really small, like a small *attaché* case, for putting in things I may want for the day, when I'm in my car. A square leather one, like yours, with B. G. S. on the lid—Oh, very nice!

Y.M.C.A.
With the Australian
Imperial Force,
1st December 1917.

Darlings,—Don't you think this paper is rather succulent? I do. I've just realised it's December. How time simply does fly, and I do wish I was going to spend Christmas with my wuggies.

The money arrived safely, *et je vous remercie beaucoup.* I am not sending the khaki cardigan back after all, it's so jolly useful under my coat. . . .

I have moved from the villa, by Col. Raw's orders, and am now ensconced at the big mess in the Maison Dacquet, known as the Daccy. I have got an enormous low-ceilinged room, with a huge bed, two huge cupboards, a huge wash-stand, and a huge mantelpiece. As a result all my photographs and ornaments are on view, and they do look nice. Uncle Lionel has given me a lovely big shell case, and the maids here have polished it till you can see your face in it. It looks fine on my table surrounded by my suede writing-case, my ribbon chocolate box, Jars' photo, my cigarette case, some cartridge souvenirs, and my Y.M.C.A. clock—*très chic.* All my other photographs are draped about the mantelpiece, and as they are never dusted, you can't say it gives anyone any extra trouble. I blow them periodically.

We have at last secured a room at the top of H.Q. for a *chauffeuses'* rest room. It's going to be no end of a boon to us, and has been christened "The Jug and Bottle." One of our men has painted a notice for the door, a large jug and bottle with a chauffeur gazing at it, and a suitable inscription underneath. The walls are biscuit colour, and we've got lovely chintz curtains and cushions, and a divan. The divan is my idea, and I stole a camp bed and a mattress and a cushion from the store room, and it's going to be covered with chintz. We've placed it under a window under a gable in the attic, and we're going to have curtains across. We've got a good stove too. When it's all *fini,* we're going to give a grand tea and house-warming, and invite the whole base. We're going to get a telephone fixed up from there down to the General Office. The only disadvantage is that it is at the top of two long flights of stairs. . . .

3rd Dec.

My car is off the road today, as there is a crack in the back axle.

I've indulged in a pair of *puttees*, and they're jolly nice and warm. There's a hard frost here today. It's frightfully cold, but lovely and sunny.

I think I've told you about Dr Macaulay. He's the director of religious work here, and is a great friend of Uncle Willie's... . While Mr Scott is away Dr Macaulay is taking his place. He is a Doctor of Divinity, and I always call him D.D. I told you about the little binges we have in a private room at the mess every Saturday evening. They are such fun. Last time but one he brought a nice R.T.O. nephew. We all change into nice frocks ... and enjoy ourselves. This time we got very hilarious and cracked nuts in a hideous new way, which the nephew taught us. You put a walnut on the table, keep it in place with the index finger of the left hand, and then smash the whole thing with your right fist. If you have enough courage to really smash, it doesn't hurt, but half measures are agonizing. After dinner we put on gum boots over our silk stockings, and overcoats, and sallied off to H.Q. to hunt for the mail. Our attire caused great excitement, and our coats were rent from us, and our clothes admired. Unfortunately the whole of the following week the D.D. was confined to bed with neuritis...

TO OUR NOBLE GUIDE AND MENTOR,
    DR MACAULAY, D.D.

Oh! Macaulay is a D.D.,
Of credit and renown.
He dwells among the Christians,
In a French and smelly town.

He probes the heart, and moulds the mind.
Of Christians young and old.
And firmly leads the straying soul
Who wanders from the fold.

With piercing look and eagle eye
He watches from his lair.
And petrifies the unemployed
With a cold and glassy stare.

.... I had asked Canon Simpson to come, and forgot to tell him that the day had been changed till the last moment, and then of course he was nowhere to be found. He preaches the most gorgeous sermons—one about being spontaneous. How if you're spontaneous you're all right, even though you do things you shouldn't, sometimes. He said he'd hate to be remembered as Albert the Good! Of course half the base were scandalized, but we loved it, and when anybody wants us to do anything, they ask if we're feeling spontaneous.

Another time he talked about the work, and said it was the Cause for which we were working, and some ideal inside us, that made the work fine. He said without this ideal it wouldn't be very illuminating to sell food behind a counter, or be held up on a wet night with motor trouble. Effie and Joyce fought for a week as to which of them he meant, as they had both been out with him and had had engine trouble, and had been soaked to the skin, and been very peevish, as a matter of fact: not a bit the heroic inner light sort of stunt. He was awfully tickled when I told him.

I really must stop now.—*Mille embraces,*

Ta Bonçe.

... On reading your letter over again, I'm struck with the feeling of what an extra nice "parr" I've got. I feel such a snipe when you're so wuggy about warm clothes, and have spent such a lot on me. I want to come and take your boots off, and pour you out some coffee, and ask for a threepenny bit, and say widdy-widdy, and all sorts of things I can't do. It's very distressing to have to love you from a distance.

CHAPTER 17

Christmas Time

To her old nurse

Y.M.C.A., A.P.O., S. 11,
B.E.F., 16th Dec. 1917.

Darling Nana,—I hope you will like this little present from Father Christmas, and I send you heaps of love and hugs with it. I wish I was going to be home for Christmas to see you all, but it can't be helped; I am a soldier now and can't do just as I like. I am so happy here. The people are all dears and I am afraid I'm being rather spoilt, but I don't think it will do me any harm. I can't remember if you saw me in my uniform, the khaki one. I'm going to have my photograph taken one of these days and I will send you one if they are good. I went to a dance at one of our Canadian huts the other night and it was such fun, it was really given for the W.A.A.C.'s There is a camp of them here and they do office work and cooking and all sorts of things; there are some jolly nice girls among them. Eighty of them had been invited to this dance and I went too. I had a lovely time and did some very stylish dancing with a nice Canadian sergeant. It was so funny to be dancing in a blouse and thick khaki skirt and out-door shoes, but I enjoyed it enormously; I think there is going to be another soon, and I hope I shall be able to go. *Au revoir* now, and hug Kathleen and Winnie for me.—
Your loving   Betty, x x x

7th Dec. 1917.
My Own Darlings,—I've been having flu' again—but I'm so happy—I'm being given a holiday from driving for a month or two, and am going to canteen. I can't thank them all enough

for being such dears. They've re-arranged everything for me, instead of packing me off home as they might have done. I am going to work in Miss B's. hut with the Canadians. I really was worn out with the car, and Col. Raw threatened to send me home. I begin work on Wednesday. I know if I went on driving I should never get really fit again, and my nerves are really on edge with the awful strain—cleaning a car on these cold mornings, and heaps of repairings.

I hope you'll like the little hanks I'm sending you for Xmas. I must fly.

Pounds of love, and I do love you so.

Gordon Hut,
27th Dec. 1917.

My Own Mammy,—I hug you all for the parcel, and the lovely things inside. The case of course is too lovely for words, and is just what I wanted. Please note my new address and act accordin'. Darling, I'm so happy here....

Y.M.C.A., Gordon Hut,
A.P.O., S. 11,
B.E.F., 2nd January 1918.

My Dear Mrs E——,—I was so pleased to get your nice long letter. Thank you so much for it, and for the lovely little cards.

I have been given a different job for a few months as you will see by my change of address. I am now canteening instead of motoring, and I am very glad of the rest and change, as I was really very tired. I am working in a Canadian hut and I am very fond of it—the men are so interesting and nice.

I have been having a few days away from the canteen with a cough and a cold, but am better now. I have such a nice room here—big and low ceilinged, with a big bed and three windows. It is in a house which has been taken over by the Y.M.C.A.—one of many with the usual courtyard and outbuildings. I and two other girls and some servants sleep here, and we have a mess of about fifty. We have built a big hut in the courtyard for our mess. The laundry for the whole base is done in one of the outbuildings. There is a sitting room for the ladies which is also a common room, and a smoke room for the men.

We have great fun here and the people are very jolly. One soon gets used to feeding in a big mess with fifty other people. There are over two hundred of us altogether in this base. We who live here have a private sitting room which is also used by the chauffeurs. It is very useful, as when we come in from driving at odd times, we can always get something to eat. In fact we are very much spoilt I'm afraid!

We had a great time at Christmas here. The two big messes each had their separate dinner—turkey and plum pudding, and then we all joined forces afterwards at a big central club we've got, and had music and dancing. In our hut we all worked for all we were worth. We decorated with holly and mistletoe and evergreens, with big red tissue paper bows and red berries. It did look so jolly. For the evening we had a Christmas tree and Father Christmas. The men love it. The hut was packed and every man got a present from the tree, a bag of sweets or tobacco, and a Christmas card. All the food and drinks were free. Then we had a band and concert and dance for them. Our hut is only one of about thirty, and they all gave some sort of entertainment, and the food was free. We had a great time, though we were all dog tired after it. But it was well worth it.

Thank you again so much for your kind letter and wishes. You say you feel proud to hear from us out here, but we are also proud to hear from those at home. Barring the soldiers, yours is much the harder job, that of "carrying on." We out here have most of the excitement and interest, and I admire the people who stick to their jobs in Blighty immensely. We all feel out here the real people at home are doing better work, very often unnoticed, than a great many people out here in the limelight. I must really stop now as it is nearly dinner time. Please give Grimmy a pat for me next time you see him, and tell him to be a good dog.—Yours very sincerely,   Betty G. Stevenson.

CHAPTER 18

The Bridge

To her father

6th Jan. 1918.

I am going back to my car when I'm fit again, and am coming home in the beginning of February. I shall either ask for indefinite leave, or hand in my permit for a month or two, I'm not quite sure when. I've never really got rid of that silly chill I got, so everyone advises me to have a good big leave, and get braced up for the Summer, so I think I shall. . . .

I'm writing such drivel, but my pen seems to be running away with me, but I don't really feel like it a bit. I feel "mentally unsettled"—what a hideous combination of words, but I can't think of a better. I suppose it's the war really—one feels one is floating about without an anchor—sounding feverishly for something definite to anchor to. "Unsettled" is really the only word I can think of. There is so much here that I see which stamps itself on my mind, and I have to think about it, and can come to no happy or definite conclusion. I long to put all of it down in writing. If only I could!

That's at the root of it. There's such a lot inside me which longs to come out in music or writing, and I can hardly bear it when I realise I can't get rid of it anyhow. Perhaps it will get so bad sometime, that I shall be able to write it away, I only hope so. Everything here seems to mean something to me, to be in inverted commas so to speak, and the most ordinary things seem to excite me in a way which I can't explain, like happiness and sadness mixed. I suppose I've got very fond of everything, and yet I often feel homesick. I find myself looking forward absurdly to driving again, and to seeing the things I know—the quayside with all the fishing boats sailing in, and the women clumping across the road, with baskets, to meet them, and take the fish to the market, and yet when they really do these things I get very annoyed, because they get in the way of the car! This is a funny sort of letter, and I don't know whether I shall ever post it. I've got what I call a "spasm"; when there's so much I want to write that I can't sort out my ideas, and I can't find words for the impressions I want to give, I think everything here is so elemental—it's like living in a dramatic situation the whole time, and you can't get away from it.

I'm awfully fond of the river here. There is a bridge over it from which you can get the most wonderful view of everything. On one side the river mouth and the sea and the little fishing boats; the quay and the big sailors' crucifix, where the women pray when there is a storm at sea. The boats anchor quite near, and they look like something hazy and unreal, sitting on a shiny wet river, with every sail and mast and man reflected in the water. I long to put my hand down and stroke them. Behind them are the houses—filthy and ramshackle, but gorgeously picturesque seen from my bridge, with the sun warming their pink, white, and grey roofs. Behind the houses again is the camp—the tents crawling up the hill like white snails, and more hills and pine trees behind them.

The whole thing is so illogical, boats and fishermen on the one hand, and on the other tents and soldiers and bugle calls. That's one of the fascinations of my bridge—the one side is peace, and the other war. I should love to be able to paint a picture of it—the boats, and the sea, and the heavenly lights in the water. The other side a railway bridge stretching across the river and a train creeping slowly over it. In the distance it looks absurdly unreal and toy-like. The train is long, and on the trucks are guns, ammunition waggons and lorries, and men are leaning out of the windows, sitting on the roofs and steps, and crowding round the open doors of goods and horse vans.

The little toy train is on the direct line to Amiens. Flat, swampy fields and ditches spread round the river, then come the hills and pine woods and the road to P. -P. I stood on the bridge the other morning and saw all this, and I wanted badly to shout or scream or do something stupid. And then some aeroplanes flew over, and soldiers and ambulances and lorries and trams and bicycles came over the bridge, and it all seemed so futile. I came back feeling I'd over-eaten myself on plain bread and butter and the very richest chocolates, two things totally unlike. Ever since I've been here I've got unhappy over unnecessary things—the gorgeous sunsets behind the hills and at sea. The huge red ball sinks lower and lower, and I try frantically to catch some idea in my mind which I can get hold of, and then the impatient sun dips into the sea, and I'm left feeling silly and small, and wondering what It was I was trying so hard to catch hold of. . . .

I'm horrified at the amount and "quality" of what I have written. I feel better, though. I'm not a bit depressed as all these ravings might seem to indicate, but sometimes the things I see hurt me so that I nearly rave with the desire to put them all down on paper. To create something out of the colossal amount of material there is waiting to be used. Perhaps I shall be able to some day.

Cutty, darling, I hug you. Don't think I've gone off my head. I've just had a spasm, and I had to write it all. I've done it before and torn it up, but this time I have put it in a letter.

Je t'embrasse de tout mon coeur.

                                                           Ta Bonçe.

A. W. T. S.

CHAPTER 19

Flying Fox

A.P.O., S. 11,
B.E.F., 10th Jan. 1918.

Mother Darling,—Just a line to say goodnight. I am beginning work again on Monday and am very glad. It's insupportable having nothing to do. . . .

I have been scribbling such a lot—a sort of diary, and I am enjoying it. I won't send any of it home because places are mentioned, and the bulk of it would attract and annoy the censor.

Have you read *Tommies Two* by Blanche Wills Chandler? I must send it to you, Dumpos—it's lovely, and I didn't send you a Christmas present because I couldn't think of anything you would like, and it seemed a pity to spend money on a useless nothing. I therefore sent you nothing chock full of love. I'm reading Locke's *Wonderful Year*—it's simply alive. The pages are covered with little bits of human existence, and thoughts and doings, and not merely printed words. I think Locke is a genius, and he does so remind me of R.L.S. If Locke rode a donkey through the Cevennes, he would write about it in just the same way—don't you think so?

I must stop now.—Good night darlings.

Betty.

T. L. L W.Y.

Y.M.C.A., Gordon Hut,
A.P.O., S. 11,
B.E.F., 13th Jan. 1918.

Darling Mother,—. . . I have just been up to the military church in the camp for the evening service, with Joyce and another girl. It was nice, and there was a packed congregation of officers and men, and sisters in their white caps and overcoats, and W.A.A.C.s—so interesting, and we all bellowed hymns and then walked back with lanterns.

This afternoon we three went for a walk in the woods. We climbed up and up, and came to a steep ladder and scrambled up to the top (in a high wind)! The view was divine. The whole of P.-P. and Étaples laid out below is in the bright sunshine . . . the white houses, and the blue sea and the two lighthouses.

I begin work again at the hut tomorrow, and I'm looking forward to it. It's horrid doing nothing. This is a rather disconnected sort of letter, but I'm very sleepy, and very full of food—oxo, ham and beans, and sponge pudding, so please excuse it. I am so sorry for all you wids at home with nothing to eat. I'm sure we've got more here. However, they've begun to be stricter now, and I think it's about time. Now we're rationed, and on rations too. We draw from the army: bully beef, jam, cheese, margarine, pickles, tea, sugar, flour, bread and biscuits, dried fruits, and dried vegetables, meat and potatoes.

In our mess, we've been having eggs and bacon every morning, now we only have eggs twice a week, but we have porridge to make up. We have condensed milk as a rule, but are allowed a very little *bon lait*. Eggs are 40*c*. each here—how much are they at home? In the town cakes are not allowed to be eaten in *cafés*, but they can be sold in shops, except on Tuesdays and Wednesdays, and the same rule applies to chocolate. But still the cakes are lovely, iced and with sugar—but it's getting more difficult now.

No milk is procurable in *cafés* after 9 ak emma; you have to put up with lemons! In some of the places they use liquid sugar—horrid sticky stuff. But still we get far more to eat than you. I think the civilians find it hard, and they have riots and queues for bread. It's not safe to go about alone carrying bread.

Didn't I ever thank you for your photo? It's lovely, and I've bought such a nice little frame for it. I'm going to have mine taken one day—and I'll send it on. . . . Goodnight, my own mammy.—Your loving daughter, who hugs you tight in spirit.

Betty.

T. L. I. W. Y.

Y.M.C.A.,
A.P.O., S. 11, B.E.F.,
1st February 1918.

Darling Dumpos,—Thanks muchly for the money order which I duly received, etc. . . .

My leave is due on the 6th, but I can't take it just at once.

It is a long time since I've written to my wids, but such a lot has been happening, which I will now proceed to explain.

I am going to transfer, and be a hut worker for the summer. I can't tell you how pleased I am. Driving has got so on my nerves, I don't feel I ever want to do it again, at least not for some time. Mr Scott has been very decent about it, and is going to try and get me permanently into the Gordon Hut, which is, of course, what I am longing for. In the meantime, I am driving for three weeks, as another of our drivers has been sent to another base for so long. It's an open Ford van, and I'm so cold, I don't know what to do—I wish I'd got that fleece lining.[1] Everything is frozen, and my face is all peeling and raw with the wind. I'm a very miserable Starkey, and I've got another cold. Thank goodness it's only for three weeks—I don't honestly think I could stick it any longer. I'm horribly homesick for the Gordon.

I borrowed an Australian's horse the other day, and had a gallop in the camp, to the intense excitement of everyone. I was so stiff the next day, I walked like a bilious drake.

In our hut there is a man who used to be head chef at the Prospect; we jawed quite a lot. There is another dear old man who comes in, and he always brings us food—maple sugar and Canadian sweets.

I have made great friends with another girl who works in the Gordon, called Avice Rhodes. She is such a dear, and we are called "the heavenly twins." Unofficially, we know that the orderlies in the kitchen call us Chubbie and Tweenie, and Budge and Toddy, behind our backs. Officially, of course, we know nothing.—*Beaucoup* love.

Bet.

From General East
8th Feb. 1918.

. . . One of my staff officers, when on leave on the 6th, saw

---

1. This was stolen in the post.

Betty at Étaples. She was driving her Archibald again for three weeks, and did not expect to get home for two or three weeks from then, which would mean the end of this month, or the beginning of next.

She was very well, but is longing to get back. She wants to get properly "introduced" into the hut, I think. Do not worry about the child. I get news of her fairly often, and I hope to be able to see her off when she goes. . . .

Y.M.C.A.,
A.P.O., S. 11, B.E.F.,
10th February 1918.

Darling One,—I was glad to get your two letters, and you mustn't be cross with it, because it won't have it, and it loves you *beaucoup*, and won't ever go so long again without writing. *Selah*.

The question of my leave was so vague and uncertain, that I purposely didn't write about it until something was definitely settled. I have now decided to leave on Thursday, 21st February, and I shall stay a night in London, and come north on Friday. Don't you worry about your Y.M.C.A. campaign, poppet beloved, because I shall get five or six weeks' leave, hurrah! Isn't it joyful?

I am afraid I'm not getting back to the Gordon, but Mr Scott is being exceptionally nice about everything, and is going to get me into a nice hut—I hope with the Canadians. I am so looking forward to it for the next few months.

I am having a perfectly heavenly time at present. Archie, my blighted Ford van, is off the road for repairs, and I am driving a horse and cart round the camp with stores! It's too thrilling for words. It's one of the Y.M.C.A.'s horses and carts, and I saw it standing outside H.Q. two days ago, and I leapt in and went off for a joy-ride. I apologised when I came back, and was greeted with smiles and cheers, and finally it was agreed that I should take over the horse till I go on leave, and there I be. I am having a *succès fou*. The cart is two-wheeled, and the market type, with painted green woodwork, enormous long straight shafts, and huge red and green wooden wheels. There is a bench with a back, sliding across the middle of the cart, and nothing between driver and horse. The latter goes by the name of Flying Fox, because it can't fly. It isn't a bad horse, and is an old artillery animal. It shies at trains, and has a habit of backing in narrow streets, and I love it. I have successfully waked up all the traffic and M.P.'s for miles. . . .

Au revoir, mon p'tit chou.—Je t'aime plus que la vie.   Bet.

The following letters, about Flying Fox, are inserted here, though they were written to us at a later date:—

Devizes, Wilts,
Sun., 23rd June 1918.

Dear Mrs Stevenson,—Her photo came this morning, and you know how glad I am to have it, and shall value it always. She always looked so happy, didn't she, and I am almost glad now not to be returning for a few months, as we always told each other all the funny little things which happened at the counter—and away from it too.

Someone wrote to me from Étaples the other day calling her the "brightest and happiest of all the workers," and the two New Zealand girls wrote also saying they had just taken her some flowers.

I expect she told you on her last leave how she drove the Stores cart and horse for about three weeks. I used to go with her whenever I could get off. We used to laugh so over it, and Betty never knew how pretty she looked sitting up in the funny old French cart with stores piled up behind.

I am here doing a temporary motor job, and can't help always remembering her coping with "Archie," the Ford, and of how once she and I charged a fence in him, to the fury of the pickets near by, and how she shouted with laughter, and they had to laugh too in the end.—Yours affectionately,

Avice Rhodes.

Ipswich, 1st August 1918.

Dear Mrs Stevenson,—... One of the things I loved best about Betty was her glorying love of her home and her family. It was lovely to hear her talk about you, and her huge thrill of excitement whenever letters came, or when she had a "spasm" and wrote reams to you.

One of the last delightful things I did with her before she went on leave was driving round with her and Flying Fox, when she sat up so brave and buoyant on that little trap, and carted stores around, bursting with delight and amusement at herself, and chuckling whenever she passed a policeman she knew, who was accustomed to seeing her only on a car!

This is not half the letter I meant it to be, but forgive me. I know so dreadfully well how the sun goes out of life, but her gallant memory will always keep you brave.—Yours,

Lois Vidal.

Diary

Maison Dacquet,
Étaples, 9th February 1918.

I've had a most amusing day, and am feeling cheery and pleased with life in general. I have also got that most pleasurable feeling of having been a small success. Archibald's magneto developed serious internal trouble last night, and I was only just able to crawl down from the Con. Camp with her, and land in the garage with a grunt and a honk. As a result she is off the road today and being doctored—I had therefore nothing to do....

We wandered along the road to H.Q., and saw standing in front of the gate the horse and cart from the Stores. Then I didn't feel bored any longer. I seized Effie by the hand and we raced along towards it. As we got to the gate Connon came out: I leapt into the cart, seized the reins, dragged in Effie and then Connon, and off we went.

Jock, the little traffic man at the corner of the Rue de Rivage, nearly jumped out of his skin when he saw us. I couldn't get used to having no horn, and nothing to make a noise with, so at the last minute I opened my mouth and yelled, and the others squealed, and Fox backed into the kerb, so no wonder poor Jock lost his nerve for a moment. He soon recovered, and then started cheering and waving his arms, which of course, muddled the other traffic considerably. We left him disentangling himself from a maze of cars and lorries. I then drove Connon to the post office where she had some cheques to see to. While she was inside, a company of Belgian artillery came past, this was too much for Fox: she turned completely round, and then began to back till I thought she would never stop, all over the road and the kerb (much to the delight of the Belgian Army), and Effie and I clinging like limpets to our seats.

At last Connon came out and held Fox till all the cavalcade

had passed. We then did a little tour of the town, and then took Fox back to the Stores where she lives. Altogether we had a successful tour.

Just before lunch I met Mr Smith and asked if he had minded. He was awfully nice, and said he didn't mind a bit. I then asked if I could have her out again, and he said yes. It was finally arranged that I should take over the driving of Fox for the Stores till I went on leave in about a fortnight's time, and that as soon as Archie was on the road again, Effie should take it over. I went away frightfully pleased with myself, and told all my M.P.'s and traffic men to be prepared. Accordingly at 2 pip emma I reported at Stores and discovered that I was to take Mr Smith out to Les Iris and Ignotus with stores. Les Iris is a hostel for officers' relatives who come out to visit their wounded people. It is a beautiful house in lovely grounds (at Le Touquet, about four miles from Staples). It belonged to a rich American in peace time, and we have taken it for the duration.

It is a gorgeous place. We drove out there in great style, and caused a great sensation, and thoroughly enjoyed it. It was a heavenly day, bright sunshine, a bit of wind, and quite a nip in the air. The whole camp was trooping out to Paris-Plage to disport itself—officers, Tommies, Waacs, nurses, and drivers. French, English, Scotch, Canadian, American, Belgian, Chinese, Portuguese, and Indian, in every sort of vehicle. The tram bulged with people, the men were sitting on the steps and on each other's knees, and standing on the coupling joints of the cars. A stream of little *fiacres* jogged along with a nice selection of officers and nurses inside, bicycles by the score, cars, and lorries giving lifts to Waacs, and two gorgeous French officers in the one and only hired car that Étaples possesses, the G.O.C. in his mighty Vauxhall with its red flag, and the A.P.M. on horseback—and Miss Stevenson and Mr Smith, plus sacks of sugar and raw meat in muslin bags, and cheese and margarine, and tea and pickles and bread, in a market cart!

We disgorged some of the rations at Les Iris, and Mr Smith looked round, and then we drove to the Villa Robinson, the *annexe*, where Mr Smith had some work to inspect, and then we went on to Ignotus. Ignotus is a medium-sized white villa, with a small garden, at Paris-Plage, a mile further on. It is a sort of rest home for Y.M.s. We go out there for odd nights and weekends when we are recovering from various diseases, or want a rest. Jock was sweet when I went home. I asked him how he liked my new car; he grinned and said he didn't quite know whether he liked me so much behind the horse as in Archie. I don't think he had quite got over my yell. Jock is a dear—he is a little short Scot with a Glengarry bonnet, and he is always on traffic duty, and at the various corners; he changes about each week. He talks the broadest Scotch with a perfectly priceless grin.

I informed him that Fox was much better than Archie because it was so nice not to have to keep on cranking her up. He then asked if I liked cranking up Archie, and in very forcible language I said no.

"I'm sure no one would ever know it then," said Jock. "You're jist the happiest person in this base, it cheers us up to look at you." I grinned, and said I thought it was because everybody spoilt me.

"*I* don't ever get spoilt—I wish someone would spoil me," Jock said with a noise between a sigh and a grunt.

"Poor Jock—I'll spoil you," I said. "We'll all spoil you—what would you like us to do?"

Jock thought deeply for a minute or two. "Well," he said, "I think I'd like you to run into me with that horse and cart. I think I'd be fairly spoilt then, wouldn't a, noo?" And we both chuckled, and I said I'd think about it. The policeman in the square had something to say about it too, and was very facetious about my charger.

CHAPTER 20

Last Leave

Betty crossed from France on Thursday, 21st February 1918. Major M. escorted her.

They had a great railway journey up from Folkestone; the carriage was full of brass hats, and Betty said they all behaved like schoolboys, and played all sorts of games.

On Friday, the 22nd, she came home. I met her, and when she jumped out of the train, I thought I'd never seen her look so sweet. She had on her long khaki overcoat, and she had two service stripes on her sleeve this time—I was so proud of her.

I had made her room look so pretty, and had made her new tablecovers, and a new lampshade, and she had a lovely new chest of drawers, and the room was full of flowers, and looked, as she said, "just heavenly."

She played so much, and as we were using the little rose room upstairs as a sitting-room, I used to sit there with the door open, and listen to the lovely music. I scribbled this one Sunday evening in April, while she was playing the piano.

BETTY

When Betty comes, the house is full of light
And warmth from her sweet heart, and bright.
You can't be sad,—the days are pure delight.
When Betty comes.

When Betty plays, and round the gallery swell
Sweet waves of music that she loves so well,
On all my heart she lays a lovely spell—
When Betty plays.

PORTRAIT TAKEN ON LAST LEAVE

When Betty goes—why, then, put out the light!
I needn't climb her stair to say goodnight.
And tie her pigtails—an imposing sight,—
When Betty goes.

She told us heaps of stories about her work in Étaples, and I often wished she could speak into a "dictaphone" so that I could hear it again when she had gone back.

I remember her describing how she had a heavy car load of people to take from Boulogne, including a nice young Highland soldier—I'll try and tell the story in her words:

> He was quite young, and a dear, and *very* shy, and had come from some far-away Highland home, and he'd been travelling for goodness knows how long, and I saw he was dropping with sleep, and his head kept on nodding. So presently his head reposed on my manly shoulder. Poor dear, I knew how awful he'd feel when he woke up, so I determined I'd let him sleep as long as he could, with his head comfortably reclining on me, and I managed to drive all right, though my left arm got a bit stiff, and when he woke up, I carefully kept my head turned the other way, so that his face had time to cool down, and I kept on talking so that he should think I hadn't noticed he'd been asleep and snoring in my ear. He was such a nice shy Scotch boy with such a lovely accent!

She told us how the "relatives" had sometimes a maddening habit of not believing she knew the way to the various hostels when she met them at Boulogne, *e.g.:* One dark and pouring night she met the boat, collected up the relatives, sternly forbade them to move from the spot where she put them, and went to wind up her car. It was pitch dark and pouring. When she came back, of course one man was missing; she hunted up and down the quay and sidings, but couldn't find him—went back to the boat to borrow a lantern from the captain, who, of course, knew her quite well. He lent her his lantern on solemn promise to return it, and with its aid, Betty at last found the missing relative, and brought him back to the fold. He was asking the way to —— from a group of people.

Betty sternly rebuked him, and led him gently but firmly back to where he'd been first set. Then she set out to find the captain and return the lantern, but this time the captain was missing. At last he was found "in a dark little house, hidden among coils of rope and buckets and things," and so the company at last started on its journey to the various hospitals and hostels.

On Friday, 15th, she and I set off in great form to have a real jaunt together in London, It was the first time she and I had gone away like this for grown-up frivolity, and we were both so excited. You see Betty was eighteen when the war began, just the age when most girls look forward to, and get, all sorts of fun and "good times," and Betty *loved* these things.

On Easter Sunday, Emil, F——, Betty and I and Jenny went to the 8 o'clock Celebration at Christ Church. That is the last time I went with her, and I shall never forget it.

From General East

22nd March 1918.

... I see your Betty is not coming back at once. Do not encourage her to stay too long at home, as she is badly wanted here. .

Grey Gables, Harrogate,
14th April 1918.

Darling Woodie,—I am so sorry I have been such a long time answering your letter, and thanking you for the sweet little egg you sent me. I have been having rather a hectic time over my permit. I was expecting it every day, and I have now been told that all permits are held up for the time being, with all this fighting. Of course I am dreadfully disappointed, as I hate to be out of it all, especially just now. I have had a perfectly gorgeous leave, and didn't really want to go back a bit, when I thought that I could—if you can understand such grammar! You know the family took such a nice house in Scarborough last year, and we are going to get the same house again. . . . I missed it all last year, and I shan't be able to bear it if I miss everything again this year. You see I must be in France four months before I get leave, and we go to Scarborough in August. However, I must hope for the best. I've had a ripping long leave this time, and haven't had a single cold, which is rather good for me. (I must tap wood!)

All this time Betty's permit was held up. The big German push which began on 21st March was in full progress, troops were being rushed across to France, and no Y.M.C.A. women workers were allowed to return to their work in France during those anxious days. However, at last Betty's permit came through. On Monday, the 6th

May, we left; as we went out of the gate, she turned and called out to Jennie, "Now remember, you're all to go to Scarborough in August, and I shall come there on my next leave."

She and I came to town together. On Tuesday, 7th May, I saw her off at Charing Cross by the midday train. She gave me a hug before she got in, and we said to each other the old parting words we always used whenever we were going away from each other. I whispered in her ear, "*The Lord is with you,*" and she whispered back, "*And with thy spirit.*" Nobody heard. And the train went out of the station. That is the last time I saw her sweet face—7th May.

There is nothing but happiness in the remembrance of that last leave—there was a great number of visitors, much loved aunts and uncles and friends on leave, and a good deal of tennis. But best of all remembrances to me is one walk across the Stray, when she said to me, "No girl ever had such understanding parents as I've got." And when I said, feeling *en veine* for original remarks, and full of pride in her, "You know. Bet, I do *like* you so, as well as loving you: you're such a good friend, even if you weren't my daughter, bless you," she was delighted with the idea of our being *friends*.

Chapter 21

May, 1918

Y.M.C.A.,
A.P.O., S. 11, B.E.F.,
10th May 1918.

My Own Darling Mammy,—I was so glad to get your letter this morning, darling.

We had quite a good crossing, and I wasn't sick. There was the most awful wind blowing at Folkestone. I was nearly blown off the quay, and was expecting a rough crossing, but there wasn't so much wind at sea. We left at 4 and arrived at 6. Halfway across it began to rain, and I retired to my cabin. A sea-bird's egg missed us by a few yards, but we didn't know till we were landed. I wish I'd been on deck all the time as I might have seen something Joyce met me and motored me back. . . .

Heaps of my old friends are still here, and it is nice to see them all again, and they've been saying such nice pretty things to me. The people who work at the Lion d'Argent with me are ever so nice, and I like the work very much, and there is heaps to do. . . .

The weather here is gorgeous; lovely sun, but not too hot.

Every evening I go to the station with Chappie and we give away food and drink to the people who are having to leave their homes in the north. It's so interesting but I can't tell you much about anything. We are all cheerful, and they were surprised to hear, of the fuss and grousing in Blighty. *They* aren't worried about anything. I knew they wouldn't be.

Goodbye, darling. Did you get my telegram.? I sent one home too.

Betty.

Y.M.C.A.,
A.P.O., S. 11, B.E.F.,
France, 17th May 1918.

My Darling Mother,—I am so glad you are going down to Devonshire with Noel. Mind you get a good rest and do nothing all the time.

The weather here is so hot we none of us know what to do with ourselves. I've bought a ripping panama hat, which is allowed, and the *tout ensemble* looks *très bien*.

Darling, many happy returns of its 16th birthday; its little present hasn't arrived, but you will receive it *anon*. I'm sending it . . . from the nice shop I told you of. I hope you will like them. They will arrive late I am afraid, but they are coming from Paris.

I simply love my new work, and I am so happy. I get two mornings off a week, *i.e.* Monday till 2.30 and Thursday till 4 p.m. The other people there are dears, and I love them. They often go away together on their mornings off, and I am in sole charge, which I love. . . . I love it all.

The other morning Chappie and I went by train to P.-P. and spent the morning sitting on the beach. It was heavenly. All the cavalry were out on the beach and tearing about and doing the most thrilling things, thousands of them, and the sun was shining on their lances, till they looked like huge twinkling diamonds. We didn't come back till lunch time. Cheerio!

Bet.

It is difficult to write of Betty's last term of service, between 7th May, when she got back to work, and 30th May, when she slipped through the Barrier. Her friends told us that she arrived back "simply bursting with happiness, even for happy Betty." She was so pleased when she got into the Maison Dacquet that she picked up Olive (a small person) and carried her round the kitchen, and finally deposited her flat on the kitchen table, to the joy of the French servants.

On Sunday, 19th May, there was a terrific air raid over Étaples. Just at this time we began to be very anxious about our son, who was very ill at Harrow. I have often had said to me, since May, "I wonder you were not more anxious about Betty while Étaples was being raided." This next letter will perhaps make it a little easier to understand why I was not anxious; it was *impossible* to be fearful where Betty was concerned. "It's a great stunt"—not a word of fear on her part, or of anything to rouse our fears.

Y.M.C.A.,
A.P.O., S. 11, B.E.F.,
23rd May 1918.

My Own Darling Mother,—I've just got your letter with the enclosure. . . . G. came down to see me last Saturday. We had great fun, though he couldn't stay very long. I went out to lunch with him, and then I went in his car to P.-P. and we strolled back on the beach, and I ordered my cabin for the season. Four of us are going to share one till the end of September—100 *francs*, which when divided among four isn't a bit bad, is it? . . . Letters are taking ages to cross now. Did you ever get my first letter about the crossing and the sea-bird's egg?

The weather has been awfully hot, and we haven't known how to exist. I don't know whether you hear much news of this part of the world—I imagine not. Anyhow we are all well and flourishing, though we don't sleep here. We all go out and sleep in P.-P. and in the woods—we find it "healthier." We are having a great time.

Chappie and I and another girl share a room in a villa we have taken over away in the woods. We leave here the last of anyone. Sometimes on bicycles and sometimes in cars. Some of us are in tents and huts, and the men in the woods and on the open verandahs of the house. It's a great stunt. I believe V—— S—— is going on leave. She will tell you all the news. I can say nothing. Our house is full of souvenirs![1] "Light Railways" and "Roads" came down the other day to see how we were. They couldn't stay long. . . .

Darling, I've lost the money order Daddy sent me. I was walking about with "Roads," and flourishing Dumpy's letter about, and when I got home the money order was *napoo*. I hunted everywhere—but of course couldn't find it. If you could bring yourself to send me another, would you send at the same time my allowance, which is due on 1st June. . . .

---

1. We saw her bedroom when we went to France in February (1919). A great hole blown out of the ceiling almost over the bed had then been plastered up; the glass and the wooden casements of the windows, which had all been blown out, were replaced by temporary oiled paper. The yard under the window still bore witness to the many raids. These were the "souvenirs."

I hope you will like the little present I am sending you. They came from Paris.—I love you.

                Bunçie.

A hug to the breadwinner, and also to the murderer. [2]

---

2. Grimmy, her dog.

CHAPTER 22

30th May (Corpus Christi Day)

On 26th May we were sent for to Harrow, and during the whole of that week we waited anxiously for our boy to be pronounced out of danger. A letter was written to Betty on Monday, 27th May, telling her of his serious condition, and promising to send for her if the doctor advised it. (The doctor had said "Yesterday (Sunday 26th) I should have told you to send for her, if you had been here; now I don't think you need, at any rate, not just now." Betty got this letter of 27th May on the evening of Wednesday 29th. She came for comfort to her dear friend Olive Stewart-Moore, who never failed her. On 30th May (*Corpus Christi* Day), before beginning her day's work, she wrote to her mother and to her brother. These were the last letters she ever wrote—full of love and concern for us three, but not a word of fear for herself. They were found next day by Olive Stewart-Moore lying on the table ready for post. Again, not a word of fear nor of the constant danger in which she and the whole base were living.

To her brother

Y.M.C.A.,
A.P.O., S. 11, B.E.F.,
20th May 1918.

Darling old Jarsy,—I am so sorry you've been on the sick list, poor little dear. I wish I could come over and hold your hand. Be quick and get well and have a good holiday, and enjoy yourself and do nothing. How lovely for you having the wids with you. I envy you.

We have been having very exciting times here, as I expect you know by the papers, but we are still alive and kicking—especially kicking—though we find it healthier to leave at nights. I shall have lots of stories to tell you when I come back. I only wish I could write them all to you, but I can't. Some of the minor incidents are, officers walking about in pyjamas and tin helmets—ladies in night attire and motor caps, and naked babies. It's all very amusing and pathetic, and I'll tell you all about it when I come home. Four of us have hired a bathing cabin for the season, and we can't think of a name. We have had many suggestions, among them—"Oh! I say," "Excuse me," "Splash me," "?" "Susan," and many others. Please suggest something. I must go and manger now.

Goodbye, little brother—*je t'embrasse*, when nobody is looking.—Your loving

Bet. x x

T. L. I. W. Y. Jarsy.

Thursday, 30th May, was her last day here; the story of that night is best told by those who shared it with her.

Étaples Administrative District
General Secretary—Adam Scott
Y.M.C.A., B.E.F.,
Friday, 21st May 1918.

Dear Mr and Mrs Stevenson,—You will have had from the Military Authorities the sad news of Betty's death last evening. I scarcely know how to begin to write you. She was the darling of the whole base staff, and was so loved by everybody that we are all sort of dazed by her loss. She had been busy all day, in the afternoon at the *Lion d'Argent*, and later, along with Mrs Stewart-Moore, with the refugees at the station.

Owing to a car breakdown, a group of workers were later than usual in starting for Les Iris, where we had been sending all our ladies to sleep recently for greater safety. A very early raid sent us all to the cellars, and after it was over we put the party of ladies on two cars to send them out of the danger zone in case the planes returned. We were held up half-way, and a second raid came over, forcing us all to take shelter under the banks by the side of the road. Everything went well until an enemy plane, just as the raid was finishing, dropped several bombs in open country near us, probably in order to get rid of them before returning.

One bomb killed Betty instantaneously, and wounded two

other workers, who are in hospital. I was by her side within a minute of the bomb falling, but nothing could be done. She could not have felt it, as she was shot through the left temple. She was taken to hospital at once.

The funeral will take place, we expect, tomorrow, and will be with full military honours as an officer of the British Army.

We cannot realise she has gone from us yet, and her place in the hearts of us all will not be filled. Only the other day we were talking of her as the sunshine of the whole place. Knowing how much she has been to everyone who knew her out here, we can have some small feeling of what her loss must mean to you both.

I can only say on behalf of us all how deep is our sympathy with you all. We mourn her as a very dear friend.

Mrs Stewart-Moore was with her all through, and will doubtless be writing you.—Believe me, yours very sincerely,

Adam Scott.

A.P.O., S. 11, B.E.F.,
31st May.

My Dear Mrs Stevenson,—I really don't know how to write you today, I am in such distress. I am Betty's little "Chappie," who loved her with all my heart, and today my heart feels as if it had been ground to pieces after our experience of last night. Through no one's fault we were caught last night in the open, five of us, and we had to shelter behind a hedge, with very little cover; we were in a most exposed place. Unfortunately, just when we prayed it was all over, a burst came just beside her (I was at the other side of the road) and got the child in the side of her temple. The doctors say she could never have felt anything. The others got slight wounds, and Mr Scott and I escaped—how, we don't know. We did all in our power—got a car and away to hospital, but all in vain.

Dear Mrs Stevenson, if you would like me to come, and if you think it would help you in any way, I would cross over and come to you at once, and I hope you will let me know, as I could tell you so much more of her than by writing. All her little treasures are safe with me, and will be until you have them. Since she came back she has been radiantly well and happy, and loved by all—never can I tell you how much. She was so upset about your boy's illness, and always came to me with all her joys and sorrows—we just shared everything.

I can't say much more as I am so shaken up and sad. I did not feel my own loss very much more than this, as she restored to me my faith and the sunshine of life.

God in His great mercy send you comfort.—Believe me, yours most sorrowfully,

Olive Stewart-Moore.

...The darkness of the night was for us then, not her. Mr Scott and I walked about all that night until dawn, as we could not rest, and I did not let him tell anyone until the morning, as we felt it was sacrilege; and when people met us and said, "Is all well?" we said, "Yes, all is well," and so it was with her then....

8th June 1918.

Dear Mr and Mrs Stevenson,—I feel that I ought to write to you as I was with Betty when she was hit. It seems useless for me to try to say how sad we have been made by her death; she was known and loved by everyone at Étaples on account of her happy smile, which never left her. She was not nervous at all. I was surprised at her calmness and steadiness.

I had done all I could to make her as secure as possible. She was wearing my shrapnel helmet, and we were well down at the bottom of the bank. She suffered no pain at all; I did not feel a tremor, but after the noise and dust of the explosion had died down I spoke to her, asking her if she was all right, and she did not answer.

We got her to the hospital at once in a car, but the doctors could only tell us that she must have been killed instantaneously and painlessly.

I am very glad to be able to say that she was smiling in death.

I was hit in the foot by a piece of the same bomb, but was able to carry on until we got to the hospital. There I was again bombed the next night, though fortunately I was not damaged this time, but the hospital was evacuated, and I, as a civilian patient, have made my own way home here. The doctor says that I shall be all right again in a few months, and I sometimes wish I had been killed instead of poor Betty.

I hope you will understand that she could have suffered no pain whatever; her untroubled smile vouches for that.

I wish above all things that I could have done something to save her, but I had already done every possible thing. If there is anything else you would like to ask me, do not hesitate; I am not too ill to answer questions.

In closing, may I say how sincerely I and all the Y.M. staff feel for you in your sorrow.—Believe me, yours sincerely,

Norman Phillips, Y.M.C.A.

... Her smile never left her; in my dreams of that awful night I still see her, smiling in an unshaken faith that all would be well, whatever happened....

A.P.O., S. 11.
1st June.

My Dear Mrs Stevenson,—We have just come back from putting the little one in her last resting-place. She had a soldier's funeral, and a beautiful service, and some lovely wreaths and flowers, and I can assure you there was not a soul there whose heart did not ache with sorrow for you.

I am sending you on some letters she wrote on Thursday, and which I found in her room since, under some things. I am going to pack up all her things and put them in a place of safety, in case the house should get hit here one night.

We did not get much sleep last night again, but were safely out from here.

I can't write much more as I feel so much, but little Miss J—— who was up at the hospital where we took Bet, and whom Bet loved so much, said she saw her last, and that the dear little face was so sweet, and as peaceful as it was always, and there was no sign of any shock or suffering.—Believe me as ever, with much love and sympathy,

Olive Stewart-Moore.

I feel her dear spirit round the place .... You see, dear, I was blessed in having her up to the end....

I must tell you about the funeral, as I am afraid no one properly did. We all went to the soldiers' cemetery and lined up at each side of the little chapel, and waited there till they carried her out, with a Union Jack rolled round just like a soldier. We went up and put our flowers and our love on the top, and the little procession started on its way down, the chaplain in his white robes in front, soldiers wheeling the little carriage; and the bugler; and then we came in twos. I walked directly behind with Effie, and then the drivers, and Lady Cooper and Mr Scott, and all the others.

The Burial Service was read and the 90th Psalm, and the chaplain spoke a few words, telling of her work, and how she had died for her country like a soldier. It was a beautiful and touching service, and was attended by her fellow-workers, people from Boulogne, her soldier friends, and the French sent a French Staff Officer from G.H.Q., to pay his respects with the others; he stood, a splendid figure, and saluted as she was carried by.

We did not have a hymn as it was a military funeral, but it was a beautiful service, and we had some verses which I have marked in my Bible to show you. And then at the last the bugler sounded the Last Post, and there was not a dry eye amongst us all, and I held on tight to my courage, and prayed so hard for you. Then they lowered her gently in, and we stepped forward and sprinkled her little bed with flowers.

Dear, it was beautiful, and it is a lovely spot with the river and the sea, and the woods all over the other side. She went home with all her courage, and a smile on her dear lips, and her lovely soul had gone without suffering. . . .

O. S. M.

CHAPTER 23

Memories

I have never seen her look lovelier than the time she came back from leave. "Joy and sunshine incarnate" she was. She and I were inseparable, and our rooms had a door between them, and the fun we used to have! She was so witty and clever, but I need not tell you what you know more of than I do.
I packed up all her dear things with my own hands, and they will be safe with me until I can get them safely to you.
She was so unselfish and thoughtful, especially after she came back, and she said, "Chappie, I do think I've grown up a little, on leave."
I go to her little resting-place, and keep it nice with flowers. People who could not come sent me money for flowers, and I take them up.... Such a lot of soldiers go up too, which I love—the men she worked for. She will never be forgotten here by any of us.

O. S. M.

...When I came to France first, I can never forget that it was your Bet who brought sunshine and laughter back to me again. No one could be with her and not benefit by the radiance.
She insisted that I should share all her little "binges" when her Uncle Lionel came, and seeing me happy again made her enjoy it doubly....
Latterly we discussed many serious subjects together, including death. We used to walk over the bridge on lovely nights after the station work was done, and then we talked a lot. That was before death and terror lurked so near us. She said the only thing that made her afraid of death was the leaving behind of you, her dear

ones, and then I said how since so many of my dear ones had faced it so fearlessly and gone over the line, it seemed so much less terrifying, and a simple thing. Little did I think then that God wanted her home to His beautiful garden.

The fateful night she missed you, and wanted me to love her as she was so worried about you and Jars, and I held her in my arms and loved and petted her.

I have never known her so happy here as she was this time. She loved her club and the work, and each night, when she had done, she rushed up to help me at the station with my refugees, and the joy of the little Scotch Mackie, the orderly, when I went out to dine perhaps, and left them to do it alone was what I called most unflattering to me.

I have had dozens of nice letters about her from people who worked here and saw us together. . . .

I will keep her treasures safely, and her little grave nice as long as I am near it.—As ever,

O. S. M.

These cards I brought away from some flowers on her grave to send you, and they are only from two of many unnamed soldiers.
. . .

It just seemed to all who knew and worked with her in the last three weeks of her life on earth, that God had already touched her with His divine hand, and that already she had a vision of the greater glory that awaited her. Everyone she spoke to she helped, and her smile was like a benediction to us all—this fact has been commented on by many, but especially by the soldiers she served in her club. It seemed as though she wanted to give us strength to carry on through the dark days that lay before us. To one who perhaps loved her best of all her many friends and fellow-workers in France, and who had watched with great interest this fine soul develop, it was a revelation, as one had seen her in many phases, but never before perhaps as "Betty the woman," and one could see and picture her in the future, happy, gracious, and kindly, never for a moment in her own great happiness forgetting those of her fellow-creatures less favoured than she.

One feels that this is so, and that God has called her to a higher and nobler work, and that He gave to all of us a glimpse of what she had attained in her higher life.

Standing by her little graveside one's heart ached and ached at the thought of one's personal loss, and the fact that not again on this earth would one see the sunny presence, and hear the merry voice and the quick wit and jest, and one sorrowed in perhaps a selfish way.

Suddenly one had a vision of the greater glory, and one saw the erect and gallant figure entering into the kingdom of everlasting light, and one heard the Master's voice as He saw her, say, "*Enter in my child, and well done thy work on earth.*"

Then with a smile of ineffable sweetness she entered in, breathing around, those who remained a spirit of courage and sweetness, and the vision passed.

One turned away hopefully, and started one's daily routine feeling that the world had been made a better place, because Betty had lived in it, and that she had left behind a fresh and fragrant spirit which would last through all time. For her sake, and for the sake of all the other glorious young lives, one must take up one's burden and answer the country's call, and do all one can with the vision of their glory and sweetness to guide us on to the end.

These are a few words very badly expressed by one who loved her so, and into whose saddened and shadowed life she helped to bring back joy and laughter, and sweetness and wholesomeness again, and in whose memory she remains for all time as a veritable "Gift of God and lore and light."

.... I wanted to tell you that as the sun was shining so beautifully this morning, I went up and got some lovely flowers, great dark red dahlias, great yellow marguerites and lovely scented carnations, and I took them up to the cemetery and put them there. I go up when I am sad and tired and perplexed, and I stay there a little, and it seems as though the spirit of peace dwelt there truly, as it helps me so, and I come away readier to go on with the problems that face one. . . .

Headquarters,
Y.M.C.A., Étaples.

It is with very great diffidence that I attempt to put on paper an appreciation of Betty—so impossible it seems to convey through the medium of the printed page any adequate impression of that bright, happy, devoted life. It is not that she was in any way abnormal or saintly or unnatural; Betty's whole charm was that she was so thoroughly natural and normal, so high-spirited and mischievous, with a delightful sense of humour, yet with a fine maidenly reserve, a deep reverence for things sacred, and a very strong sense of duty.

She came to us along with a young friend when neither of them was more than twenty. They were our youngest workers and were immediately dubbed "The Babies." Everyone was interested in them and loved them. Betty's work was to drive a car, sometimes with stores to the huts, at other times with lecturers, concert parties, and entertainers. She also took her share in the transport to and from the hospitals of relatives of dangerously wounded officers and men who were here as our guests. It was amusing to note how—while the senior drivers planned to relieve Betty and Joyce of the long runs, especially at night—the two "Babies" would spend any spare time they had in conspiring to do the longest, hardest runs of the day, and in persuading the others to allow them to take over the night journeys. And then, when the number of "relatives" increased, and all the drivers had to make these long night runs, great was their joy. They felt that at last they were carrying their full share and being allowed to take a real part in the sacrificial service in which the men they sought to serve were engaged.

Everywhere Betty made friends; the orderlies at the huts all loved to see her, the military police on point duty all felt that she was their little friend, and the workers at the Stores were always ready to load and unload Betty's car. She had a way of getting even the garage boys, who were badly overworked, to find time "just to come and *look* at" her car when it wasn't going well. On the day of her funeral I found that the men in charge of the mortuary and cemetery were her devoted friends. They had seen her comforting the wives and mothers she brought to the gravesides of their menfolk. In the *Lion d'Argent*, where she was latterly engaged in canteen work, she had many friends; she had a smile and a cheery word for everyone who entered the building.

Among her fellow-workers, too, Betty was always a favourite; one has no hesitation in saying that she was the most popular of all. Wherever she went she carried sunshine with her. Full of mischief and pranks, and humour and jokes at the expense of all of us, yet so gentle and sympathetic with anyone in trouble, she had no enemies and no rivals. The mess brightened up perceptibly on the dullest and rainiest day when Betty entered.

During the retreat in May, when French women and children, driven from their homes, were passing through Étaples in thousands, Betty was one of the two ladies who, night after night, gave food and drink to these poor refugees on the station, after her day's work at the canteen was over, and it was there she had been working until ten o'clock on the fatal night. When the raids came she was just the same happy girl, brave and calm in the midst of danger, bright and cheerful up to the last moment, and then died with her beautiful smile still on her lips. Happily, death was instantaneous, and she was spared the agony of wounds and suffering. I do not think there was one of all her fellow-workers who would not willingly have been her substitute in order that she might continue that rich, young life so full of promise. On every side we asked the same question—"Why *Betty?*"

She was a true Englishwoman; more than that one cannot say. She was worthy, well worthy, of the race of heroes who have ungrudgingly given their lives in this great struggle.

Adam Scott.

The *Croix de Guerre avec Palme* was bestowed on her.
Le Maréchal de France, Commandant en Chef les Armées Françaises de l'Est, cite à l'Ordre de l'Armée:
Mademoiselle Stevenson, Betty, de *l'Y.M.C.A.*:
A fait preuve, dans ses fonctions de chauffeuse et de dame de cantine, de beaucoup de courage et de dévouement. A été mortellement blessée au cours d'un bombardement aérien.
Au Grand Quartier Général, le 17 Février, 1919.
    Le Maréchal,

Commandant en Chef les Armées
Françaises de l'Est,
Petain.

Leonaur Editors' Notes

There were many, many more personal letters received by the family regarding the love, appreciation and admiration for Betty but these have been omitted in this modern edition.

www.ingramcontent.com/pod-product-compliance
Lightning Source LLC
Chambersburg PA
CBHW030229170426
43201CB00006B/159